Voice and Vote

Voice and Vote

**DECENTRALIZATION AND PARTICIPATION
IN POST-FUJIMORI PERU**

Stephanie L. McNulty

Stanford University Press
Stanford, California

Stanford University Press
Stanford, California

Printed in the United States of America on acid-free, archival-quality paper

Library of Congress Cataloging-in-Publication Data

McNulty, Stephanie L., author.
  Voice and vote : decentralization and participation in post-Fujimori Peru / Stephanie L. McNulty.
        pages cm
  Includes bibliographical references and index.
  ISBN 978-0-8047-7397-3 (cloth : alk. paper)—ISBN 978-0-8047-7398-0 (pbk. : alk. paper)
  1. Decentralization in government—Peru.   2. Political participation—Peru.
3. Democracy—Peru.   4. Peru—Politics and government—2000–   I. Title.
  JL3429.D42M39   2011
  323'.0420985—dc22   2011000526

Typeset by Westchester Book Group in 10/14 Minion

For Ramón

CONTENTS

ILLUSTRATIONS

ACKNOWLEDGMENTS

I AM HIGHLY indebted to so many people, without whom this study would not have been possible. I simply cannot name them all in these pages. I do, however, want to single out some people as having played especially crucial roles over the eight years that it took to complete this project.

First, I would like to thank my mentor and friend, Cynthia McClintock. She has provided countless hours of patient assistance as these pages progressed from an idea about Peruvian politics to an actual book. She is a true role model, and I thank her for all that she has taught me. Several other professors at The George Washington University helped enormously during the research and writing process, including Jennifer Brinkerhoff, Nathan Brown, Chris Deering, Bruce Dickson, Gina Lambright, Forrest Maltzman, Lee Sigelman, and Susan Wiley.

I would also like to extend my gratitude to all the Peruvian scholars, professionals, and activists that generously provided their time and information during my visits to Lima and the regions. Almost all the people I interviewed showed an admirable dedication to improving their country. I hope and pray that their efforts pay off. Although there are too many people who contributed to this effort to name individually, several people went way above and beyond the standard call of duty, including Frida Bera, Yolanda Díaz Callirgos, José and Edita Delgado, Luis Chirinos, Carlos Contreras, Aldo Panfichi, Tom Reilly, José López Ricci, Gerardo Tavara, and Emma Zevallos Aguilar. I would also like to thank the political science department of the Pontificia Universidad Católica del Perú, which provided me with the opportunity to teach and publish in Peru. And, of course, thanks to the students of Latin American

Political Processes (2004), who taught me as much about Latin American politics as I taught them.

Several good friends and colleagues have provided invaluable assistance with various pieces of this book, including: Chanya Charles, Sarah Chartock, Lan Chu, John Donaldson, Tasha Fairfield, Beth Franker, Lee Ann Fujii, Carolina Garay, Maiah Jaskoski, Maria Beatriz Orlando, Andrew Selee, Alejandra Vallejo, Connie Veillette, and Tamara Walker. Thanks, too, to the members of the 2009 Midwest Political Science Association "Participation in Latin America" roundtable in Chicago, Illinois the participants in the 2006 Latin American Studies Association "New Forms of State-Society Relations" panel in Puerto Rico, and the participants in the 2003 Institute for Qualitative and Multi-Method Research in Tempe, Arizona, all of whom gave me very useful feedback on different versions of this work. Much of the research for this book was made possible by the generous financial support of the Peruvian Fulbright Commission and the Department of Education's Fulbright-Hays Doctoral Dissertation Research Award.

I am grateful to my editor, Stacy Wagner, and her assistant, Jessica Walsh, for making this book a reality. I am also grateful to two external reviewers for their extremely helpful comments that strengthened my logic, argumentation, and organization. Delphine Martin and Amanda Blewitt helped me with the technical aspects of publishing. Of course, all errors are mine alone.

Since I arrived in 2008 at Franklin and Marshall College, my colleagues in the government department and the institution have also incredibly supportive. I would like to especially thank Dr. Robert Gray for his mentoring during my first two years at F&M as the manuscript became the book.

Finally, I would like to thank my family and friends, for their love and encouragement during this long process. Most of you know who you are. My mother, grandmother, and sister have been incredibly supportive of this effort, and I am so lucky to be one of them. Our friends and family in Peru have made my multiple visits not only possible and productive but extremely fun as well. Special thanks go out to the fantastic caregivers who helped me work knowing that my girls were happy in loving environments.

Most important, I would like to thank my wonderful husband, Ramón Escudero, and our two beautiful daughters, who have supported me in countless ways, especially by providing endless amounts of love and joy. Without them, this book simply could not exist.

**INTRODUCING PERU'S
DECENTRALIZATION EFFORT**

Part 1

1 PERU'S FRAGILE DEMOCRACY

IN LATE 2000 and early 2001, Peru faced a political crisis. The former president, Alberto Fujimori, had fled the country in disgrace and faxed his resignation to Congress after evidence surfaced that he and his chief of security had bribed legislators, judges, and the media. Congress rejected his resignation and then ousted him, calling him "unfit" to govern the country. Allegations of corruption and human rights violations by party politicians dominated the headlines. The international media followed the crisis closely, noting that videos of the corruption "scandalized" the country and calling Peru "crisis-ridden" later that year.[1]

After Fujimori left, Peruvians were extremely dissatisfied with their political system. Congress and the judiciary struggled to regain legitimacy and autonomy after ten years of authoritarian rule. Many argued that the future of democracy in Peru partly rested on its ability to decentralize its highly centralized government and incorporate new actors into decision-making processes. Peruvians were not alone. Their neighbors in Ecuador and Bolivia were also clamoring for change. Farther away in Africa, Asia, and Eastern Europe, citizens of the Philippines, the former Yugoslavia, Haiti, and Tanzania were calling for the end of politics as usual. Representative political institutions no longer met the demands of citizens who wanted their voices to finally be heard.

In Peru, a newly elected government decided to meet the crisis head-on. Influenced by participatory models of governance, such as the experience with participatory budgets in areas of Brazil, local councils in the Philippines, and town hall meetings in the United States, the newly empowered political elite designed a comprehensive decentralization[2] reform that explicitly mixes representative and participatory democratic institutions. As one Peruvian congressman stated during Congressional debates:

> This proposal defends participatory democracy within the regional governments by establishing an adequate *combination* of representative democracy by those who have been elected and participatory democracy with the presence of civil society (December 17, 2002; italics mine).

By 2002, the reform—an example of what I call "participatory decentralization reforms," or PDRs—had been finalized.

Peru's PDR restructures the state in several ways. In addition to empowering several levels of new governments—including regions (akin to states in the United States), provinces (akin to counties), and municipalities (akin to cities)—the reform also creates new ways for civil society[3] to participate formally in regional and local decision-making processes. As such, it is one of the most ambitious examples of a participatory decentralization reform in recent history.

Peruvians designed and implemented several new participatory institutions (PIs)[4] at the regional and local level. These institutions are also starting to appear around the world. As Brian Wampler (2007a, 57–58) writes, "directly incorporating citizens into participatory decision-making venues has been a central feature of institutional innovations in Brazil, South Africa, Spain, Venezuela, Indonesia, and other new democracies over the past two decades."

This book focuses on two PIs in the newly created regions: (1) a mandatory participatory budgeting process, in which civil society actors participate in regional budget planning;[5] and (2) Regional Coordination Councils (Consejos de Coordinación Regional, or CCRs), which bring together mayors and elected civil society representatives twice a year to discuss development plans and budgets. These new participatory institutions are considered by some to be the real success stories of the reform (PRODES 2007a, 2009).

THE ARGUMENT

The Peruvian experience presents a multilayered story about why countries decentralize, why particular designs are chosen, and the constraints that these designs put into place. It also demonstrates the power that local factors can have in overcoming these constraints once the reform starts to be implemented around the country. The book begins by addressing national-level design issues. Specifically, Part 2 tackles three questions:

1. What explains national policy-makers' decision to devolve power to regional governmental and societal actors through constitutional reform?
2. What factors help us understand the particular design of the participatory institutions?
3. How does this design then condition the implementation of the reform?

The analysis highlights the important role that electoral strategies and domestic politics play in the origin and outcome of PDRs. In answering the first question, I argue that the post-Fujimori democratization process provided the right context, or opportunity structure, for this kind of reform. A window of opportunity opened for reform-minded agents. National politicians, specifically presidential candidates, then made strategic electoral calculations to push through a constitutional decentralization reform very quickly after Fujimori fled the country. Thus, the case suggests that in countries like Peru, with weak political parties and few subnational political elites, strategic calculations by national political elites explain the decision to decentralize.

What led these same reformers to embrace participation in the early phases of the reform? Again, the return to democratic rule provided the opportunity structure. Three additional factors combine to help us understand the emergence of a PDR in this case: (1) experiences with corporate structures in the 1970s and 1980s; (2) the experiences of some participatory planning processes in a few localities in Peru during the 1980s and 1990s, some of which implemented by these very reformers; and, in the case of the participatory budget, (3) institutional relations between the Ministry of Economy and Finance and Congress.

Debates in Congress also help us understand the specific PI designs that emerged during the reform process. Congressional debate surrounding the PIs became politically charged at times, especially as regional elections approached. When debating the CCR design, a group of politicians intervened to grant civil society voice but no vote. Some resisted granting civil society more power for ideological reasons; others worried that the CCRs might grant too much power to potential competitors in the regions. The participatory budget, however, was viewed widely as a technical process and never seen as potentially threatening the power of elected officials. As a result, civil society retained voice *and* vote. The analysis demonstrates the power that political strategies—motivated by both ideology and the fear of losing power—have when undertaking specific PI design issues.

When we explore the outcomes of the PIs, we see that design does matter. A national-level analysis of the participatory budget shows that it has emerged in most cases as an institution with the potential to help democratize Peru and increase participation. In contrast, the CCRs are weak and ineffective in most regions of the country. Thus, to understand PDR outcomes we first need to look at the genesis and evolution of the design. Politics affect design, and design affects outcomes.

Part 3 of the book explores the implementation of the reform in more detail. It asks two additional questions: (1) How are the newly created participatory institutions unfolding in six of Peru's new regional governments? (2) What factors contribute to the successful implementation of participatory institutions in these cases?

When we look more closely, we see that some regions have overcome design constraints and are implementing the participatory institutions better than others. In some regions, the CCRs are actually emerging as a dynamic and innovative space for collaboration between civil society and the state. In other regions, governments are restricting participation in or manipulating the budget process to fund their own projects. Using data from six regions of Peru, this book explores the factors that allow these more successful regions to overcome design constraints or avoid legal requirements when implementing these new institutions. I argue that in the most successful cases, two regional factors—leadership and a collaborative and organized civil society—create a virtuous cycle of participation that leads to the successful implementation of the CCRs and the participatory budget.

Analyzing the Peru case both confirms previous research and adds new findings and research debates to scholarship on decentralization. Studying Peru's experience builds our knowledge of the strengths and limitations of decentralization generally and of participatory decentralization reforms more specifically. This book's extensive data on regional politics in Peru—a level of government often overlooked in most existing studies about participatory institutions—moves the discussion beyond conventional wisdom in several ways. It demonstrates that not only leftist leaders implement these institutions; rather, politicians from the entire political spectrum use these institutions to improve their image and expand their electoral base. Further, although it is true that successful institutions necessitate some level of cooperation and co-ordination within the regional civil society, this cooperation and organization can be relatively new. This finding goes against some arguments about social capital that suggest that the benefits of organizing can only be seen after long periods of time.

This book also provides useful information about the successful implementation of participatory institutions in general—whether part of a decentralization package or not. Similar innovations exist in several other Latin American countries (for example, Guatemala, Mexico, the Dominican Republic, and Brazil) and around the world (for example, France, Spain, and Canada). Neighborhoods in Los Angeles, Chicago, and Philadelphia are experimenting with new ways of involving citizens in decision-making at the local level. The 2009 military coup in Honduras took place in part as a response to the desire to implement participatory democracy in this small Central American country. We will surely see a rise in these efforts in more countries around the world as participatory models of governance are seen as potential solutions to the problems with representative democratic institutions. In many ways, this study helps us understand the conditions that will increase the chances for success for the institutions that emerge from these efforts.

These issues are important to policy-makers and international development organizations, such as the United States Agency for International Development (USAID), the World Bank, and the Inter-American Development Bank. USAID is actively supporting Peru's decentralization efforts—and similar efforts around the world—through several projects. Similarly, multilateral development banks spend billions of dollars promoting decentralization reforms around the world. According to the World Bank's website, from 1997 to 2003 more than 190 projects, totaling more than 2.5 billion dollars, had decentralization components (World Bank "Bank Projects"). Donors tend to assume that decentralization improves democracy and governance and that participatory institutions will ensure accountability and transparency in the developing world. Yet, more data are needed to assess this assumption. The conclusion of this book provides policy recommendations that can help strengthen similar experiments in other parts of the world.

PARTICIPATORY DECENTRALIZATION REFORMS

How is a participatory decentralization reform differentiated from other reforms that devolve power to subnational governments? In many ways they are part and parcel of the wave of decentralization reforms taking place around the world. However, two necessary dimensions characterize PDRs: decentralization *and* mandated participation. Reformers must devolve new powers to subnational levels of government and mandate new forms of citizen participation in these governments. Reformers generally design new institutions to channel citizen participation and give citizens decision-making power in governmental processes. In other words, these reforms find new ways to give both voice *and* vote in subnational decision-making processes to societal actors.[6]

There are several similar cases of this kind of reform. In Bolivia, reformers coupled decentralization with efforts to increase civil society's participation. The Popular Participation Law, passed in 1994, grants formal power to "territorial base organizations," including indigenous, *campesino*, and neighborhood groups, and assigns them important functions in municipal government processes. Additionally, representatives of these organizations form oversight committees to monitor and control the use of local funds.[7] Another effort took place in the Philippines, where the government formally institutionalized the participation of civil society organizations (CSOs) at the local level as part of its 1991 local government reform. Accredited organizations participate in development councils, work on councils that set up local contracts and bids, deliver social services, and manage local projects (Angeles and Magno 2004). Other cases of PDRs include the Dominican Republic, Nicaragua, South Africa, and Uganda.[8] By including both participatory budgets and coordination councils (as well as other PIs that are not studied in this book), Peru has passed one of the most ambitious examples to date of a PDR.

PDRs, therefore, represent one kind of decentralization. Their key features are top-down, mandated participation in subnational governments as part of a legal framework. The newly empowered governments are required to implement the PIs. These cases can be distinguished from cases where innovative new forms of participation emerged after a decentralization reform, such as the participatory budget in Brazil and in municipalities around Mexico. The Brazilian and Mexican experiences stemmed from grass-roots local innovations that encourage citizen participation *after* a reform.[9] PDRs set up these channels as part of the actual reform package.

This innovative policy mix is heavily influenced by democratic theories that stress direct, or participatory, democracy. Inspired by the thought of political philosophers such as Jean-Jacques Rousseau and James Harrington, several political theorists have pointed to the need for citizen participation beyond elections.[10] They argue that a country can hold competitive elections, but citizens may still not adequately participate in the system (Avritzer 2002; Barber 1984; O'Donnell 1994). Scholars, activists, and policy-makers, especially since the 1970s, have come forth to call for complementary strategies: implementing participatory approaches to complement and strengthen representative institutions. Binding decision-making power is devolved to these new actors through institutions that formalize society's participation.

However, the Peru case demonstrates that mandated participation, when stemming from top-down national political forces, does not always translate to meaningful citizen participation in practice. It is no surprise to those who study the developing world that laws are not always implemented as intended after passage. Thus, in many countries these new forms of participation are working well in some areas of the country, yet barely functioning in others. Decisions to design and pass PDRs as well as their implementation are the main topics of this book.

LAYING THE GROUNDWORK

This book contributes to two major strands of theoretical analysis: the extant literature that explores the decision-making process that leads to decentralization reforms, as well as an emerging body of literature on participatory institutions.

Decentralization Reforms

There is an extensive debate, going back to the early 1990s, that explores the puzzling decision to design a reform that empowers new levels of government (and, as a result, new political elites).[11] This decision is counter-intuitive because national politicians devolve power to their subnational political counterparts— counterparts that could eventually emerge as competitors. When examining this issue, early literature tended to stress three variables as explaining the reforms: (1) international pressures, such as pressure by donors and/or foreign investors (Doner and Hershberg 1996; Fox 1992; IDB 1997; Wong-Gonzalez 1992); (2) economic crisis and/or reform (Bresser Pereira 1993; Manor 1999; Rondinelli 1989); and (3) socioeconomic development or modernization, measured in light of economic growth and urbanization (Bahl and Linn 1986; Campbell 2003).

A second wave of studies convincingly shows that these variables do not explain the majority of cases.[12] For example, in terms of donor pressure, Montero and Samuels (2004, 17) note that "[d]ecentralization emerged as a major theme in the [international donors'] discourse in the region only *after* [italics in original] 1988 . . . well after political, fiscal, and administrative decentralization were under way [in many countries]." Sabatini (2003) correctly argues that international support probably reinforced these trends, but did not cause them.

Socioeconomic factors do not always lead to decentralization either. Alfred Montero and David Samuels bring this point home when writing, "quite simply, both developmentalist and neoliberal governments have historically decentralized *and* recentralized" (2004, 14; italics in original). As O'Neill (2004) points out, in Bolivia there is no relationship between decentralization and the fiscal deficits associated with Latin America's economic situation. Eaton and Dickovick (2004) show that in Argentina the government actually began to recentralize power to promote economic stability in the 1990s. Finally, Escobar-Lemmon's research on decisions to decentralize shows that "urbanization did not have a statistically significant effect on the level of fiscal decentralization" (2001, 30). Thus, the extant literature on this issue shows that economic crisis, reform, and development do not hold explanatory power.

Another set of findings points to decentralization as a result of the wave of democratization that has taken place around the world (Bird and Vaillancourt 1998; Nickson 1995). However, it is difficult to demonstrate a causal relationship between democracy and decentralization. In a seventeen-country statistical analysis of the motivations behind decentralization in Latin America, Escobar-Lemmon (2001) finds that this relationship is not statistically significant. Eaton's comparative historical analysis shows that "there is no simple or straightforward relationship connecting regime change with either decentralization or re-centralization" (2004a, 16). His research on Chile (2004a and 2004b), for example, documents how decentralization took place during Pinochet's dictatorship.[13] Oxhorn argues that decentralization contributed to Mexico's democratization process, noting that although decentralization and democratization are "intimately intertwined," they are not necessarily causally related (2004, 3). Rather, as David Samuels (2004, 67) cautions, we must "explore the particulars of every country's transition to understand why politicians decentralized" in a given situation.

More recently, a consensus has emerged that domestic political variables help us understand this counter-intuitive decision. Willis, Garman, and Haggard's (1999) important study first came out to argue that domestic political variables best explain the scope and pace of decentralization in Latin America. Based on research on Brazil, Venezuela, Argentina, Colombia, and Mexico, they argue that decentralization has a "discernable political logic that has important consequences for the success or failure of [these] efforts" (Willis, Garman, and Haggard 1999, 8). They go on to argue that bargaining between subnational and national political elites often explains these reforms.

Recent studies by Escobar-Lemmon (2003), Eaton (2004a), Montero and Samuels (2004), O'Neill (2004), and Selee and Tulchin (2004) have further developed this argument with additional evidence from Bolivia, Brazil, Mexico, Colombia, Argentina, Guatemala, and Venezuela. Although acknowledging that processes are complex, Montero and Samuels (2004, 20) argue that "incentives of politicians at all levels of government and the resulting relationships between national and subnational politicians" often help us understand the decision to decentralize. They focus on national and subnational political elites, mostly affiliated with political parties, making strategic calculations about the electoral benefits of decentralizing.

Although the literature about why countries decentralize is relatively extensive and a consensus regarding the importance of domestic political aspects has emerged, two issues remain under-theorized. First, existing studies tend to privilege partisan or elite political dynamics between national and subnational actors. It is not clear how these dynamics play out in countries with weak political parties and/or few subnational elites. In some cases, subnational elites are not strong and cannot participate in bargaining processes. In other cases, there is no competitive party system or the political parties are quite weak. For example, Chile decentralized in an environment with few subnational political elites and a noncompetitive party system. In this case, conflicts and debates about decentralization tended to take place at the national level (Eaton 2004a and 2004b). Because subnational politicians were relatively "unimportant within their parties," national political calculations guided the decentralization process (Eaton 2004a, 197).

This book expands this analysis to another case with weak parties and few subnational elites: Peru. As the discussion of Peruvian politics will demonstrate, Peru represents a case with both few subnational political elites and weak political parties. What variables should we explore when trying to understand decentralization in a case like this? Do national political strategies explain outcomes? This book explores this question in more detail.

A second under-studied issue is the strategic decision-making process that leads to a *participatory* decentralization reform. Although scholars agree that the decision to decentralize is puzzling, I argue that the decision to design a PDR is even more so. In these cases, politicians not only devolve power to political counterparts, but also to societal actors such as nongovernmental organizations (NGOs), labor unions, community groups, and business associations. These groups are less understood and less predictable. They operate on a variety of different logics. Yet, they have been given formal power in subnational decision-making in Peru. What explains this decision? There is a dearth of research on this issue.

Only recently have scholars begun to address the issue of participation as a necessary component of decentralization. Specifically, there is a small but important body of literature that stresses the need for participatory institutions to ensure the success of decentralization reforms. To understand this argument, it is important to remember that for years it was assumed that decentralizing the state would improve democratic governance. These assumptions flow from Tocqueville's arguments about the importance of local governments in the American democratic experiment. Tocqueville's thought has influenced generations of scholars, who argue that local governments are more efficient and effective. Fiscal federalists[14] and research by scholars such as John Ackerman (2004), Harry Blair (2000), and Jeff Hunther and Anwar Shah (1998) demonstrate that local government can be more effective and responsive to citizens.

Skeptics, however, counter that Tocqueville and his followers may be overly optimistic. Often, those who support decentralization qualify their findings (for example, Grindle 2000). Other scholars and policy-makers have increasingly uncovered a series of *negative* effects of decentralization reforms, such as increased rent seeking and inefficiency (Bardhan and Mookherjee 1998, 2002; Oxhorn 2004), higher levels of corruption at the local level (Warner 2003), and a weakening of political parties (Sabatini 2003). As George Peterson (1997, 1) notes for the World Bank,

> [D]ecentralization does not guarantee that local governments will listen to the voices of ordinary citizens.... Decentralization created an opportunity for greater citizen control in governance, but other reforms must occur simultaneously if this opportunity is to be realized.

To mitigate these mixed results, a new wave of studies has come forth to argue that reformers should both decentralize *and* institute means of increasing participation in order to improve democratic governance. As Cheema (2007, 174) notes in his review of experiences in devolving power (one aspect of decentralization),

Both supporters and opponents of devolution agree that without adequate mechanisms for accountability and for combating corruption at the local level, devolution could lead to inefficiencies, misuse of resources, and loss of citizens' trust in the local political process.

Several countries, including Peru, are setting up participatory institutions in order to prevent these problems.

Two studies demonstrate the importance of participatory institutions in newly decentralized states. In their study of India, Bangladesh, Ghana, and Côte d'Ivoire, Crook and Manor (1998) explore government performance after decentralization reforms. They find that although citizen participation increased in all cases after a reform, government performance varied. Governments performed better where they enacted specific initiatives to increase participation. They find that "increased participation had a positive impact on the performance of decentralized institutions" (Crook and Manor 1998, 21). Dele Olowu and James Wunsch's (2004) work on seven African countries (South Africa, Botswana, Nigeria, Uganda, Ghana, Chad, and Kenya) puts forth similar conclusions. Their volume, which compares experiences with "democratic decentralization" in Africa, finds that two factors that facilitate strengthened democracy after decentralization are having effective local institutions that allow for collective action and having open and accountable political processes at the local level (Olowu and Wunsch 2004, 238–9). Participatory institutions could be one way of ensuring both.

Reformers seem to be listening to this argument and we are starting to witness an increase in participatory decentralization reforms around the world. Yet, there is very little scholarship on this particular type of reform. Several questions are left unresolved, such as: What is the best reform design? How effective are these reforms? When do they work well and when do they fail? Although this book cannot answer all of these questions, it does examine why national politicians stress participation in this reform as well as the factors that facilitate successful implementation.

Participatory Institutions

A small but growing body of literature—the second that this analysis complements—on participatory institutions does provide a useful starting point when looking at implementation issues. Several scholars have found that PIs can affect participation and democracy at the local level. For example, Rebecca

Abers's (2000) work on the participatory budget in Brazil has found that this experience has, in fact, empowered previously marginalized citizens, such as the poor and women. Her scholarship supports findings about New England's town hall meetings, such as Frank Bryan's (2004) ethnographic study of more than 1,500 meetings, which argues that these institutions do in fact foster democracy. Building on this work, several scholars have documented additional positive effects of participatory institutions, such as increased social spending in poor neighborhoods (Bruce 2004), increased associational activity at the local level (Baiocchi 2005; Bruce 2004), reduced clientelistic relations (Wampler and Avritzer 2004), engaged disempowered citizens such as women and the poor (Nylen 2003), increased participation over time (Bruce 2004), improved service delivery (Wagle and Shah 2003), and changed political culture (Baiocchi 2003, 2005; Bruce 2004; Nylen 2003; Wampler 2007a). Yet, as Brian Wampler (2007b) argues, many of these effects are contingent upon the successful functioning of the institutions.

In reality, not all PIs function well, and in many cases, these institutions have been implemented with varying degrees of success. Existing studies of PIs in Brazil and Bolivia have documented this variation (see Avritzer 2009; Goldfrank 2007b, forthcoming; Van Cott 2008; Wampler 2007a). The growing literature on PIs and governmental effectiveness points to at least five explanatory factors that could help us understand this variation.[15]

First, we might look to economic factors. The importance of this variable is brought to light by Benjamin Goldfrank's (2007a) comparative study of three cities (Montevideo, Uruguay; Porto Alegre, Brazil; and Caracas, Venezuela) that set up participatory budgets after a decentralization reform took place. In these cases, the degree of decentralization of resources and authority, measured partly as per capita municipal budget, explains why some cases worked better than others. In Peru, although the participatory budgets and CCRs were mandated as part of the decentralization reform, the amounts of the regional budgets do vary. Thus, we should explore whether richer regions are more participatory.

A second and related variable that emerges as potentially important to explore is the institutional capacity of the government. Do governments that function better implement better PIs? Although this variable rarely is discussed explicitly in the literature on PI experiences, it is worth considering due to the increased emphasis on institutions in political analysis. I explore this variable in light of how well regional governments spend their budgets.

A third variable that might explain variation is political party support. Most of the well-researched cases of PIs are put in place by leftist leadership (see Chavez and Goldfrank 2004). For example, one of the earliest cases of participatory budgeting, in Porto Alegre, Brazil, was designed by the leftist Workers' Party in an effort to make municipal decision-making more transparent. Several other examples of participatory planning, such as Villa El Salvador in Peru,[16] Kerala in India,[17] and the participatory budget process in Ecuador,[18] have all been promoted by the left. Thus, some might posit that leftist leadership would promote the more successful cases of PI implementation.

However, as this practice expands no clear link between leftist parties and successful experiences is emerging in comparative studies of a larger number of cases (see, for example, Avritzer 2002; Nylen 2003; Peruzzotti and Selee 2009). In Brazil, the participatory budget began as a Workers' Party initiative (see, for example, Avritzer 2002; Bruce 2004; Gret and Sintomer 2005; Wampler 2007a), yet the practice has expanded to municipalities run by politicians from political parties across the political spectrum and in some cases is working well. This contradictory evidence renders the Peru case even more important. Peru's reform took place under what some would call a centrist administration (Toledo), and although the left in Congress promoted the PIs, they were not the only groups supporting their institutionalization. Further, regional presidents represent a variety of ideological and partisan backgrounds, allowing us to explore the role that political party affiliation and leftist politics play in explaining successful outcomes.

Several recent studies are starting to argue that leadership, a fourth potential explanatory variable, explains successful PI implementation. For example, Donna Lee Van Cott's (2008) recent comparison of Ecuadorian and Bolivian PIs finds that leadership holds explanatory power when looking at why some are more successful than others. Merilee Grindle's (2007) comparison of thirty Mexican municipalities, representing a variety of party affiliations, also demonstrates that leadership, or what she calls "state entrepreneurship,"[19] has the strongest effect on local governance performance. And, as Grindle's (2007) study demonstrates, leaders are not always promoting a partisan agenda. These two recent studies join a growing list of scholars who have been pointing to the important role that committed leadership has played in ensuring PI success (Abers 1998, 2003; Avritzer 2007; Conterno n.d.; Fung and Wright 2003; Malena 2009; Wampler 2007a, 2008).

Finally, Avritzer (2009, 2007), Baiocchi (2005), Heller (2001), and Wampler (2007a, 2008) also encourage us to explore the nature of civil society when trying to explain variation in outcomes.[20] This can be divided into two aspects: (1) historical experience with organizing; (2) more recent organizational experiences within the subnational civil society sector. The first aspect, historical experience with organizing, emerges from a growing body of literature on social capital. This literature suggests that over time, organizing can build networks that foster trust and "norms of reciprocity."[21] Some literature on social capital suggests that historical experience with organization and the emergency of social capital might explain varied levels of governmental performance. The most important study supporting this finding is Robert Putnam's (1993) study on efficacy of government in Italy. He argues that the historical tendency to form civic organizations in the north led to higher levels of social capital (as compared to the south), which then explains variation in subnational government effectiveness. Do his findings translate to the Peruvian experience with participatory institutions?

Other studies focus on more recent levels of organization and coordination in contemporary civil society, which might also help us understand variation in PI experiences. Several studies point to the important role that the civil society sector has played in ensuring these institutions' success. For example, in his comparative study of participatory decentralization reforms and the institutions that are set up in Kerela (India), Porto Alegre (Brazil), and South Africa, Patrick Heller (2001) finds that civil society is "critical" to the process. Brian Wampler (2007a) argues civil society (and citizen) response to participatory institutions partly explain variation in experience in Brazil. Does some aspect of the current-day civil society sector help us understand PI success?

Later chapters in this book borrow from, build on, and, in some cases, correct all of these scholarly findings. The Peru case allows us to test the explanatory potential of all of these variables as well as compare PI implementation as part of a mandated, top-down decentralization reform. Most of the literature on PIs focuses on experiences that emerge *after* decentralization. Few works ask if the same conditions might be at work even given different legal contexts. For now, in order to understand Peru's attempt to mix participatory and representative democracy in one system, we must look more closely at several aspects of national-level Peruvian politics.

PERUVIAN POLITICS: A PRIMER

Peru's political system is often characterized as a fragile democracy with in-effective and weak state institutions, high levels of corruption, and severe leadership problems. It has a long history of centralized power and resources. Societal actors have distant relations with the national government.[22] And political parties and citizen participation have historically been quite weak.

As Peruvian historians Carlos Contreras and Marcos Cueto (2004) document, like most Latin American countries, after independence "high classes" governed Peru, and the general population was excluded from politics. Charles Kenney (2004, 7) writes that participation from 1895 to 1914 "was quite limited: the percentage of the total population casting votes rose from just 0.1 percent in 1895 to . . . about 4 percent in 1908." In the nineteenth century, oligarchic families were, to some extent, spread around the country. Over time, as regional economies weakened and resources began to be centralized in the capital city, wealth and power began to slowly concentrate in Lima. People moved to Lima in search of education and jobs. Lima's population doubled from 1908 to 1930, primarily due to migration from Andean areas. By 1950, migration from the Andes led to 40 percent of Peru's population living in Lima and the more hospitable coastal cities (Contreras and Cueto 2004). Yet participation in political life remained quite low (Kenney 2004, 7).

In the early 1900s, social movements began to emerge in opposition to the oligarchy's rule, such as an indigenous, student, and worker movements. Another important movement, with origins in Mexico—the Alianza Popular Revolucionaria Americana (American Popular Revolutionary Alliance, or APRA)—emerged to unite students and workers to pressure for a more democratic political system.[23] APRA emerged as a more powerful social force as it organized labor and *campesinos* to pressure the oligarchy, now running the state, for more rights. By the 1930s, APRA formalized into a political party and continued to press for change in the oligarchic system. Yet it was not allowed to fully participate in the political sphere until 1962 (Kenney 2004). As the political system slowly opened up in the 1930s and 1940s, class struggles began to take place in many areas of Peru. Several additional political parties were created during this period, including the Acción Popular (Popular Action, or AP) on the center-right and several smaller parties on the left.[24]

As the century progressed, the political system expanded even more. In the 1960s, student organizations became more active in national life, and the first NGOs emerged (Portocarrero et al. 2002). Yet, as Contreras and Cueto (2004) note, these movements emerged in the context of a society with deep social divisions and weak institutions.

Fernando Belaúnde Terry was elected president in 1963 with a mandate to respond to these movements' demands. Because many felt that Belaúnde was not moving fast enough, in 1968 the military, led by Juan Velasco, overthrew Belaúnde's democratically elected government to implement some of the more progressive reforms that he had promised but not delivered. A rare example of a leftist military government in Latin America, the Velasco regime undertook a comprehensive land reform that restructured peasant-landowner relations.[25] This reform also served to push former landowners and regional elites to migrate to Lima in search of new economic opportunities, further centralizing the economic and political resources in the capital city (Díez Hurtado 2003).

During this period, the military government also began to promote organizational initiatives to increase popular participation (Arce Espinoza 2004; Remy 2005). The roots of the regime's philosophy lay in the corporate model, which was gaining popularity around the hemisphere.[26] For example, as part of the agrarian reform, the government organized *campesinos* into cooperatives that managed and worked the land.[27] Although most of the cooperatives eventually broke up, this organizational initiative did slightly empower some emerging civil society movements during the period of military rule.

Because the military regime did not succeed in meeting many of its goals, a transition to democracy began in 1978.[28] A Constitutional Assembly rewrote the constitution and paved the way for democratic elections in 1980. Fernando Belaúnde Terry was reelected and Peru transitioned back to democratic rule.[29]

During the early and mid-1980s, scholars document a "weakly institutionalized" party system, which included the "populist" APRA, the AP in the center, and the Popular Christian Party on the right (Levitsky and Cameron 2003; Kenney 2004). The left also grew in numbers and strength—forming a coalition called the Izquierda Unida (United Left, or IU). At the same time, organizational activity increased even more.[30] Although this trend did not take place evenly around the country, in many regions organizational initiatives increased dramatically in response to several economic and societal crises plaguing the country.[31] As later chapters describe, IU leaders encouraged citizen participation in several cities around the country, thereby laying the foundation for many of the participatory institutions that exist today. However, these initiatives could not stem the continued migration to the city. Rural masses as well as regional elites continued to move to Lima seeking safety from the violence, jobs in the growing national state apparatus, and/or educational opportunities.

In 1985, APRA's leader, Alan García, was elected the first *aprista* (a member of the APRA party) president. The García years proved extremely difficult. García overspent state funds and could not control inflation, and the economy slid into crisis (especially after 1987).[32] He angered the international and domestic finance community when he suspended Peru's debt payments and nationalized banks. In addition to these severe economic problems, the Shining Path, one of the region's most violent leftist guerrilla organizations posed an increased threat to Peruvians.[33] The García regime was also plagued by allegations of corruption, culminating in his leaving the country almost two years after stepping down in 1990.

One of the only policies García managed to implement was the country's first decentralization reform, discussed in more depth in the next chapter. This reform allowed for regional elections for the first time in history (1989 and 1990)—some would say as a last-ditch effort to improve APRA's popularity and status around the country. However, decentralization could not begin to rectify the myriad problems facing the country, and Alberto Fujimori cut short the effort just a few years later.

By the late 1980s, the political party system had collapsed due to the economic crisis and increased violence as well as weak organizational structure, poor leadership, and citizens' increased distrust in the party system.[34] The IU coalition also dissolved, due to ideological and personal conflicts. Independent movements began to play a more important role in channeling citizen demands.

As the 1990 presidential elections approached,[35] Peruvians were searching for a solution to their numerous social, economic, and political problems. In 1990, Alberto Fujimori—a political outsider—ran on an anti-elite, antipolitics platform. His movement won the presidency by a landslide; the Peruvian electorate sent a clear message that they were tired of the traditional political class, primarily residing in and ruling from Lima, and sought change.[36]

The Fujimori years proved detrimental to most organizational initiatives and Peru's already weak civil society. For example, labor organizations were systematically weakened (Contreras and Cueto 2004; Larco and Mejía 1995), and his regime co-opted many grassroots organizations, especially women's organizations that existed to feed their communities (Blondet 1999). Fujimori distrusted NGOs and other professional organizations that he considered potential sources of political competition and/or leftist activities (Castillo 1996; McNulty 1996). Further, the party system "decomposed to a degree that surpassed even the most notoriously fragmented systems in Latin America" (Levitsky and Cameron 2003, 1).

After implementing one of the most severe structural adjustment packages in Latin America—called "Fuji-shock"[37]—Fujimori continued ongoing efforts to rid the country of terrorism. In 1992, as conflict with Congress intensified, Fujimori shut down his own government, ostensibly to fight terrorism more forcefully, in what is commonly referred to as his *auto-golpe* (self-coup).[38] For many analysts, this act sounded a clear warning that Fujimori himself valued centralized rule and stability more than democracy (Burt 1992; Mauceri 1995; McClintock 1993). However, the Peruvian public supported this move, and Fujimori continued to enjoy high levels of popularity, especially after Abimael Guzmán, the leader of the Shining Path, was captured later that year.

After his self-coup, Fujimori quickly oversaw the writing of a new constitution, which reorganized Congress, reformed the judiciary, and recentralized government.[39] The fledgling regional governments, recently empowered by García, were replaced by authorities appointed by Fujimori. Years of anti-democratic reforms and repression ensued as Fujimori implemented his own "direct democracy," creating changes that superseded all existing institutions to work directly with the populace.[40] "Fuji-shock" increased poverty and reduced the time and resources that people could commit to organizing. Thus, Fujimori's structural adjustment and anti-democratic practices created severe challenges for the already weakened civil society sector.

Fujimori was easily reelected in 1995 and immediately began to push his reelection project.[41] He would run again in 2000, arguing that his 1990–1995 term should not count against the two terms (the legal limit) under the new constitution. The 2000 elections were shrouded in the government's manipulation of media, public works, and other elected officials (Conaghan 2002, 2001). International and domestic election monitors reported irregularities in the electoral process. In the final weeks before the election, the Organization of American States sent a high-level election observation mission to monitor these problems.[42] The first round took place as scheduled, even as international observers voiced concern.[43] Irregularities ensued. Even as exit polls reported that Alejandro Toledo—a Stanford-educated economist and self-professed "Indian"—was running neck and neck with Fujimori, many feared that the

National Elections Board (controlled by Fujimori) would report a majority of votes for Fujimori.

Amid international pressure, a second round was called. However, it was clear that the playing field was not even and Toledo withdrew from this round in protest. Domestic and international election observers followed his lead. Because he was the only candidate, Fujimori easily won the second round. Upon his taking power, a high level of opposition to his third term already existed. For example, Toledo's newly formed political party, Perú Posible, and several regional and national civil society actors coordinated the Marcha de los Cuatro Suyos (March of the Four "Suyos"[44]), a well-attended protest that took place on Peru's Independence Day—also the day of Fujimori's inauguration. Yet, even given the domestic discontent and international skepticism, Fujimori still assumed power for a third five-year term in July 2000.

Shortly thereafter, scandal erupted. Allegations of arms trafficking and the release of videos capturing Fujimori's right-hand man, Vladimir Montesinos, bribing a congressman came to light.[45] Later that same year, Fujimori left the country and faxed his resignation from Japan. Congress immediately declared him unfit to govern and removed him from office. These events opened the path for desperately needed democratic reform for the first time since Fujimori took power in 1990.

As those who study transitions to democracy would expect, civil society did organize during the push to topple Fujimori.[46] Regional organizations reactivated (for example, Loreto and Moquegua) or formed (for example, Cusco), and national level protests—such as the Marcha de los Cuatro Suyos—became more frequent. Thus, in the late 1990s, civil society became more organized and active in Lima and in many regions around the country. However, in accordance with many scholars' predictions about transitions (for example, O'Donnell and Schmitter 1986), after the activity died down, the high levels of organization did not continue. At the same time, political parties remained weak and independent movements gained even more momentum.

Immediately after Fujimori fled, Valentín Paniagua, the head of Congress, assumed the presidency for a one-year transition post. The transition government immediately set out to address Peru's weak civil society, pervasive corruption, and citizens' disillusionment with representative democracy. Because of his extensive experience in Peruvian politics and his unassuming demeanor, Paniagua enjoyed high levels of popularity and political support during his transition government. He quickly assembled a transition government with a diverse group of professionals, many of whom hailed from the civil society sector. His government began to systematically rebuild democratic institutions and attack corruption by passing reforms that stressed transparency, participation, and accountability.

Meanwhile, candidates prepared for another election in 2001. This time, Alan García, still popular due to his charismatic style, returned to Peru and threw his hat into the ring. In a hotly contested second-round race, Toledo—with 53 percent of the vote—beat García. He immediately promised to implement several reforms to strengthen Peru's fragile democracy and to continue to clean up the government. He vowed to attack an extremely centralized political and economic system. This would prove difficult, as Lima's population made up 31.9 percent of the nation's total population and generated approximately 50 percent of the nation's GNP (Gonzales de Olarte 2004). Power, resources, and people were inordinately located in the capital city, thereby draining resources. Peruvians living in areas outside the capital felt isolated and ignored by the national government. Hundreds continued to arrive in Lima, seeking basic services and jobs. Thus, Toledo faced several challenges—including a fragile democracy, widespread corruption, and extreme centralization of power and resources in the capital city.

Toledo's inauguration marked an important moment in Peru's recent history. Analysts expressed great hope for his government. Unfortunately, his performance did not always live up to these inflated expectations. His government was plagued by extremely low levels of public support, perhaps the lowest in the country's recent history. Toledo and his government were shaken by scandal after scandal—hyped by what often was called the Fujimori-Montesinos "mafia"[47]—including allegations of illegitimate children, nepotism, corruption, forgery, Cabinet crises, and drug use. The only major reform that subsequently made it through the political maze was the decentralization reform analyzed in this book.

The 2006 elections did little to raise the public's hopes. García and Fujimori—two of Peru's most corrupt ex-presidents—often did surprisingly well in the polls. Name calling and insults among the candidates dominated the elections. A political "outsider" Ollanta Humala, leader of the Peruvian National Party and affiliated with the *etnocacerista* movement,[48] ran with increasing support from the poor and disempowered in Peru. In the end, Alan García resumed his place as president of Peru amid uncertainty about whether he would resort to his old ways or whether he was truly a "reformed man."[49]

November 2006 also marked the end of the first regional governments' administrations as new officials were elected and took power in 2007. Regional movements gained even more strength in these elections, and Peru's national political parties had a very poor showing (Ballón 2006; Leyton 2006). This trend continued in the October 2010 regional elections. These elections demonstrated that national political parties do not represent the nation and that regional voters prefer those with local and regional experience in tackling their specific problems.

The second García administration has sent mixed signals about its commitment to both decentralization and participation. In 2007, García announced a "decentralization shock" to push the process forward; however, critics noted that his plans did not encompass strengthening the new forms of participation. Of course, most of the same problems continue to plague the country, including weak political parties, weak state institutions, and widespread poverty. The new participatory institutions, designed as part of the 2002 decentralization reform, are some of the very few in place that could help rectify these problems.

RESEARCH METHODOLOGY

Two methodological devices guide this work. First, I rely heavily on the case study method, which is considered a particularly effective means for identifying causal mechanisms in situations of causal complexity.[50] As Robert Yin (1994, 1) writes, "Case studies are the preferred strategy when 'how' or 'why' questions are being posed, when the investigator has little control over events, and when the focus is on a contemporary phenomenon within some real-life context." Peru is a particularly interesting case of a participatory decentralization reform as it sets up several means to increase civil society's participation in the new subnational governments. Because the decentralization reform is an ongoing process in a complex social environment, the case study allows us to effectively delve into several "how" and "why" questions.

The second methodological device employed throughout this study is the structured, focused comparison. A common criticism of the single case study is that findings are hard to generalize due to lack of variation in the dependent variable and the fact that only one unit is studied. To overcome these problems, scholars propose the structured, focused within-case comparative method, which consists of asking similar questions across smaller units within a single case (George 1979; George and Bennett 2005; Lijphart 1971; Snyder 2001). Peru's twenty-five regions provide an excellent opportunity for comparative research on the implementation of PDRs. Comparing regions in Peru allows us to hold constant some key variables across cases while searching for explanatory factors when we see divergent outcomes.

The third part of this book, therefore, presents an in-depth look at six regional experiences in Peru. I used several case selection criteria when deciding what regions to study. First, following Peruvian custom, I wanted to represent each of the diverse geographical areas in the country. Peru is generally divided into the coast, the Andean highlands, and the jungle. Also based on Peruvian custom, I further divide the highlands region into north, central, and south and include a region from each.

When deciding where to go within each geographical region, to the extent possible I chose my cases using what John Stuart Mill (1925) coined the "method of difference." Within the geographical regions, I looked for cases with similar socioeconomic characteristics. The Andean and jungle regions—including Cajamarca, Ayacucho, Cusco, and Loreto—are similar in many regards. Each region generates a very small percentage of the country's GDP in any given year. Their citizens are relatively poor and less educated than those who live in larger cities such as Lima. The two coastal regions—Lambayeque and Moquegua—have fewer people living in poverty, which is typical of coastal areas, but still generate a very small percentage of the annual GDP. Their citizens' education levels are higher than those of the Andean and jungle areas, but still low relative to those who live in the country's urban center, Lima. Table 1.1 captures the different aspects of each of the cases that contributed to its selection.

Table 1.1. Case selection criteria

Region	Population (as of 2005)	Percent total poverty (2004)	Percent literacy (aged 15 years and older) 2003	Percent secondary education in 2003	Percent GDP (2007)
Ayacucho	619,338	64.9	71.84	75.53	0.9
Cajamarca	1,359,023	74.2	77.81	56.58	2.4
Cusco	1,171,503	59.2	83.74	68.11	2.4
Lambayeque	1,091,535	46.7	90.2	81.33	2.5
Loreto	884,144	62.7	92.01	64.83	1.8
Moquegua	159,306	37.2	93.09	93.28	1.3
Lima Metropolitan	6,954,583	N/A	96.93	95.68	47.0
National	26,152,265	51.6	89.7	80.42	100.0

SOURCES: All data, excluding percent poverty and GDP, are available at http://www.mesadeconcertacion.org.pe/indicadores.php (accessed June 18, 2008); Percent GDP is taken from "INEI: Cuentas Nacionales del Perú: Producto Bruto Interno por Departamentos 2001–2007," http://www1.inei.gob.pe/biblioineipub/bancopub/Est/Lib0784/index.htm, p. 20 (accessed September 8, 2009).

All of the regions are governed by the same legal framework that increased their powers as part of Peru's PDR. Yet, as my fieldwork in the region shows, the outcome, that is, each region's experience with participatory institutions, varies. When trying to understand this variation, we can safely assume that economic and educational differences are not explaining variation in experience with the new institutions. Part 2 of this book explores the factors that do explain this outcome.

DATA COLLECTION

This book is the product of almost fifteen years of researching Peruvian politics. I began to study Peruvian politics in 1996 when I traveled there to document the nonprofit sector during Fujimori's regime. During 2004 and 2005, I spent eighteen months in Peru undertaking fieldwork for this book. During this time, I traveled periodically to the six regions, spending approximately three weeks in each region's capital city, where I interviewed politicians, activists, nongovernmental organization employees, academics, international development professionals, and state government officials. I visited local libraries and found studies of local politics that were not available in Lima. I observed participatory budget sessions and located and interviewed elected members of the new Regional Coordination Councils. In all events I attended, I was the only outside observer present. Over this period of eighteen months, I interviewed more than 120 people familiar with regional politics[51] and observed several days' worth of participatory events. Few scholars have traveled this extensively around the country documenting political life.

After leaving Peru in 2005, I followed events and conducted a follow-up research trip in late 2007. During that trip, I gathered additional documents and interviewed several experts on the topic. Through 2008 and 2009, I continued to correspond with my contacts in the regions to update the information I had gathered on the participatory institutions. And finally, in 2010, I interviewed former president Alejandro Toledo in Washington, D.C.

OVERVIEW

The chapters that follow help us understand the 2002 reform and how it unfolded in the four years following its passage. Chapter 2 places the reform in the historical context of decentralization in Peru. It describes the reform in general and the participatory aspects of the reform specifically. It provides the first comprehensive English-language description of decentralization in Peru that includes the legal framework of the 2002 reform.

Part 2 of the book analyzes the reform's design and implementation at the national level. Chapter 3 explains why politicians passed one of the most ambitious participatory decentralization reforms in history by reforming Peru's constitution. Chapter 4 documents the political strategies that explain the particular design that governs the two participatory institutions studied in this book. It links political strategies to design outcomes, then documents how the ensuing design constrains effectiveness in the case of the Regional Coordination Councils.

Part 3 of the book explores and analyzes the implementation of the reform in six regions of Peru. Chapter 5 documents the PIs in the six regions to explore how the CCRs and participatory budgets unfolded in the first regional presidents' administrations (2003–2006). The chapter demonstrates that despite a common legal framework, the PIs are being implemented in very different ways. For example, in Lambayeque and Cusco, the regional government complied with the legal framework and is responding to citizens' needs. In Ayacucho and Loreto, the regional government did not comply with the reform's mandates and showed little interest in doing so. In the remaining cases, Cajamarca and Moquegua, the outcomes are somewhat mixed.

Chapter 6 explores this variation in more depth and offers a better understanding of the factors that condition the successful implementation of participatory institutions. This chapter then analyzes the six variables, introduced earlier, that might explain successful implementation of PIs in the six regions. Part 4, Chapter 7 concludes with some thoughts regarding the implications of these arguments.

Overall, Peru's experience has surprised many. Peru continues to push decentralization forward, slowly transferring more power and resources to the new governments. Participatory institutions grant societal actors both voice and vote in regional decision-making, marking a radical change from politics as usual in this country. These participatory institutions, especially in places like Cusco and Lambayeque, are emerging as one of the most successful aspects of the reform. Peruvians are participating in unprecedented numbers, in part due to the institutions described and analyzed in this book (PRODES 2007c). These efforts have the potential to help stem the crisis of governance that is facing countries throughout Latin America and around the world. By analyzing this experiment in depth, this book elucidates the possibilities and limitations of the decision to restructure political systems in a way that promotes formal participation.

2 PERU'S 2002 PARTICIPATORY DECENTRALIZATION REFORM

IN 2001 AND 2002, newly elected politicians faced several challenges, including how to move power and resources to other parts of the country and how to clean up the political system. A consensus existed regarding the need to decentralize, but the specifics were lacking. This chapter describes past efforts and the present decentralization package that emerged by late 2003. It lays the foundation for the questions that are addressed in the following chapters, such as why politicians decided to pass this particular reform and how it is unfolding in the regions.

DECENTRALIZING PERU: AN ONGOING PROCESS

Like most Latin American countries, Peru has a long history of highly central-ized government.[1] The Spanish colonial system centralized power, and during much of Peru's republican history, the oligarchy and the country's economic sys-tem reinforced this system. As noted in the previous chapter, by the late 1900s, political elites, power, and resources were highly concentrated in Lima. Before the mid–twentieth century, there had been some attempts to decentralize ad-ministrative powers; however, these generally failed.[2] By the end of the twentieth century, Peruvians had stepped up their efforts to decentralize their administra-tive and political structures. However, as Peruvian analyst Manuel Dammert (2003b) argues, these efforts are also best described as "unfulfilled promises."

Almost every Peruvian constitution has made some formal nod to the importance of a decentralized state,[3] yet the most prominent efforts to codify this process have taken place in the latter part of the twentieth century. Since 1979, the constitution has maintained that the state should be "unitary, representative, and decentralized" and makes at least passing reference to regional and local governments.[4] The most recent efforts, analyzed in this book, build on or modify language in the 1979 and 1993 constitutions.

In 1979, as part of the transition to democracy, the Constitutional Assembly formally set up regional and local governments in the new constitution.[5] Nickson (1995: 239) argues that this push to decentralize came from two primary actors: the political left, which "saw strengthening of municipal authority as a mechanism both for promoting citizen participation and for obtaining better service provision"; and technocrats "who hoped for a more efficient, cost-effective, and coordinated provision of basic services through stronger municipal structures."

From the democratic elections in 1980 until 1984, there was little movement toward pushing decentralization forward. This changed in 1984 when the Belaúnde government developed a National Regionalization Plan and Congress passed several laws to clarify the nature of subnational governments (for example, Laws 23,853, 23,878, and 24,030).[6] Although the laws were general in nature, they did specify basic functions of regional and local governments and allowed municipalities to generate some income (Ojeda Segovia 2003; Zas Friz Burga 2004). The local governments were set up formally for the first time; however, they had very little real power and were administratively weak.

Peru's First Regionalization (1987–1992)

The biggest push to move decentralization forward took place under Alan García's first administration (1985–1990). Although this study does not explicitly compare García's efforts with the 2002 reform, there are several aspects of this experience that help us better understand the current efforts. In many ways, the 2002 reform picked up where this early effort left off. And in other ways, reformers made a conscious effort to learn from the mistakes made in the late 1980s. Thus, a brief description of the first regionalization is important to the analysis of the current reform.

García's first step toward implementing decentralized government began with the modification of the regional legislation in 1987. Law 24,650 established twelve regions based on economic corridors and proximity.[7] In 1989, five regions elected governments, and in 1990, the remaining seven held elections (Adrianzén 2003). APRA—García's political party—and the left won most of the regions (Contreras 2002). This was the first time in history that Peru's regional governments were elected and installed.

The design of this reform influenced the 2002 efforts in several ways. The combined legal package that emerged from 1979 through the end of the García administration set up a parliamentary system with a regional assembly, a regional council, and a president (Bensa Morales 2002; García 1989). The regional councils were made up of the president and his or her secretaries and functioned like a cabinet (Zas Friz Burga 2004, 65). Regions held assembly elections, then the assembly members elected the regional presidents and vice presidents. The assembly consisted of directly elected officials (not to exceed 40 percent of the body), provincial mayors (who were also elected in a separate election), and representatives of civil society organizations, primarily social and cultural institutions (not to exceed 30 percent and in proportion to the rural population of each region). CSOs elected representatives for the assembly. The types of organizations that could participate in these elections included: *campesino*, agricultural, university, cultural, professional, neighborhood, parent, and women's organizations (Bensa Morales 2002). This parliamentary-style system created a system in which the executive branch (the president and the regional council) depended on the assembly to get their work done.

Why did the reformers include these civil society organizations in the assembly? Two factors contributed to this decision. First, historical trends in Peru stressed a loosely adapted version of corporatism and not liberal or individualistic perceptions of citizenship. For example, during his military regime in the 1970s, Velasco set up self-managed cooperatives to run the newly restructured *haciendas* and farms. Thus, the design built on the corporatist model that had already been implemented in Peru during the military regime and was gaining popularity in other Latin American countries.

Second, the design fit with the political interests and ideology of two prevailing political powers of that period, the APRA and the left. It conformed to official APRA doctrine—as expressed by Víctor Raúl Haya de la Torre, the founding father of APRA, and even García himself—which stressed increased popular power and granting more political space to the masses.[8] And many of these social organizations, such as the agricultural organizations and labor unions, were either formally or informally *aprista*, that is, aligned with the APRA party. The growing leftist movement in Peru also recognized that many leftist activists participate in social organizations. And including civil society tended to correspond to their ideological leanings as well. Thus, interests converged and social organizations assumed formal powers in the regional governments set up under García. This experience partly influenced debates about participation that took place in Congress when designing the current decentralization reform.

García pushed forward the issue largely due to his own political interests. The APRA is the oldest and most institutionalized party in Peru and is one of the few parties with a relatively strong organizational base outside of Lima (especially in the north). Thus, as García was losing popularity in Lima during the second half of his tenure, he was aggressively transferring power and resources to regional governments—many of which he correctly anticipated would eventually be in the hands of APRA. This represented a last-ditch attempt to strengthen his power base even as he was losing support at the national level. In addition to boosting his regional support, the reform would provide APRA with a concrete achievement to flaunt during the 1990 presidential elections.

Most agree that García's decentralization efforts failed miserably. Johnny Zas Friz Burga (2004: 84–90), a Peruvian legal scholar, highlights two sets of problems: the legal framework and the political context during this period. Problems with the legal framework included the following:

- There was an overlap of functions among the different levels of government;
- Regional assembly members were elected in different ways (some were directly elected, some were elected by CSOs, and others were elected as mayors), which led to competing constituencies and tensions among these officials;
- The central government did not transfer sufficient funds, and regional and local governments were not able to generate their own financial resources;[9]
- The central government had very rigid demands in terms of the administration of the few programs that were devolved to the regions;
- The reform re-created centralism in regions by setting up new governments in the regional capitals;[10]
- There was no body to resolve conflicts that emerged during the process;[11] and
- There were no mechanisms to coordinate activities or programs that took place at both the local and regional levels and/or in two or more regions.

Other problems directly resulted from the multifaceted crises that were facing the country. Zas Friz Burga (2004) highlights the following:

- The national context, including a crisis of political parties, political instability, political violence, and economic instability;

- The population's unsatisfied expectations regarding how regional governments should be able to improve quality of life (unsatisfied primarily because of the lack of resources and inefficient administration of the new governments);
- The regional politicians' (and their technical teams') lack of experience; and
- Weak alliances and/or coalitions—typically needed to effectively govern in parliamentary politics—in the regional assemblies.

When interviewed for this study, governmental and nongovernmental officials agreed that the first regionalization failed. Furthermore, most noted an additional problem: the reform was entirely too bureaucratic. The presence of both an assembly and a council—with potentially overlapping responsibilities that never were clarified in later legislation or in practice—made the governing process too difficult. Many interviewees noted that there were so many levels of government that it was hard to actually get anything done. One congressman, a high-level APRA official, stated that the problem of too many assemblies and no concrete results, that is, *asambleísmo*, was a "total nightmare." To further complicate the system, the reform granted the national executive veto power, adding another layer to the bureaucratic structure. However, as one Peruvian expert noted in an interview, Fujimori cut short these efforts too soon to judge whether they would have worked in the long run. It is clear that when Fujimori made the decision to recentralize the state structure (see below), the public did not clamor to keep the regional governments intact.

The reform attempts in the 1980s set an important institutional precedent for the reforms that are taking place today. In some respects the differences are striking, as the present design package makes a concerted attempt to avoid the mistakes of the past (such as the overly bureaucratic structures and the problems inherent in parliamentary systems) by setting up a presidential system in the new regions. The regional assembly was dropped from the institutional design and reformers opted instead for the much smaller regional council. The regional council is very different as well. Members are directly elected and are tasked with the legal and fiscal duties that the assembly undertook in the previous reform. Also, instead of immediately forming twelve macroregions through a top-down decision, the macro-regionalization process will take place over time. Yet there is also continuity—especially evident in the decision to institutionalize the role of civil society in subnational governments.

Fujimori: Recentralization in a Neoliberal Regime

Through his *auto-golpe* (self-coup) and the 1993 constitution, Fujimori reversed these embryonic regionalization efforts. Part of Fujimori's *auto-golpe* in 1992 included closing down the regional governments and replacing them with seven-member Consejos Transitorios Administrativos Regionales (CTARs), or Transitory Regional Administration Councils. The CTAR members, appointed by Fujimori, reported directly to the president's Ministry.[12] Municipal governments also suffered under his regime. As Catherine Conaghan (2005, 79–80) documents:

> To reduce the resources in the hand of potential rivals, Fujimori tightened the central government's grip over discretionary public spending. In December 1994, [the Fujimori-controlled] congress passed Legislative Decree 766, the Municipal Tax Law, which completely restructured municipal finances. The law ... made municipal governments more dependent on the central government via the Municipal Compensation Fund. .... Under the new system, Lima's share of transfers from the central government dive-bombed; municipal income decreased by 40 percent in 1994.

Slowly Fujimori recentralized power and weakened subnational governments.

Fujimori also centralized power through his economic reforms. Efraín Gonzales de Olarte (2000) argues that Fujimori's structural adjustment policies reinforced "neo-centralism" by weakening the economies of cities and areas that were not part of the "center" (that is, Lima and its immediate areas).[13] Furthermore, as noted in the previous chapter, Fujimori systematically weakened all intermediary agents that existed between him and the populace, such as political parties and civil society organizations. For example, labor organizations lost many of their members after legislation made the labor pool more flexible and increased reliance on short-term contracts. NGOs faced new restrictions and regulations that governed their development projects as well. In the end, these legal, political, and economic structures led to dependent regions and a highly central political system.

"Direct Democracy" and Innovations at the Local Level

In spite of the economic and political recentralization that took place in the 1990s, several initiatives did emerge to stimulate citizen participation at the local level. After the coup, international actors pressured Fujimori to democratize, and he adopted some ways to increase citizen participation. Specifically, the Citizen Participation Law (Law 26,300), passed in 1993, stipulates that citizens are legally allowed to initiate referenda and recall officials at the local level.[14] As part of Fujimori's "direct democracy," the regime encouraged direct participation in development activities, such as social projects, the "glass of milk" program, and soup kitchens supported by the state. This meant that some grassroots organizational activity did take place at the local level during his regime.[15]

During this period, several local initiatives emerged to encourage citizen participation. These experiences also shaped the institutions that were designed in the most recent decentralization reform. Local initiatives tended to take one of two forms. First, several community roundtables, called *mesas de concertación* (hereafter referred to as *mesas*), sprang up in several municipalities around the country. The *mesas* brought together representatives from the government and civil society in a formal space to discuss and come to agreement, or *concertar*,[16] on community issues.[17] For example, governmental representatives from the health, education, and environment sectors met regularly with NGOs and/or grassroots organizations to discuss programs in a particular sector.

One of the most successful examples took place in Cajamarca, where the municipal government, led by Luis Guerrero—who was later elected to Congress and served on the committee that designed the current decentralization reform—organized a *mesa* to address local development issues in a coordinated and participatory way.[18] During the 1990s, similar initiatives emerged in regions such as Cusco, Huancavelica, and San Martín (Grompone 2004; Panfichi 2007). Although these were often locally driven, implementers also relied on technical assistance from national NGOs with funds from international donors. Advocates argue that these roundtables coordinate development efforts and, potentially, improve state-society relations by bringing diverse actors to the same table to discuss policy.

Second, means of local participatory planning, such as developing strategic plans and experimenting with participatory budgeting, became more prevalent. Several communities had interesting experiences with participatory planning (discussed below) that were taking place completely independent of the central government. These were emerging in Peru at the same time that participatory governance methods were becoming more prominent around Latin America. Thus, while the macro-political context was stressing the concentration of power in the central government, several local experiences with citizen participation in governance were taking place around the country. It is important to note, however, that these experiences were mostly very local and never expanded beyond the subnational level.

As discontent about Fujimori's anti-democratic practices increased, discourse about the need to decentralize increased as well. According to surveys in the late 1990s in several cities around the country, including Lima, respondents considered Fujimori's government highly centralized and blamed the lack of development in other areas of the country on him (Adrianzén 2003). Several national leaders from the civil society community advocated, through publications, conferences, and articles, for a decentralized state. The regional movements that existed also began to call for decentralization. For example, in 1998, regional activists and intellectuals in Cusco began to meet and discuss several issues, including the need to democratize and decentralize. Over time, they developed a formal decentralization proposal in conferences and fora and presented it nationally at the Conferencia Nacional Sobre Desarrollo Social (National Social Development Conference, or CONADES), an annual forum that brings together civil society and government representatives to talk about issues of national importance.[19] During the 2000 campaign for the presidential elections, decentralization became one of the main slogans.

The Transition Back to Democracy

Although Valentín Paniagua, the transition president, recognized the importance of decentralization, he could not actively promote it because of the transitory nature of the regime and the immediate need to clean up the state that Fujimori left behind. Paniagua did, however, set up a commission to study the issue—along with several others—in order to inform the constitutional reform process after the elections. He also instituted several means of encouraging dialogue among state and civil society actors. His most important achievement in this vein is the 2001 institutionalization of the local roundtable experiences described above in the national Mesa de Concertación para la Lucha Contra la Pobreza (Roundtable for the Fight Against Poverty), hereafter referred to as the MCLCP.[20] The MCLCP, led by a representative of the Catholic Church, focuses on issues surrounding poverty reduction around the country and has become an important national and regional actor.[21]

During the transition to democracy, two trends converged to provide the political context for the current decentralization reform. First, as noted above, examples of state-society collaboration and civil society participation in governing, such as the MCLCP, had become increasingly popular.[22] After the 2001 elections, several politicians who had implemented these local experiences during the 1980s and 1990s were now placed in national positions, including in Congress and as officials in the Paniagua administration. Further, widespread agreement about the need to reduce corruption and increase public sector accountability also emerged in Peruvian political and societal circles. As the media released video after video showing the corruption in the Fujimori-Montesinos government, the public became aware of the pervasive problem at various levels of government. The public manifested disgust with this situation, and during the Paniagua administration, politicians quickly moved to increase public sector transparency.

During the 2001 campaign, both leading presidential candidates, Alan García and Alejandro Toledo, promised to decentralize the country, call immediate regional elections, and incorporate ways for civil society to participate in the new regional and local governments.[23] Although not all of their campaign promises proved viable, decentralization did emerge in post-Fujimori Peru. The next chapter explores the factors that made the reform a reality.

THE LEGAL FRAMEWORK (2002–2003)

As soon as Toledo became president, it was imperative to adapt the legal framework to create stronger regional and local governments. Congress immediately began to draw up legislation that would govern the process. It emerged as one of the most ambitious participatory decentralization reforms in the world. This section details the specifics of the reform, with an emphasis on the participatory aspects.

The decentralization reform is, in actuality, a constitutional reform followed by a series of laws, decrees, and presidential resolutions. The legal framework is evolving; Congress continues to pass new legislation to refine and push forward the process.[24] From 2002 to 2003, Congress and the executive wrote and passed more than twenty-six legal initiatives. The remainder of this chapter focuses on the five most important pieces of legislation that set up the original legal framework for regional governments and new forms of participation:

1. The constitutional reform;
2. The General Decentralization Law (Ley de Bases de la Descentralización), which lays out a broad framework;
3. The Organic Regional Government Law (Ley Orgánico de Gobiernos Regionales, or LOGR);

4. A modifying law that clarifies the Regional Coordination Councils; and

5. The Participatory Budget Law (Ley Marco del Presupuesto Participativo).

Constitutional Reform, March 2002

The first step in the decentralization reform lay in reforming the 1993 constitution through eleven articles. The constitutional reform (Law 27,680), ratified in March 2002, creates a regional, unitary state (not a federal system).[25] The reform sets up several levels of subnational government: macro-regions (which combine several regions to make a larger political unit), regions, provinces, districts, and *centros poblados* (very small towns).[26] It grants all of these levels new powers and resources and allows for the direct elections of new authorities.

The reform is designed to gradually take place in four overlapping and "parallel" phases:[27]

- Phase One: Install and organize the regional and local governments (2002).
- Phase Two: Consolidate regionalization process by creating macro-regions (ongoing).
- Phase Three: Transfer sectoral powers (for example, housing, natural resource management, and environment) to regional and local governments (ongoing).
- Phase Four: Transfer health and education sectoral responsibilities to local and regional governments (ongoing).

The first phase set up twenty-five political regions based on the already existing departments in Peru. The second phase called for a referendum—held on October 30, 2005[28]—to set up macro-regions that combine several regions into one political entity. During the last two phases, the national government transfers several powers—called *competencias*—to the local and regional governments.[29] Peru is currently undertaking these last two phases as powers are increasingly being transferred to the new governments.[30]

The law sets up three institutions that, combined, govern the regions. It declares that the structure of each regional government will consist of the president, who serves as the leader of the region (much like a governor in the United States) and is directly elected for a four-year term; a regional council, which serves as a legislative body and has council members who are directly elected for four year terms); and the Regional Coordination Council, which is one of the participatory institutions studied below.

The constitutional reform itself is very vague about the participatory aspects of Peru's decentralization efforts. The exact language regarding the CCR states that it is "comprised of provincial mayors and representatives of civil society, serves as a consultative and coordinating body with municipalities, with functions and attributions that the law will determine" (Law 27,680, Article 191).

The constitution also states that regional and local governments need to implement additional mechanisms to increase citizen participation in politics and increase citizen oversight. First, each region must develop a strategic plan, or *planes concertados de desarrollo* (hereafter referred to as regional development plans). The constitution states that the regional government shall "formulate and approve the regional development plan with municipalities and civil society" (Article 192). Second, regions need to develop their budgets with citizens' participation and hold periodic open meetings (*audiencias públicas*) twice a year to provide information about the execution of the budget. Specifically the constitution states in Article 199 that "the aforementioned governments formulate their budgets with the participation of the population and publicly disclose their execution annually according to the law." However, the reform fails to include details about these particular initiatives. Instead, future legislation would need to do so.

Immediately following the adoption of the constitutional reform, regional elections were set by the Law of Regional Elections (Law 27,683). This law stipulates that a regional president, vice president, and council are elected every four years in November, at the same time as municipal elections. With the constitution laying out the basic framework, Congress needed to pass more specific legal framework in the first half of 2002 before the first regional election in November 2002.

General Decentralization Law, July 2002

The next step lay in passing the General Decentralization Law (Law 27,783), which is longer (with fifty-three articles) and more comprehensive than the constitutional reform. In addition to outlining the powers of each level of government (national, regional, and local), it creates the National Decentralization Council (Consejo Nacional de Descentralización, or CND), accountable to the president, to implement and oversee the decentralization process and outlines the reform's four phases in more detail. The law also explicitly states the principles of decentralization, including the ideas that decentralization is permanent, dynamic, irreversible, democratic, and gradual (Article 4). In terms of fiscal decentralization, several additional principles are outlined, including definition of powers, transparency, predictability, neutrality as it relates to transfer of resources, and fiscal responsibility (Article 5). Next, the law moves to the specific objectives of the reform, which are broken into political, economic, administrative, social, and environmental. These nineteen objectives stress the ideas of efficiency, modernization, coordination among levels of government, sustainable development, and citizen participation.

One key objective is to increase citizen participation in the management of public affairs and oversee the fiscal responsibilities of each region and locality. The law states that citizens will participate "in all forms of organization and social control" (Law 27,783, Chapter 3, Article 6). Chapters 4 and 5 (Articles 17 through 20) most clearly outline the forms that this participation takes. Chapter 4 states that regional and local governments must promote citizen participation in the development, debate, and consensus building (*concertación*) of regional development plans and budgets. They must ensure access to information about the plan and the budget as well as the mechanisms that ensure accountability. This participation should be channeled through the spaces for consultation, coordination, consensus (*concertación*), and oversight that the regional and local governments establish in accordance with the law.

Chapter 5 deals with the annual budget. It is participatory and decentralized. The annual participatory budget serves as an administrative and management instrument. The budgets should be based on the corresponding development plan. Both the plan and the budget should be based on the support and participation of the private and public sectors, regional and local society, and international donors. The Ministry of Economy and Finance (MEF) will emit annual instructions that regulate the participatory budget process, and the budgets must meet the requirements of the National Public Investment System. Only public (or capital) investment costs are subject to public debate; operational/fixed costs are not.

Although the General Decentralization Law does set out more specifics about the participatory institutions, it includes few details about the nature of the CCRs and the actual process of the participatory budgets. After clarifying the territorial limits of the regions (Law 27,795), Congress set out to define even more aspects of the regional governments through the Organic Regional Government Law.[31]

Organic Regional Government Law, November 2002

The Organic Regional Government Law (LOGR) fleshes out even more details of the specific principles (Article 8), powers (Articles 9 and 10), and almost 200 functions (Articles 45–64) of the regional government. It clarifies the nature of Lima, classifying it as its own administrative entity that does not pertain to a region. It also sets up a process of accrediting regions for the eventual transfers of powers (Articles 79–85). As the next chapter discusses in more detail, the debate and passing of this law became much more politicized than the previous law. As regional elections approached, the members of Congress had more to lose (or gain) as societal actors were empowered with voice and vote in the regional governments.

This law does not focus on the participatory aspects of the reform. It does state that the "regional government's management is ruled by the development plans and the participatory budget" in Article 32. As a result of the extreme politicization during congressional debates, the initial LOGR removed the CCR from the regional government structure, going directly against the constitution. To rectify this problem and ensure the constitutionality of this law, a modification law had to be passed to clarify the role of the CCR.

Law to Modify the LOGR, January 2003

Like the constitution, the law that modifies the LOGR (Law 27,902) stipulates that the basic structure of the regional governments includes a regional council, the presidency (the president and vice president), and a CCR. The CCR in each region is defined as an "entity in the regional government that consults and coordinates" (Law 27,902, Article 11). It is made up of "the regional president, who will preside (or his/her vice president if asked), provincial mayors, and representatives of civil society." The law (see Articles 11.A–11B) further states that:

- The proportion of mayors to civil society representatives is 60 percent and 40 percent, respectively. This is calculated based on the number of provinces in the region. Provincial mayors automatically make up 60 percent of the body, and the 40 percent is then calculated accordingly.[32]
- At least one-third of the civil society representatives should come from the business or the agricultural (*productores*) sector.[33]
- Civil society organizations with legal status register with the regional government. In order to register, an organization must have a legal representative and prove a minimum of three years' existence.

- The registered organizations hold an election every two years. The appropriate number of delegates is then elected by these organizations to represent civil society on the CCR.[34]
- The civil society organizations that can participate include (among others): agricultural organizations, business and professional associations, labor unions, neighborhood groups, universities, churches, indigenous and *campesino* organizations, roundtables, and women and youth groups.
- Each CCR meets two times per year for ordinary sessions and can also be convened by the regional president for extraordinary sessions.[35]
- Members of the CCRs do not receive payments, daily fees, or other types of remuneration.
- Members of the CCRs emit opinions about the annual plan and the annual participatory budget and other issues if requested by the regional council.
- The CCRs do not have binding power. The absence of a consensus will not impede the regional council from deciding how to move forward.

With this framework in hand, regional officials could elect CCRs and formalize civil society's participation in regional government.[36] As the law states, regional governments would need to first inform civil society organizations that they could participate in this institution. The government would then need to open a process whereby legally accredited organizations could register to participate in the election. Next, each regional government would need to hold the CCR election, in which all registered groups could elect a certain number of representatives.

Since this legislation was passed, several more recent laws have reinforced the role of the CCRs (Defensoría del Pueblo 2005c). For example, the law that regulates investments in the regions (Law 28,059) states that the CCRs must be consulted about projects that promote private investment. The regional government is also required by law to consult the CCRs about regional integration plans when forming macro-regions (Law 28,274). Thus, Congress has continued to formally incorporate the CCRs into the regional government structure.

Participatory Budget Law, 2003

Congress's next step lay in developing a more comprehensive legal framework for the participatory budget process at the regional, provincial, and district levels. As briefly noted in Chapter 1, participatory budgets devolve decision-making authority to new actors, who debate and vote on what projects to fund. It is widely believed that participatory budgets can give citizens or organizations a more direct role in subnational decision-making processes. Increasing participation in budgetary decisions empowers more actors to be involved in the development process of their communities. When implemented, this process becomes part of the intricate web of checks and balances in subnational governance as new actors are given both voice *and* vote in subnational processes.

Participatory budgeting can be an important tool for oversight and accountability. As Anwar Shah (2007, 1) writes:

> [When done well,] it offers . . . an opportunity to learn about government operations and to deliberate, debate, and influence the allocation of public resources. . . . Participatory budgeting also strengthens inclusive governance by giving marginalized and excluded groups the opportunity to have their voices heard and to influence public decision making vital to their interests.

He goes on to add that it "can improve government performance and enhance the quality of democratic participation" (Shah 2007, 1). All of these outcomes were desirable to post-Fujimori politicians struggling to strengthen democracy in Peru.

Most discussions of participatory budgets start by mentioning one of the first and best-known experiences with this form of decision-making—that of Porto Alegre, Brazil.[37] In 1989, citizens in Porto Alegre, frustrated with the lack of transparency and democracy in their government, elected a mayor from the Workers' Party. To address the fiscal problems that they had inherited, the municipal government allowed citizens to participate in discussions regarding how to spend scarce municipal resources. The experience proved successful, and over time, the municipality opened the process to more massive participation and began to share their experience in global fora.

In Peru, participatory planning and budgeting at the local level took off in the late 1990s.[38] Some of the actors involved in the national-level design process had instituted similar processes at the local level. Some municipal leaders attended conferences, heard about the experience in Brazil, and decided to implement this idea in their city. For example, in Ilo, a port town in the south of Peru, CSOs and local leftist leaders, such as former mayor Ernesto Herrera Becerra, implemented participatory planning processes and budgeting. Herrera was elected to Congress in 2001 and served on the committee that designed the decentralization reform. In Villa El Salvador, a shantytown outside of Lima, elected leaders from the IU began to undertake participatory planning in the early 1980s.[39] In 1999, they launched a formal participatory budget process. Thus, by the time the decentralization reform was passed, several Peruvian cities had experience with participatory budgeting.

In an effort to ensure more accountable and transparent use of public funds, the Paniagua government and the Ministry of Economy and Finance became interested in these experiences and decided to experiment further with this process. The MEF, working with the MCLCP, began a pilot project to launch the exercise at the national level in 2002. The pilot program involved designing regional development plans in a participatory and consultative manner, which would then serve to guide that year's budget-making process. In other words, regional budgets should reflect regional development priorities as outlined in the plans. Twenty-two regions undertook the first step, designing development plans and budgets by convening and consulting civil society actors, and nine regions eventually qualified for regional funds for development projects.[40] The pilot program was viewed as a success, and Congress' Budget and General Accounts Committee worked closely with the MEF to develop the legislation that would govern this process at the national level. Participatory budgeting is now mandatory in all districts, provinces, and regions of Peru.

The Participatory Budget Law institutionalizes this experience at the national level. The current legal framework for the process is a compilation of several laws, decrees, and official instructions. As noted above, the constitutional reform, the General Decentralization Law, and the LOGR all reference citizen or civil society participation in regional and local budgets. From 2003 to 2008, the process was regulated by the Executive Decree D.S. 171-2003-EF, which outlines some definitions and the phases of the process. The Participatory Budget Law, or Law 28,056, passed in mid-2003, states that the goal of the process is to strengthen civil society–state relations and to promote the just, rational, efficient, and transparent use of resources. It also intends to ensure society's control over the use of resources. The law stipulates that the process is regulated through annual instructions developed by the MEF's National Public Budget office.

The instructions that defined the process in all years under study (2003–2006) clearly outlined eight phases (paraphrased below) that took place over the course of a calendar year at the regional level.[41]

Phase One defines preparation. First, regional actors should disseminate information about the process and the existing laws in order to prepare participants for the process. A timeline for the process should be developed and materials for the regional workshops prepared. According to the instructions, the CCR should spearhead this process.

Phase Two defines the call for participation. After the preparation process is complete, the regional government should publicize information about the participation process. The regional president and council develop and publish a regional ordinance that outlines the process for accrediting the organizations' participation, their responsibilities, and a timeline of activities.

Phase Three defines how to identify and register participating agents and the formation of the technical team. After the call for participation is complete, the regional government should open a registry for organizations that are qualified to participate, called participating agents, or PAs. These agents can include members of the Regional Council, CCRs, and CSOs that are registered by the government.[42] Participating agents have a voice and also vote in the process. At the same time, the government should form a technical team to support the process. The team should consist of regional government officials who work in the budget office and experienced members from civil society. The technical team assists with the process and has a voice, but no vote.

Phase Four defines the training of the PAs. Training includes holding training events, also called workshops (*talleres*), for the PAs. The training should be sponsored by the MEF, the CND, NGOs, and the regional government officials.

Phase Five defines the meetings (also called workshops) that the regional government holds with the government officials, the technical team, and participating agents. To ensure that the budget is linked to the regional development plan, one of the goals of these events should be to discuss the development plan and budgetary progress and results from the year before (*rendir cuentas*[43]). During these events, participants should also identify regional problems and propose programs that need attention. Several specific workshops are suggested in the MEF's instructions, such as a meeting to present the development plan and bring it up-to-date and meetings that go over the criteria for judging project proposals. In order to facilitate project evaluation, the MEF offers sample criteria and a point system that could be adapted to each regional context as deemed necessary. Governments should inform the PAs as to how much they expect to spend in investment projects the next year.

Phase Six defines technical evaluation. While Phase Five is going on, the government should receive proposals (also called project "profiles") from key regional actors (for example, regional government teams, provincial and/or district mayors, and civil society organizations).[44] The technical team should then evaluate the proposed projects and help strengthen the proposals in order to meet MEF requirements. They can discard proposals that do not meet the basic criteria. They can also give preliminary points to the projects based on the criteria and point system developed in the earlier workshop.

Phase Seven defines how agreements are to be formalized. At this point, a final regional workshop should be held at which the regional president presents the project proposals, as prepared by the technical team, to the participating agents to discuss, modify, and approve. The workshop participants should debate the projects, modify the points, and develop a final list of priority projects. The final list of projects (signed by PAs) should then be sent to the CCR, the president, and the regional council for approval.[45] Once finalized, the regional government should then send a copy of the final budget to the MEF, Congress, and the General Accounting Office. The budget should also be published and posted on the Internet.

Phase Eight defines accountability and oversight (*rendición de cuentas*).[46] Participating agents should form oversight committees to monitor the execution of the budget during the upcoming year. These committees can denounce officials to the Ombudsman's Office, the General Accounting Office, Congress, and/or the Public Ministry. Oversight committees should have four members, whose role is to: (1) oversee the implementation of the participatory budget process as well as the government's adherence to the agreements reached during the process; (2) ensure that the prioritized projects become part of the region's budget; (3) regularly inform the CCRs about budgetary spending to date; (4) ensure that the regional government provides information to the public as the law establishes; and (5) oversee timelines and project execution. Governments should inform the public on a regular basis regarding spending to date. They should post the information on their websites. Governments also need to make sure that the oversight committee has data on the budget, including revenue and investment spending, on a quarterly basis.

The MEF and Congress continue to adapt the legal framework with the goal of improving the implementation of the process and the resulting budgets. For example, in 2009 Congress passed Law 29,298 which reduced the number of phases from eight to four and requires the regional governments to inform the public in advance the amount of the total regional budget that will be debated in the participatory process.[47]

As the instructions demonstrate, the process is meant to be orderly and technical. The design reduces possibilities for manipulating the process, corrupt practices, or the government's cooptation of the organizations. Governments do not receive their budgets unless they can demonstrate that meetings have been held. Therefore, concrete incentives for compliance are in place. There is still room for interpretation, and Chapter 5 describes the way in which the legal framework for both the participatory budgets and the CCRs is interpreted by different politicians once elected.

It is important to clarify that giving voice and vote to participating agents does not mean that the budget that leaves the workshop is the final budget. Rather, as the above discussion indicates, the proposed list of projects then goes through a multifaceted approval process. Regional officials and the national government (specifically, the MEF) have a chance to change the final budget. The budget might change for several reasons. The amount of money that a region actually receives the next year can change (increase or decrease); a project that is passed in the participatory budget workshop might be declared unviable later in the year; regional presidents—for political reasons—might fund different projects.[48] Thus, this participatory process becomes one of many steps in the complex budgeting process, typified by several layers of checks and balances.

Skeptics might ask, considering the complex process that the budget goes through after leaving a prioritization workshop and the many actors who can then change the budget, how truly empowered are these agents? Is their voice and vote really meaningful? Or is the participatory budget a mere exercise in delivering false hope and expectations to civil society?

There are several ways to explore this issue. First, we can ask: are governments actually funding the programs that are agreed upon in the participatory budget workshops? If not, why? Second, we can ask participating agents themselves if they feel that their participation is meaningful. Finally, we can explore the number of participating agents who attend meetings. Is the number increasing over time? If so, this might indicate that PAs find the experience important and meaningful.

Data on the Peru case, while scarce, do exist. In an effort to explore this issue, the Mesa de Concertación para la Lucha Contra la Pobreza undertook a comprehensive monitoring of the 2007 regional budgets. First, it surveyed participating agents who attended workshops in 2006. Second, the MCLCP monitored the regional governments' compliance of the eight steps outlined by the MEF guidelines. And finally, in 2008, the MCLCP compared the projects that the regional governments actually funded in 2007 with the original proposal from the final workshop. Additional data regarding the number of participants is available through the MEF's participatory budget online portal.[49] The World Bank (2010) recently published an analysis of the data on the portal to help the MEF analyze the impact of the process. Although none of these sources are comprehensive, combined they should give us a good picture of the overall quality of PA participation.

The overall evaluation of the process shows that, in fact, PA participation *is* meaningful. PAs do make both their voices and their votes heard. First, the MCLCP finds that fourteen regional governments funded at least 50 percent of the approved projects during the 2007 fiscal year (MCLCP 2008). When compliance was low, the MCLCP went back to the regional teams and asked why. Because elections had just been held, most reported that the low compliance resulted from budget changes related to a change in government (MCLCP 2008). Thus, this year was atypical in many respects and it is difficult to draw conclusions as to why budgets change after the participatory process.

Second, when asked to "grade the process," 50.5 percent of the respondents reported that the process was "regular," 35.1 percent "good," and 5.4 percent "excellent" (MCLCP 2007, 51).[50] Eighty-two percent of the PAs responded that "civil society's predisposition, or inclination, to participate" was "regular" or "good" (MCLCP 2007, 61). When asked to rank the role of civil society in general in the participatory process, 61.9 percent responded that it was "regular" and 28.2 percent called it "good" (MCLCP 2007, 69). In addition, the majority (69.4 percent) of the respondents said that the process is improving with time (MCLCP 2007, 53).

Finally, we can explore the number of PAs. Are people showing up to participate? Is this number increasing or decreasing over time? The MEF's participatory budget portal provides data regarding the number of PAs in the 2005–2009 regional budgets.[51] The portal documents a significant and increasing number of participating agents that discuss the 2007, 2008, and 2009 budgets. According to my own analysis of the data, to vote on the 2007 budget, 1,850 PAs participated in twenty regional workshops. The next year, 2,592 PAs attended twenty-two regional workshops.[52] For the 2009 budget, 3,596 PAs participated in all twenty-four regions (see Table 2.1).[53]

One thing to keep in mind about these numbers, however, is that a PA can represent the regional or local government or a registered CSO. Fortunately, the

Table 2.1. Data on participating agents

	2007*	2008**	2009***
Number of PAs	1,850	2,592	3,596
PAs representing CSOs	892	1,635	2,130
Percent CSOs (as percentage of total PAs)	48	63	59

SOURCE: http://presupuesto-participativo.mef.gob.pe/app_pp/db_dist edit.php (accessed May 15, 2009).

*Data available for 20 regions
**Data available for 21 regions
***Data available for 24 regions

MEF data also show us the kind of organization (governmental or nongovernmental) that the PAs represent each year. Are these PAs really representing regional civil society or are the meetings packed with government employees? An analysis of these data shows that the number and percentage of CSOs represented is also increasing over time.[54] For the 2007 budget, only 892 (or 48 percent) of the PAs represented CSOs. For the 2008 budget, that number almost doubled, and 1,635 PAs (63 percent) represented CSOs. And, when discussing the 2009 budget, 2,130 (59 percent) PAs represented civil society organizations.

The MCLCP concludes that, although not perfect, the process is becoming more and more "settled" and participants are pleased with the quality of their participation (MCLCP 2007). Most governments funded at least 50 percent of the agreed-upon projects. And a significant number of regional CSOs participate every year. Most important, observers expect the process to continue to improve over time. Thus, given the short amount of time that this process has been in place, we can conclude that civil society has, in fact, been empowered through this institution with voice and vote in subnational governance.

CONCLUSIONS

By the end of 2003, Congress had clarified the legal aspects of the CCR and participatory budget.[55] Table 2.2 summarizes the key characteristics of both the CCR design and the regional budget process outlined in this legal framework. As the table notes, in terms of "who" participates, the participatory budget process is actually more open than the CCR. "Agents" are often defined more loosely by governments and can include individuals who are interested in participating (although they generally are not given a vote). CCR members automatically are considered agents as well. Details about participation, that is, the specifics about which groups can participate, will vary by region.

Table 2.2. Comparing key characteristics of participatory institutions

Characteristic	CCR	Participatory budget
Who can participate?	Registered civil society organizations vote in a special election for the CCR members who will represent civil society	Registered participating agents (includes members of the CCR, government officials, and representatives of civil society)
Who can register?	Organizations with a regional or provincial presence that are legally registered, have legal personnel, and can prove three years' existence	Regulated by regions (generally must demonstrate the legal existence of organization)
Nature of decision-making process	CCR approves the regional development plans and the budgets but decisions are not binding	• Participating agents given voice and vote in the final product (budget); budget then sent to regional council, CCR, and president for final approval; list of final projects then sent to the MEF • Process is part of an extensive budget-making system that purports to improve transparency and accountability
Other key characteristics	• 60% mayors, 40% representatives from civil society • Meets twice per year • No salary or fees for participants • Approve annual plan and budget and other functions as necessary	• Must be linked to the regional development plan • Technical team (made up of government and nongovernmental officials) evaluates proposals, has active role • Only capital investment costs (*gastos de inversión*) debated • No salary or fees for participants • After regional workshop, list of projects is sent to CCR and regional council for final approval • Projects must meet National Public Investment System requirements to be funded by MEF

Now that we understand the reform and can place it in its historical context, we can tackle our first three research questions. What explains national policy-makers' decision to devolve power to regional governmental and societal actors through a constitutional reform? Which factors help us understand the particular design of the reform? And how does this design then condition the implementation of the reform? The answers to these questions are the subject of Part 2.

ANALYZING THE REFORM

Part 2

3 EXPLAINING THE DECISION
TO EMPOWER NEW ACTORS

WHAT EXPLAINS national policy-makers' decision to devolve power to regional governmental and societal actors? Why would these politicians pass a reform that could eventually reduce their own power? This chapter serves to improve our theories regarding why national politicians decentralize power. It also expands our theoretical framework to include the motivations behind participatory decentralization reforms. This final question is not addressed in the existing decentralization scholarship.

The chapter unfolds in two sections. The first section tests prevailing hypotheses regarding the puzzling decision to devolve power to subnational governments. It systematically discusses each of the five explanatory variables discussed in the literature on decentralization and presented in Chapter 1. The discussion improves our understanding of decisions to decentralize in countries with weak political parties and few subnational political elites. The second section analyzes the even more surprising decision to empower societal actors.

When we think about why reformers decided to go forward with this reform, it is important to remember that the decentralization reform in Peru is part of a much larger wave of decentralization reforms taking place around the world. These reforms are becoming possible due to the general consensus that decentralization can solve myriad economic, social, and political problems. Peru is no exception. The Peruvian reform occurred when the interests of three key nationally important actors—actors who are typically at odds—converged around the need to decentralize the state.

First, as mentioned in the previous chapter, civil society leaders, typically from the center-left or left, argued for the need to decentralize power and bring government closer to the people. They advocated for direct democracy mixed with the representative institutions that already existed but that had failed the average citizen of Peru. Further, the technocratic and neoliberal class pressured for a similar reform agenda as part of the second-generation reforms that stress stronger institutions, accountability, and efficiency. For institutions like the World Bank, concepts such as increased citizen participation and decentralized states are ways to ensure more efficient governments and check corrupt leaders (Burki 1999). Finally, national political elites such as García, Toledo, and representatives in Congress also viewed the reform as necessary. Their role in this process is discussed at much more length in this chapter.

Even with this high level of political support by normally competing actors, it is still remarkable that national politicians passed a reform that could reduce their own political power. Even more surprising is the decision to cede formal power to civil society actors. What factors explain this outcome?

CREATING STRONGER SUBNATIONAL GOVERNMENTS

More and more scholars are grappling with the seemingly irrational decision by national politicians to cede power voluntarily to subnational officials. As introduced in Chapter 1, the literature points to several competing variables that explain similar efforts around the world:

1. International pressures;
2. Economic crisis and/or neoliberal reforms;
3. Socioeconomic conditions, measured in light of urbanization and economic development;
4. Democratization; and
5. Domestic political factors, such as electoral strategies and elite bargaining.

The literature tends to agree that the last variable, domestic political factors, holds the most explanatory power. However, as noted in Chapter 1, this finding is mostly based on cases with strong party systems and/or subnational actors who participate in the debate and design process. Does this finding apply to cases such as Peru where the political parties are weak and regional elites barely exist? In this section, I briefly consider these variables as they apply to the Peru case. I undertake this analytical exercise recognizing that these events took place in a complex social and political environment. The analysis is meant to tease out the factors that help us better understand the outcome—Peru's PDR—and contribute to scholarly analysis on decentralization.

International variables did not drive the decision. Although international institutions are supporting the decision to decentralize and are funding programs to push the reform forward, there is no evidence to suggest that the decision to decentralize is the result of pressure from international actors. When interviewed, Alejandro Toledo stated emphatically that international pressure and actors did *not* drive this decision. He noted, "It was a political decision, and I am solely responsible for that.... In no case did the World Bank, Inter-American Development Bank, or USAID tell us that we should decentralize."[1] The United States Agency for International Development, the World Bank, and the Inter-American Development Bank (IDB) gave loans or grants during the Toledo administration to fund the initiative *after* the reform process began. Additional evidence lies in the notable absence of discussion of international finance institutions or donors in congressional debates, media reports, and during my personal interviews with experts. When asked to explain the decision to decentralize, interviewees stressed that domestic, not international, factors explain this process. It appears that the Peru case supports Christopher Sabatini's (2003) argument that international donor "enthusiasm for reversing the centralization of government through devolving power and responsibilities to local governments helped *reinforce* this trend within the countries" (2003, 139; italics mine). Although the Peruvian case certainly reflects a global trend to decentralize power, international pressure did not cause these efforts.

Nor did economic crisis or neoliberal reforms drive the decision. Although the Peruvian economy has always been considered weak, it was not in crisis during this period. According to the World Bank,[2] GDP growth rates also increased slightly or remained stable during this period. The economy grew 1 percent in 1999; 3 percent in 2000; 0 percent in 2001; and between 4 percent and 5 percent in 2002, 2003, and 2004. Nor was a new neoliberal reform package being implemented after Fujimori's regime.[3] Fujimori had implemented one of the most radical structural adjustment reform packages in the hemisphere, yet had also cut decentralization efforts short and recentralized his political power in the national government.

To what extent do other socioeconomic factors explain the decision to reform? Scholars tend to analyze urbanization and economic development rates (in light of per capita GNI) when assessing this relationship. Peru has not experienced notable changes in economic growth or rates of migration to urban centers since the late 1990s when decentralization began to take on renewed importance in national politics. According to World Bank data, gross national income per capita remained relatively stable from 1998 to 2004 when using the current U.S. dollar. Specifically, GNI per capita was $2,220 in 1998; $2,100 in 1999; $2,050 in 2000; $1,970 in 2001; $2,030 in 2002; $2,160 in 2003; and $2,380 in 2004. The urbanization rate has been steadily increasing since 1940 and did not markedly increase or decrease around the time of the two major decentralization reforms.[4] Thus, similar to other findings, outlined in Chapter 1, the Peru case does not suggest that socioeconomic factors explain this reform.

The remaining two variables, democratization and domestic political factors, do help us understand the emergence of this reform in the Peru case. In terms of democratization, there are different ways to unpack the role of this variable in light of decentralization reforms. When discussing the "democratization promotes decentralization" hypothesis, Montero and Samuels (2004, 17) write that scholars sometimes claim that "democratization opens up 'bottom-up' pressures for decentralization by creating new political spaces and providing for direct elections." Thus, "several scholars have suggested that as democratization progressed, pressures for decentralization followed close behind as citizens expressed a demand for more responsive government" (Montero and Samuels 2004, 17). Others might put forth a top-down notion that democratic governments promote decentralization.

Neither interpretation applies to the Peruvian case. As the discussions in Chapters 1 and 2 demonstrate, Peru has transitioned back and forth from democratic to nondemocratic systems throughout the twentieth century. Yet there is no linear or sequential relationship between the two forces (democratization and decentralization) in this country. The democratically elected governments before the military regime made no effort to empower subnational governments. Further, although the 1979 constitution referred to Peru as a decentralized state, the democratically elected Belaúnde made no move to push decentralization ahead. It was only late in García's first administration that the regional governments were actually created. Nor did the reform result from "bottom-up" pressures. Although national civil society intellectuals— convinced that decentralization was necessary and holding high government positions in the Paniagua and early Toledo governments—did play an important role during this period, they were mainly based in Lima. When asked who pressured for this reform, one expert responded that "it was mainly the intellectuals and NGOs. It was never a grass-roots initiative." Although some organized social movements and CSOs voiced support for the reform, there was no groundswell of support. As Tanaka (2002a, 18) argues, although protest and discontent with the Fujimori regime increased in the late 1990s in the regions, regional movements and grassroots organizations were, in general, "fragile and vulnerable." They were not a determinant cause of the reform described above.

Yet we cannot discount the role of the post-Fujimori transition to democracy. Although democratization did not *cause* decentralization, it provided an important *opportunity structure* for the reform.[5] I borrow this concept from social movement theory, which often refers to political opportunity structures as the broader political system that shapes and encourages prospects for change. Social movement theorists, such as Doug McAdam, Charles Tilly, and Sidney Tarrow, use this concept to explain collective action. We can also use this concept to explain the opening up of reform opportunities that political agents then take advantage of. The opportunity itself does not cause the outcome, rather it allows for it and/or structures it.

The fall of Fujimori opened a unique window of opportunity. In this case, public disgust for the behaviors associated with Fujimori, for example, extreme centralization of power, corruption, and the lack of transparency in the public sector, helps explain the success of current efforts. Fujimori's decision to cut short decentralization was fresh in the minds of those who pressured for change. Thus, decentralization, in conjunction with the need to democratize the country, became popular slogans during the public's efforts to prevent his reelection. National politicians, also fed up with the extreme centralization and authoritarian nature of Fujimori's regime, took advantage of this opportunity and pushed forward the reform agenda. Decentralization became an important symbol of the need to clean up Peruvian politics. Without the extreme authoritarian experience fresh in the minds of many and the urgent need to reform the political system, a reform like this might not have passed.

A more determinate variable lies in the electoral strategies of national political elites. A World Bank (2002, 84) report on Peru confirms Toledo's assertion when stating, "The dominant force behind decentralization is political." Interviews with members of Congress and those close to the design process also expressed this view. As one lawyer who participated in the design team noted, "The reform was the result of political objectives. We were handed this mandate. The [regional] elections [were called] first, and later we elaborated the design. There were political pressures to make this happen quickly." Unlike the other cases documented in the decentralization literature, however, these elites were not necessarily "party brokers," as political parties were almost completely discredited during this period.

In the Peru case, electoral strategies mattered, but they were linked to national political elites' electoral calculations, not to party strategies. National presidential candidates' electoral strategies in the 2001 presidential and 2002 regional elections explain the push to decentralize. By the second round of the 2001 elections, both presidential candidates, Toledo and García, had promised to decentralize the state. Both hoped that holding regional elections would provide opportunities for them to consolidate their own power around the country. Martín Tanaka (2002a, 24) describes the electoral stage well:

> In the 2001 elections Toledo raised the decentralization flag again as a campaign strategy, with even more emphasis than the 2000 election. This time Alan García, who could also present himself legitimately as an advocate of decentralization, was his principal adversary. In his speeches, García reminded people that it was during his Presidency that the regional governments were first created and Fujimori then intervened and deactivated them in his self-coup of April 5, 1992. Finally, Toledo was elected and he had given his word to be a decentralizing president.

In his first presidential speech, on July 28, 2002, Toledo stated, "I am from the provinces and am a rebel *with* a cause against centralism." In this speech he promised to create a National Decentralization Commission (CND) and called for regional elections in November.

Once Toledo settled into office, he expressed concern about the rapid pace of decentralization. García, the principal public opposition figure, continued to push the issue and accused Toledo of faltering on his promise. When interviewed, Toledo noted that this was a difficult moment in his presidency:

> For a moment I thought that we should postpone the election for one more year. . . . What was the rationale for the delay? . . . I personally felt very strongly that we should wait a year to very aggressively strengthen the managerial capacity of the regions, of the provinces, and of the districts. They had never had any real power and all of a sudden we said: "Now you can decide about your education, your health, your roads, and here, you have money."

Toledo went on to note that he "paid a political price for that decision."[6]

Martín Tanaka (2002a, 25) argues that calling elections so early was a "gross miscalculation on the part of the president." Tanaka (2002a) goes on to argue that Toledo's rush to decentralize was primarily the result of two factors. First, he was operating in the shadow of APRA's reforms in the late 1980s. If Toledo did not go forth with his promises, he would cede some power, and perhaps popularity, to his principal source of organized opposition—APRA and Alan García. García was publicly pushing the reform and even goading Toledo to go forward. Second, he was hoping that the regional elections would help him consolidate his support around the country and prevent a decline in his popularity. His very new and loosely organized party, Perú Posible, had candidates running in the regional presidential elections later that year.

In the end, APRA won twelve regions, and independent parties or regional movements took seven. Other parties, including Unión por el Perú Social Demócrata and Somos Perú, won five, and Perú Posible won only one regional presidency. The results clearly demonstrated that Toledo and his newly formed political party did not enjoy widespread support and that APRA's power base continued to be relatively strong in many areas outside of the capital.[7]

Thus, the Peruvian case confirms work by political scientists who point to domestic political factors, specifically electoral strategizing, as explaining decisions to decentralize. Both candidates appealed to the electorate by promising to decentralize during the presidential campaign. They both hoped to consolidate power bases around the country immediately following the presidential election.

However, as discussed earlier, this case is slightly different from most of the cases that are well documented by decentralization scholars. Most scholarship points to electoral dynamics between national politicians and subnational political elites when explaining reforms (see Willis, Garman, and Haggard 1999; O'Neill 2004; and Montero and Samuels 2004). Thus, much of this work presupposes the existence of national and subnational political elites and relatively strong political parties.

Peru is unique in two ways. First, as noted in Chapter 1, Peruvian political party organizational structures are weak and extremely centralized and most political parties have weak organizational ties to other parts of the country. Once elected, members of Congress do not have especially strong ties to their regional constituents.[8] Thus, strategies are not necessarily partisan, but are tied to consolidating power bases through movements that are usually personality-based at the subnational level.

Second, there are very few political or economic elites in most regions of Peru. As one scholar in Peru stated in an interview, "There are no real elites with power in the regions. There is no political elite, no commercial elite, no middle class, and no bureaucracy." As a result, we do not see national elites bargaining with regional elites to increase their power. Rather, Peru's reform reflects purely national-level electoral strategy primarily dictated by leaders such as Toledo and García. In that sense, it supports Eaton's (2004a) finding that in the absence of regional elites, we should expect political bargaining to take place in the national arena among national level elites.

In sum, the transition to democracy post-Fujimori provided an important opportunity for a reform of this nature to be passed. The Peruvian public embraced any effort that might democratize and clean up the country. This coincided with national political elites recognizing that a reform of this nature could help them increase their power bases around the country. National electoral strategies help us understand the reform in the context of a country with few regional elites and weak political parties.

CREATING PARTICIPATORY INSTITUTIONS

Perhaps a more interesting question in light of this particular reform is the decision to institutionalize civil society participation. Do the same factors prove decisive? Because few existing decentralization studies have explored this issue, we cannot test a set of variables that might explain this outcome. Rather, we can borrow from existing studies on decentralization and test the same variables' explanatory power in the decision to create a PDR. I also explore institutional factors, which emerged as important in my interviews with experts on the budget process.

Again, for the same reason mentioned above, international, economic, and socioeconomic factors do not explain the decision to design a *participatory* decentralization reform. International actors did not pressure the reformers to include participatory institutions in the design.[9] As one interviewee noted about the participatory budget, "We had the idea. International experiences did not affect the decision-making process at the national level." Further, given the economic data provided above, it is clear that economic crisis and changing economic development rates did not influence this decision.

As in the decision to empower subnational governments, the transition to democracy and slightly different domestic political factors explain the fact that reformers mandated participation at the subnational level as well. Three factors merit additional discussion.

First, as is true for the reform in general, the recent democratic transition and the backlash from the Fujimori regime also help us understand the decision to open up space for civil society's participation in subnational governments. In this case, the importance of this unique moment went beyond favorable public opinion and support for an attempt to restructure power. After Fujimori fled, several local activists and leaders who had set up roundtables, participatory budgets, and/or participatory planning now held important political positions. Several were elected into power. For example, Ernesto Herrero, former mayor of Ilo, presided over Congress's Decentralization Committee during the 2004–2005 session, and Luis Guerrero, former mayor of Cajamarca, led the committee while drafting the constitutional reform in the 2001–2002 session. Both are avid proponents of participatory democracy as a cure for the ills of representative democracy in Peru. Paniagua had also appointed several national civil society leaders to political positions, such as Cecilia Blondet from the Institute of Peruvian Studies who became the Minister for the Advancement of Women and Human Development in Peru. Many of these same officials, or others from similar backgrounds, continued to hold high-level positions during the early years of the Toledo government, where they actively promoted citizen participation. These leaders viewed participatory institutions as a solution to some of the problems in the political system.

In addition to the civil society professionals who had been recruited to or won positions in the national government, the CCR idea gained currency and was actively promoted by civil society actors who were involved in the public policy debates during this period, especially Lima-based NGOs involved in decentralization issues (for example, Grupo Propuesta Ciudadana and Red Perú) and the national consortium of CSOs (the Asociación Nacional de Centros de Investigación, Promoción Social y Desarrollo, or ANC). Representatives from these organizations attended open meetings hosted by the Decentralization Committee to debate and discuss this model. They provided language for bills and helped organize public fora for debate around the country. Thus, the context of democratization opened up political opportunities for the PIs and gave civil society professionals increased space to advocate participatory approaches during the design process.

Second, the decision to include the CCR in the regional government structure was heavily influenced by the historical experiences that stressed civil society participation in governance processes. The reform built on and adapted the corporatist model for civic participation that was codified in the 1979 constitution. As noted in Chapter 2, this model privileged organized groups over individual citizens as a means to channel demands. Regional

CSOs participated in the regional assemblies that existed briefly in the late 1980s during García's regionalization efforts. Thus, civil society, not citizens, emerged as the agent for change in this particular context.

The decision to set up a mandatory participatory budget process was slightly influenced by historical experience. In some ways the reform replicates at the national level local experiences with participatory budgeting—such as Cajamarca, Villa El Salvador, and Ilo. As noted above, some of the leaders of these processes were now in Congress and participated on the Decentralization Committee. As one interviewee who designed the participatory budget noted, "the make-up of congress was 'pro-participation.' This meant that many congressmen and women really liked this idea."

However, a third factor—institutional political dynamics—emerges as especially important in explaining the decision to implement a nationwide participatory budget process. Specifically, the Ministry of Economy and Finance initiated the program as a means to control corruption and clientelistic politics. The highly technocratic MEF became frustrated with the lack of transparency behind funding decisions and instigated a participatory budget process, starting with a pilot program in 2002. As one interviewee stated, "our goal was to improve public spending at the local level and make sure that public funds were being spent well. The typical mayor was corrupt and did not understand public policy." Another expert noted, "The political class was disconnected from its constituents." They were promoting projects that served their own interests and not necessarily their constituents. For this expert, it became a "control mechanism."

The problem went beyond mayors and local officials. According to interviewees who work on the budget, before the participatory budget program was in place, Congress changed the regional budgets to serve its own interests. Now that the regions in Peru had their own budgets, they are submitted to the MEF directly. Congress no longer needs to approve them.

In a published interview, excerpted below, in *El Comercio* on October 10, 2004, Nelson Shack of the MEF described why the ministry supported the participatory budget so strongly.

> SHACK: We are giving citizens more control over public finances. We are not only looking to improve efficiency, but also exercise more control over political authorities . . . with this [reform] we gain a degree of control over the authorities and avoid decisions that are guided by political criteria. This is one of

the most important steps in the fight against corruption because the best form of control is citizen oversight.

INTERVIEWER: How did the idea to implement a participatory budget emerge?

SHACK: At the end of 2001 a series of conceptual discussions began about how to improve state-society relations and to look for ways in which citizens could participate in decisions about assigning public resources in investment projects. After reviewing experiences from other countries, we launched a pilot program in nine departments.

INTERVIEWER: And what was the result?

SHACK: It was so successful in a short amount of time, only two years, that it was implemented in the entire country. . . . Now Peru is the worldwide leader of this issue. At first it was only a best practice in terms of participation, but now it is a formal obligation.

In sum, the MEF in its oversight role had an institutional interest in ensuring that government funds were well spent. Led by Shack himself, the MEF designed this process to control regional spending, prevent corruption, and reduce pork barrel politics in Congress.

CONCLUSION

This chapter makes important contributions to a common question that decentralization scholars ask: what explains the national policy-makers' decision to devolve power to subnational governments? The chapter also tackles a previously unexplored question: what explains the national policy-makers' decision to devolve power to subnational nongovernmental actors? As such, it presents the first systematic analysis of the motivations and calculations behind a *participatory* decentralization reform.

The chapter demonstrates that democratization processes, in this case a transition to democracy after ten years of authoritarian rule, did provide an important context, or opportunity, for this particular reform. Public disgust for the corrupt and authoritarian practices of Fujimori's regime provided a perfect political environment for an ambitious reform. In the case of the participatory institutions, the transition to democracy meant that several proponents of participatory democracy had now ascended to elected or appointed positions in the new government. Thus, they pushed these reforms ahead from within Congress and the executive branch.

However, the transition to democracy does not fully explain this reform. Instead, when we examine national politicians' motives, we see that political factors—specifically electoral strategies of national political elites—play a decisive role in explaining the outcome. The presidential candidates in 2001 made strategic calculations about the potential to increase their personal power bases in the regions. These candidates were not necessarily representing political party strategies, since political parties were still weak in Peru. Rather, they sought to consolidate their own power bases in different parts of the country.

The Peruvian case study helps us understand the emergence of decentralization in countries with weak parties and few regional elites. Unlike previously studied cases, bargaining between regional and national political elites did not factor into the process, primarily because there are few regional political elites in Peru and those who did exist were not power players during these years. Thus, the case suggests that in countries with few regional political elites and weak political parties, the electoral strategies of national political elites can still lead to comprehensive decentralization reform.

The same factors do not help us understand why the participatory institutions were included in the original language of the reform. When we look at the genesis of the PIs, history and institutional factors help us understand this outcome. Peru's historical experience with corporate bodies that channel societal demands (such as cooperatives during the military regime and the regional assemblies during the first regionalization experiment in the late 1980s), as well as several experiments with local participatory planning, influenced this particular design. Political dynamics between national-level institutions, in this case the MEF and Congress, also led to a mandatory participatory budget exercise in the new regional governments. These factors combine to explain how societal actors gained voice and vote in subnational decision-making processes.

Most of the people in power agreed that decentralization was needed. They often supported the decision to include participatory institutions as well. However, when it came to designing the specific nature of the PIs, this consensus broke down. Politicians began to argue heatedly about the exact details regarding civil society's voice and vote. The next chapter delves into these debates in order to expose the interests behind this dissent. It also shows how the politics behind the debates ended up creating designs that constrained participation in some ways.

4 THE ROLE OF POLITICAL INTERESTS IN CONSTRAINING PDR OUTCOMES

PERUVIAN POLITICIANS agreed that representative democracy had fallen into crisis during the Fujimori regime. They agreed that several policies would be needed in order to rebuild the political system. One solution lay in a comprehensive decentralization reform that created new institutions to incorporate civil society organizations into the decision-making process of the new governments. Actors across the political spectrum supported this reform effort. However, one aspect of this reform proved more difficult to agree upon. Specifically, reformers did not completely agree about what the participatory institutions should look like.

The previous chapter explored several aspects of the design of Peru's participatory decentralization reform. It helped us understand why this particular PDR was pushed forward by national politicians and political elites. This chapter explores the design of the two PIs under study in more depth. It asks two questions about the Regional Coordination Councils and the participatory budgets. First, how do political interests influence the design of both the CCR and the participatory budget? It is important to note that the design debates discussed in this chapter primarily took place in Congress as each piece of the decentralization legislation was debated and passed. It then takes the analysis one step further and explores a second question: how does the design, debated and passed by national politicians, then condition the implementation of the reform at the subnational level?

The first two parts of the chapter revisit the congressional debate in order to better understand the specifics of the design of Peru's PIs. Although the strategies of national political elites converged to push Peru's PDR forward, they did not converge around the design specifics. On the one hand, there was heated debate about the role and function of civil society participation in the CCR. On the other hand, there was very little debate surrounding the codification of the participatory budget process.

This chapter contributes to a large body of literature that argues that design is very important when we explore the success or failure of participatory institutions specifically and decentralization more broadly in the developing world. Olowu and Wunsch (2004) emphasize the importance of institutional design when exploring the extent to which decentralization actually democratizes several countries in Africa. They argue that "[i]nstitutional design issues are critical for local governance" (Olowu and Wunsch 2004, 268). Goldfrank (2007a, 2007b, 2009, forthcoming) draws the same conclusion with regard to designing participatory budgets in Latin America. When comparing experiences in Brazil, Uruguay, and Venezuela, he finds that "the right institutional design is vital" (Goldfrank 2009, 2). Bardhan and Mookherjee (2006) argue that the overall impact of decentralization depends partly on design. Wampler (2007a) documents the importance of design in explaining variation in the participatory budget process in Brazil. Avritzer (2009) echoes this argument when linking participatory budget design to the effectiveness of the budgets in several cities in Brazil. Because the design does not vary substantially in Peru, we cannot use it as a potential explanatory variable in the analysis in Part 3. However, we should still explore the process and impact of design in a top-down reform such as Peru's participatory decentralization reform.

To document the impact of design on PI implementation and results, this chapter presents national-level data on PIs since 2003. These data are based on reports by three sources that monitor PIs around the country: (1) the Defensoría del Pueblo's (Human Rights Ombudsman's) Good Governance Office, which monitored the CCRs around the country from 2003 to early 2006; (2) the Grupo Propuesta Ciudadana (GPC), a nonprofit organization that has monitored several aspects of regional governments, including their spending, transparency, and citizen participation, in up to fifteen regions around the country since the reform began;[1] and (3) the Ministry of Economy and Finance's portal, which hosts data on the participatory budget processes presented in Chapter 2.[2] The chapter outlines how political strategies—motivated by both ideology and the fear of losing power to competing actors—affect PI design and how that design then affects PI implementation.

REGIONAL COORDINATION COUNCILS: POLITICIZED DEBATE

When researching the PIs in Peru, I was often struck by the interesting and unique nature of a decentralization reform that institutionalized civil society's voice and vote in subnational governments. I often wondered why reformers decided to create a council that mixes elected actors from civil society organizations and political parties in one institution. Interviewees explained that the final CCR design was not what many proponents originally had in mind. During the extensive consultations that took place as the constitutional reform was debated, different proposals emerged regarding what the CCRs should look like. The earliest debates centered around whether participation should be mandated from above, as reformers had done when setting up popular councils in Bolivia, or allowed to emerge in more spontaneous, innovative ways, like the participatory budget in Brazil. Most agreed that mandating participation would be most effective because, as one interviewee noted, "if it was not mandated from above, it would never happen."

The next issue, then, lay in what a mandated council that included civil society should look like. Some argued that it should expand the powers of the Mesa de Concertación para la Lucha Contra la Pobreza (Roundtable for the Fight Against Poverty) and be part of the roundtables that already existed around the country. These *mesas* could work with the regional government more directly and formally in decision-making. One interviewee called this the "external model," that is, the CCRs would exist outside of the regional government structure, thereby bridging civil society and the state. However, critics of this proposal argued that the *mesas* were too weak; they relied on volunteers and their mandate was very open-ended. Politicians who did not support participation could ignore or weaken them. Instead, the argument went, a civil society council with binding decision-making authority might be the best model.

Although the idea of an institution as part of the government (that is, the "internal model") gained support, interviewees pointed out that it quickly became apparent that elected officials would want to participate in this particular institution as well. High-level officials noted in interviews that political parties "resisted" granting civil society unlimited powers; thus, the CCR emerged as an institution that included both elected political and societal officials. In the end, the constitutional reform states that each CCR is "comprised of provincial mayors and representatives of civil society [and] serves as a consultative and coordinating body with municipalities, with functions and attributions that the law will determine" (Law 27,680, Article 191).

As the regional elections approached in November 2002, decisions about the role and functions of the CCRs had to be decided upon. At this point, the consensus in Congress about the existence of the CCR largely dissolved. As noted in Chapter 2, language about the CCR was even left out of the original Organic Regional Government Law, debated in November, a month before the regional government elections. A closer look at congressional debates sheds light onto the controversial aspects of this PI.

According to plenary debate transcripts,[3] two design issues almost prevented the CCR from making it into the final reform legislation. The first major debate concerned its functions, specifically whether it would have voice and vote, that is, binding decision-making power. APRA, a group of representatives from the National Unity party (Unidad Nacional, or UN), and a handful of right-wing politicians remained adamantly against ceding decision-making power (vote) to civil society in the regions. The debate raged in Congress in discussions about whether the body should *concertar*.[4] Originally, the Decentralization Committee proposed language stating that each CCR should *concertar* with the regional governments about certain issues. Should the word appear in the legislation, the CCRs would have binding decision-making authority. When this language hit the floor, it sparked intense debate.

The APRA bench was firmly against granting binding power to civil society through the CCRs. As Congresswoman Judith de la Mata Fernández de Puente of APRA stated, the CCRs "should only be consultative. . . . It should only provide opinions and not '*concertar*' . . . because '*concertar*' means that the regional governments cannot do anything. . . ." (October 31, 2002). Representatives from a faction of the right-wing UN agreed, arguing that "with respect to the Regional Coordination Council . . . it cannot be to '*concertar*'. . . . It should be a purely consultative entity, to give opinions and ideas" (October 31, 2002). Another congressman, Carlos Infantas Fernández, from the right-leaning party Independent Moralizing Front, concurred, commenting:

> In terms of the Regional Coordination Council, unfortunately it is already approved in the constitution in a way that, in a certain form, it is going to share power with the Regional Council. I would then suggest to the president of the committee that they revise its functions, with the purpose of restricting them

to solely issues of consultation, so that the Regional Council does not lose the power that it needs nor does the regional president lose his power to govern. (October 31, 2002)

Another congressman (independent) signaled that nongovernment organizations should not participate and to allow them would be unconstitutional. He stated:

In terms of governance, I'd like to remind you about the case of Spain and Chile. Who participated in the Moncloa pact? Five parties. Who participated in Chile? Four parties. Did Manuela Ramos of Spain, Flora Tristan[5] of Spain, or the NGO against the sexual harassment of women [participate]? No sirs. (December 3, 2002)

Thus, several representatives from the right, as well as the APRA party, strongly opposed granting civil society voice and vote in the CCR.

Several members of Congress, mainly a loose coalition that had joined the president's Perú Posible bench in Congress, continued to defend the need to open up Peruvian politics to new actors in order to increase trust in government and ensure more transparent politics. Many of them were staunch advocates of participatory democracy and had experience with participatory institutions in their own regions. For example, Congresswoman Paulina Arpasi Velasquez (PP) lamented,

As the sole *campesina* congresswoman, I worry about why the participation of civil society is not being considered. . . . Why do we fear the people, the social organizations? This is why people are in the street calling for immediate solutions. If they could participate and dialogue from a position within the government, there would be no marches and protests in the streets. (November 7, 2002)

Congressman Herrera Becerra stated, "How do we strengthen democracy? . . . We can give it strength through participatory democracy" (November 7, 2002).

In the end, party politicians from the APRA and the right prevented the term "*concertar*" from appearing in the final legislation by refusing to vote for text that included it. Instead, the institution emerged with purely consultative functions and civil society was given voice, but no vote in regional decision-making.

Second, critics voiced concerns about creating new bureaucracies and falling in the trap of the *asambleísmo,* or the problem of setting up too many bureaucracies that meet often, yet rarely lead to concrete results. This problem existed in the previous regional governments. As Congressman Jorge del Castillo argued, "APRA undertook an important effort to regionalize in its time and this had—among other defects, we admit—a cancer called *asambleísmo,* and now they are trying to incur this crass error again" (November 7, 2002). These concerns manifested themselves as opposition to the CCRs in general and then a call to limit the number of civil society members in the CCRs.

APRA was most vocally and consistently in favor of drastically limiting the number of representatives. Early in the debate, APRA suggested putting a limit on the percentage of representatives from civil society. On October 31, 2002, Congresswoman Mercedes Cabanillas Bustamante de Llanos stated, "I suggest that the number of [civil society representatives] be proportional to the number of district and provincial mayors. Mayors have popular sovereignty because they are elected by the people." Later that day, APRA clarified its position. Congressman César Alejandro Zumaeta Flores stated, "Our suggestion is that the civil society representatives should be a proportion of the mayors who participate in the Regional Coordination Council." He argued that 30 percent of the CCRs should be made up of representatives from civil society and 70 percent should be mayors.

Members of parties on the right expressed similar concerns. Congresswoman Emma Paulina Vargas de Benavides (UN) argued, "By not being precise about the number of representatives from each organization, their representation could become unmanageable" (December 3, 2002). Eventually the legislation was passed with a compromise 40 percent / 60 percent proportion, thereby ensuring that civil society representatives never outnumbered the mayors elected by popular vote.

Did Toledo have an official position on this issue? According to one media outlet, he recognized that unlimited participation would never happen and favored restricting the number of civil society representatives in the CCR to 50 percent.[6] This opinion differed from the invited Perú Posible members who were pushing for a more empowered CCRs. While few published documents or press accounts elaborate on his position, Prime Minister Luis Solari did speak to Congress to encourage it to push the modification law through on

December 3, 2002. Congressional transcripts document that after noting confusion about what was keeping Congress from coming to agreement, since most had agreed on the constitutional language, Solari put forward a moderate position. He stated:

> In the project that the Executive has remitted, it is conceived that in no case should the representatives of civil society exceed the number of provincial mayors. Why, Mister President? Because we need to protect representative democracy. Thus, the number of elected representatives cannot be surpassed by the number of nonelected so that there is a clear hierarchy among those who emerge from the popular vote and those who have not.

Peruvian political analysts tended to blame APRA for refusing to cede formal powers to civil society actors. However, the debate transcripts show that although APRA was most consistently and vocally against this institution, especially when other politicians agreed to put forth a compromise position later in the debate process, the political interest that intervened to weaken the CCRs stretched beyond the APRA party. Resistance to these mechanisms also existed among right-wing politicians. These politicians prevented the CCRs from emerging as powerful because they then could reduce the power of elected officials.

Congressional voting records from the November 7, 2002 vote on the Organic Regional Government Law (Ley Orgánico de Gobiernos Regionales, or LOGR) indicate that APRA was not the only party to block language about the CCRs in the original LOGR. Of the twenty-three members of Congress who abstained (no one voted against), one hailed from the left (Unión por el Perú Social Demócrata), two were independents, and the rest (thirteen) were *apristas* or center-right and right parties, including: Somos Perú (two), UN (three), Cambio 90 (one), and Acción Popular (one). If those who abstained had voted in favor, language about the CCRs would have remained in the bill. To best understand the reasoning behind both groups, let us examine them separately.

Why was APRA so adamantly opposed to these aspects of the CCRs? Their position is especially puzzling considering they had implemented a similar design in the late 1980s, giving civil society voice and vote in the regional governments' regional assemblies, and had raised no objections to the CCR design when it was included in the 2002 constitutional reform. The entire political party, moreover, was built on encouraging participation of the masses. Obviously one concern was purely political—APRA knew it would win many regional presidencies and did not want their politicians to share power with nonelected officials from civil society. Another part of the explanation lies in many *apristas'* conviction that civil society organizations are controlled by the radical left and communists. Jorge del Castillo expressed this paranoia in the debates when attacking his fellow members of Congress who supported unlimited numbers of civil society representatives in the CCRs. He stated, "I knew that some *ex-reds* had evolved into other colors . . . and that the *radishes* had transformed into *watermelon*, that is to say that now they are green on the outside but red on the inside" (November 7, 2002, italics in original). To him, support for expanding the power of the CCRs meant supporting the extreme left.

Why did right-wing party politicians hesitate to implement more participatory democracy in the regions? Peruvian politicians on the right rarely come out to support participatory politics as an alternative to problems with representative democracy. They view civil society with skepticism, as it is not formally elected to represent citizens. Yet the reasons also lay in political calculations. These politicians believed that granting binding power to CSOs would give power to leftist sectors in the regions. Because elections were near when the CCR design was being debated, these politicians did not want to risk reducing the power of their own parties' candidates (weak as they might be) in the regional and local levels, especially if that power would be given to their political enemies on the left.

Thus, political strategies—motivated by both ideology and fear of losing power—intervened to constrain the design of the CCR during the reform process. Did the same political debates take place when the time came to design the specifics of the participatory budget process?

PARTICIPATORY BUDGETS:
AN APOLITICAL DEBATE PROCESS

The legislative process surrounding the participatory budget provides a stark contrast to the highly charged political environment surrounding the CCR design. For example, in Congress, no one publicly objected to the legislation when debating the Participatory Budget Law in permanent commission on July 10, 2003. The bill passed easily and quickly, keeping the proposed language intact.

Why did this PI escape politicized debate about civil society's participation? The timing of the debate played an important role in facilitating the legislative process. Regional elections had taken place, thus politicians were not making as many electoral calculations during this period. Furthermore, Congress was running behind schedule. Therefore, the date for plenary debate was pushed into July 2003 when Congress was not in session. As one high-level congressional staffer noted in an interview, "There was not very much congressional debate. The bill passed easily in committee. Then we sent the bill to the permanent commission. Congress was not in session, and the permanent commission can sign bills." The permanent commission voted, and the law passed with no debate or modifications.

Yet a more determinate factor that explains the lack of conflict around this institutional change is the role that the MEF played in spearheading the process. Most of my interviewees noted that the MEF has a lot of power as an institution, and legislation that it supports generally passes with few changes. One member of congress stated, when interviewed, that "the MEF is a very strong actor and has a lot of credibility in Congress." Owing to the MEF's leadership, it was largely viewed as a technical, not political, reform. The language suggested by the MEF focused on steps, phases, and technical criteria. From the beginning, it placed investment costs (which tend to fund public works) under public scrutiny. Fixed costs, such as salaries and operating costs associated with the governments, are not debated in the regional participatory budget workshops.[7] And, ultimately, the process leads to a series of recommendations that in the end are subject to the approval of the regional president and council. The MEF hoped, however, that by including several monitoring and oversight mechanisms, such as the oversight committees and the public town hall meetings, regional officials would be deterred from changing projects after the regional budget workshops.

Thus, the participatory budget was viewed in Congress as a technical process, spearheaded by a powerful institution, that did not directly threaten the power of elected officials. One important outcome of this apolitical process is that the incentive structure that was originally proposed by the MEF remained intact in the final legislative framework. Specifically, the regions must demonstrate that they have undertaken the process in order to qualify for funds. This contrasts with the nonbinding nature of the CCRs. Further, participatory agents emerged with voice *and* vote in the budget workshops when prioritizing investment projects. Thus, a reform with potential to radically alter power structures in the regions passed easily in a congress that had spent days debating civil society's participation in the CCRs.

This difference surprised me, especially as it became clear that the participatory budget was quickly becoming an important institution in many regions of Peru. Had the same politicians who resisted civil society's participation in the CCRs ignored a powerful venue for participation in the participatory budget process? What is the broader impact of political strategies on actual participation? It is worth taking some time to explore the effectiveness of these PIs using the national level data that exist. The next section explores some indicators of how well the PIs were implemented in the early years in the newly formed regions.

THE BROADER EFFECTS OF DESIGN DEBATES

When we compare the implementation of the two participatory institutions at the national level, it becomes immediately clear that design debates, or the lack thereof, also affected the eventual effectiveness of the institutions in Peru. This section briefly demonstrates that the politicized debate, led by APRA and right-wing parties, severely hampered the effectiveness of the CCRs. The participatory budget, on the other hand, has emerged a more powerful institution with real possibilities of changing the nature of state-society relations and subnational governance in Peru.

CCRs: The Weak Link

Several indicators illustrate the problematic nature of the CCRs. First, in some cases, regions are not even holding timely elections of the civil society representatives in the CCRs. All twenty-five regions held CCR elections in mid-2003 and representatives from civil society were elected for two years (Defensoría del Pueblo 2003a). By law, another election should have been held in each region again in mid-2005. However, Defensoría del Pueblo (2007) reports show that by the end of 2005, five regions still had not held the legally mandated elections for the civil society representatives. Although the exact reasons for regions not holding elections are unclear, my research shows that in some cases it is due to a lack of interest in the institution. However, in at least one case the delays were caused by the decision to expand the CCR's powers. Thus, the lack of timely elections is not always an accurate indicator of a weak CCR.

The number of meetings is another indicator. Once elected, are CCRs meeting at least twice a year as the law stipulates? The monitoring organiza-

Table 4.1. Number of CCR meetings (2003–2006)

Region	2003	2004	2005	2006
Ancash	3	3	2	1
Arequipa	2	3	5	6
Ayacucho	1	1	2	0
Cajamarca	5	1	3	1
Cusco	4	2	3	3
Huancavelica	4	3	13	5
Ica	1	2	1	0
Junín	1	2	3	1
La Libertad	2	2	0	0
Pasco	0	0	6	4
Piura	5	1	1	1
San Martín	0	0	0	0
Ucayali	3	0	4	3

SOURCE: GPC 2007a.

tion Grupo Propuesta Ciudadana documents the number of meetings in thirteen regions. Its data show that in 2003 (the first year of the CCR), almost 40 percent of the governments monitored failed to meet the minimally required number of meetings. In 2004, the percentage of regions that failed to comply with the law reached almost 50 percent. In 2005, more regions convened their CCRs, and only approximately 30 percent failed to hold meetings. Yet by 2006, the end of the administration of the first elected regional presidents, 61 percent of the regions had not held the mandated meetings. Table 4.1 presents the GPC data by region.

Finally, when held, are meetings well attended by the CCR members? In many regions, CCRs are having problems with attendance rates. It is especially hard to get mayors to attend—often preventing a quorum (GPC 2005b). For example, in Cusco only seven of the eleven mayors attended the first meeting in 2004 (Asociación Arariwa and CBC 2005). In the thirteen regions monitored by the GPC, an average of 45 percent of the mayors attended meetings (GPC 2007a). In three regions (San Martín, La Libertad, and Pasco), not one mayor showed up for a meeting at least 50 percent of the time from 2003 to 2006 (GPC 2007a). The GPC writes (2005a) that "[provincial mayors] do not attend sessions because, it seems, they do not consider that it is an important space for decision-making." Mayors are not convinced that the meetings are worth their time because they are purely consultative.

Civil society members' participation is also problematic. GPC data on the thirteen regions demonstrate that on average, from 2003 to 2006, only 63 percent of the civil society representatives attended meetings (GPC 2007a). In all six regions studied in this book at least one member from civil society is not actively participating.[8] The lack of participation is due to several factors, including disinterest and a lack of understanding regarding the role of this institution in the regional government. Moreover, the cost of attending meetings can be prohibitive. As one interviewee noted, "Participation can make you poor!" In some regions, traveling to the capital can take days, and the costs are impossible to assume. In a 2005 workshop of seventeen CCR civil society members, members argued:

> Participation has various costs (transportation, material, time, etc.), which are very important because they can lead to exclusion. If the costs are not assumed, the poorest sectors are going to see limited participation and have a smaller role in the CCR, particularly in extensive regions with problems with communication, such as those regions in the jungle. (Defensoría del Pueblo n.d., 8)

Because the CCRs do not have binding power, the lack of reimbursements or honoraria for CSOs has created a problem that negatively affects participation rates. There is no incentive structure in place to ensure assistance and participation of these members—in contrast to mayors who are elected and are subject to more standard means of accountability, such as recalls and elections.

Thus, several problems with the CCRs are apparent. As a 2005 evaluation states, "The functioning of the CCR continues to be characterized as precarious, to the point that it can be defined as the weak link in the institutionalization of the regionalization process" (GPC 2005b, 41). Regional presidents form them to comply with the law, but there is not enough interest on the part of either the regional government or civil society in the region to actively promote them in most cases. This has led the CCRs to be weak and ineffective in the regions, leading one Peruvian political scientist to call it "irrelevant" (Tanaka 2007). Interviewees directly attribute these problems to the restricted participation that emerged after the politicized congressional debates about the CCR design.

By contrast, the participatory budget process has been much more successful. Analysts and citizens alike agree that, "there is a general recognition that the participatory budget is the most valid mechanism in the decentralization framework" (World Bank 2010, 38–39). Grupo Propuesta Ciudadana (2009, 5), writes that "that the participatory budget is the most important participatory mechanism that has been established since the return of democracy and decentralization in our country." An academic analyst writes, the "participatory budget experience is probably the initiative that can produce the most radical changes in terms of civil society's decision-making in the context of the decentralization process" (Grompone 2005b, 5).

Reports by independent monitors and the Peruvian government show that all regional governments comply annually with the minimal requirements to hold a participatory budget process since it was made mandatory. This is probably because a regional government cannot receive its budget without demonstrating to the MEF that the specific steps were undertaken.

Governments are also holding public meetings (*audiencias públicas*) to divulge information about what programs are being funded and spending to date. The budget process is not tied directly to the public meetings, but this is an important aspect of ensuring citizen oversight of the budget process. The LOGR stipulates that regional governments should hold these meetings at least twice a year. In 2003, four regions of twenty-five failed to hold the two obligatory meetings. The Defensoría del Pueblo (2006a) notes that they were often rushed and late in the year. In 2004, all regions held the required meetings, and the Defensoría reported that governments publicized the events earlier than the previous year (Defensoría del Pueblo 2006a). In 2005, all but three regions (Puno, Pasco, and Tacna) called the required two meetings. When the meetings were called, they were called in advance and publicized more widely than previous years. One congressional report states after 2005, in general the meetings were "taking place in the regions" (Comisión de Descentralización, Regionalización, Gobiernos Locales y Modernización de la Gestión del Estado 2008, 36). Thus, more regions are holding meetings to inform their citizens about spending than are calling CCR meetings.

Although interviewees always discussed ways in which the process could improve, they consistently stressed that since 2003, the participatory budget process has made great strides. Actors are more familiar with the eight-step process and consistently learn more about it each year. Regions tend to devote more time to the meetings, they organize the different budgetary discussions (district, province, region) better, and they have seen an increased number of PAs over time. And, as noted in Chapter 2, according to the MEF's statistics, PA participation has increased over time.

Important civic learning processes are also taking place. CSOs are gaining a better understanding of how the state works. For example, civil society actors now regularly discuss technical aspects such as the National Public Investment System (SNIP), project profiles, and scoring criteria. This vocabulary and knowledge was not part of the civil society collective consciousness just a few years ago. And some state officials—especially those who work on the budget teams—are becoming more open to transparent processes. Several bureaucrats from regional governments who had also worked in the regional governments during the Fujimori regime, as members of the Consejos Transitorios Administrativos Regionales, mentioned in interviews that they thought this is a much better process for making budgetary decisions. During my own observation of the 2004 process in Lambayeque, described in more detail in Chapter 5, it became clear that the participating agents underwent a learning process.

Overall, the regional participatory budget process seems to be on its way to becoming an important institution in Peruvian politics.[9] It is improving over time and becoming a constant part of the regional governments' agendas. All regions are undertaking the basic process, and almost all regions are demonstrating a willingness to inform the public about spending activities through public meetings. Interviewees consistently assured me that the process was "institutionalized" in the regions, and they do not expect this to change.

Of course, the budget process is not without problems. There are some technical difficulties facing regions. For example, because the budget tools and workshops are in Spanish, non–Spanish speakers (the estimated five million to six million indigenous who speak Quechua or Aymara and native communities where Amazonian languages are spoken) cannot fully participate in the process (PRODES 2005). As is true for CCR meetings, another problem lies in the costs of attendance. This has led to a strong urban bias among the PAs in the regional budget fora, especially when they are held in the capital.

A more complicated problem, however, lies in the National Public Investment System, which is not a user-friendly system. The MEF installed the SNIP in 2000 to verify and approve investment projects. To meet SNIP requirements, a project profile has to include reliable statistics about its impact, have information about cost-share, and be ready for a feasibility study (if that had not already been done).[10] Yet statistics are outdated, and regional actors are hard-pressed for the time and resources that go into developing a technically sound project. Slowly, Peruvians are now starting to reform the SNIP to make it easier to manage and use.

Finally, the original point system used to rank projects during the participatory budget workshops during the period under study was slightly biased toward infrastructure projects. Infrastructure projects garnered more points on the scorecard than projects of a social nature, such as health and education (O'Brien 2004). This can lead to a tendency that John Cameron (2008) calls an increase in "cement projects," or small-scale infrastructure projects such as wells and bridges, instead of regional projects that address more social issues. Thus, one active debate about the budget process is how to revise the scorecard to put more weight on social programs.

Although these technical problems are serious, several actors at the national level are working to improve them. The MEF seems open to making the process as user-friendly as possible, as long as the quality of a project is not threatened. They have sponsored annual evaluations of the process to receive input regarding how to improve the process. Civil society actors regularly provide feedback on the process and relations between these actors are fluid. By ensuring that the legal framework is evolving, through annual instructions that are treated as binding, the process has the potential to overcome more problems than the CCRs.

A more pressing problem lies in the fact that regional budgets are small and the amounts that are debated (investment costs) are even smaller. As Table 4.2 shows, the amounts designated to the regional governments remained the same in 2003 and 2004, and only increased slightly in 2005, due to increases in fixed costs (mainly salaries), not public investment costs (GPC 2004c). By 2007, the amount had increased to 18 percent of the national budget, but still too little to undertake the number of projects needed to attack the problems in the regions.

Perhaps the bigger problem, however, is not the total budget, but rather the percentage of that budget that is allocated to capital investment costs (that is, the part of the budget that is debated in the participatory workshop) in the regions. According to the GPC (2007a, 22), in 2004 89 percent of the regional budgets was fixed costs while only the remaining 11 percent was capital investment costs that could be debated by participating agents. This percentage increased slightly in 2005—13 percent of the regional budgets was open to

Table 4.2. Percent of budget by level of government (2000–2007)

Budget	2000	2002	2003	2004	2005	2006	2007
Central government	87.3%	82%	80%	77%	77.5%	75%	68.6%
CTAR or regional government	N/A	13%	15%	15%	15.7%	17%	18.0%
Local governments	12.7%	5%	5%	8%	6.8%	8%	13.5%

SOURCES: Centro de Investigación de la Universidad del Pacífico 2001; López Ricci and Wiener 2004; GPC 2004b, 2006, 2008.

Table 4.3. Revisiting the comparison of Peru's participatory institutions

Characteristic	CCR	Participatory budget
Who can participate?	Registered civil society organizations vote in a special election for the CCR members who will represent civil society	Registered participating agents (includes members of the CCR, government officials, and representatives of civil society)
Who can register?	Organizations with a regional or provincial presence that are legally registered, have legal personnel, and can prove three years' existence	Regulated by regions (generally must demonstrate the legal existence of organization)
Other key characteristics	• 60% mayors, 40% representatives from civil society • Meets twice per year • No salary or fees for participants • Approve annual plan and budget and other functions as necessary	• Must be linked to the regional development plan • Technical team (made up of government and nongovernmental officials) evaluates proposals, has active role • Only investment costs (*gastos de inversión*) are debated. • No salary or fees for participants • After a regional workshop, a list of projects is sent to the CCR and the Regional Council for final approval. • Projects must meet National Public Investment System requirements to be funded by MEF
Nature of congressional debate	Four days of politicized debate	Apolitical, no floor debate
Civil society's decision-making power	Civil society members have voice but no vote when approving regional development plans and annual budgets. Decisions not binding	Participating agents have voice and vote in the budget debate process
Incentives for regions to comply	None	Regions cannot receive their budgets until they demonstrate that the steps have been undertaken

debate (GPC 2006). Again, this is not a significant amount, and PAs often complain that they are spending a lot of their time and resources to participate in a process that debates relatively small amounts of money.

Table 4.3 restates many of the basic components of the PIs as discussed in Part 2. It reflects the additional components that emerged in the debate process: (1) the nature of the debate process; (2) the constraints that politicians put on civil society's decision-making power; and (3) incentives for regions to comply with the legislations.

CONCLUSION

This brief comparison of the two institutions documents the wider-reaching effects of political strategies on institutional design. Political interests affect design and design affects outcome. When political strategizing became a factor, Peruvian reformers unleashed a process that constrained participation down the line. Congressional debate surrounding the CCR design was highly charged and political, whereas the participatory budget took on a technical nature and did not spark controversy. Although hardly a perfect process, the participatory budget process is emerging as an experience with longer-term potential to engage citizens and keep local government officials accountable. In 2004, for example, 28 percent of the regions did not comply with the most basic requirement regarding the CCRs—electing the civil society representatives two years after the first election—while 100 percent of the regions complied with the minimal requirements for the participatory budgets and holding town hall meetings.

Figure 4.1 illustrates this process. The comparison suggests that when politicians perceive that a PI might constrain their own power (either immediately or eventually) and expand power of competing actors, they get more involved in the debate process. Increased involvement then translates to a decline in the transfer of real power to civil society actors.

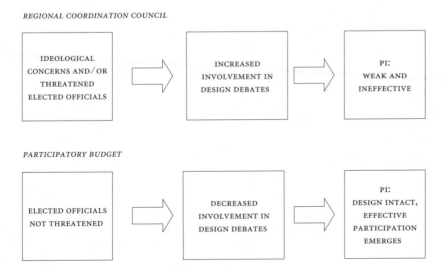

REGIONAL COORDINATION COUNCIL

| IDEOLOGICAL CONCERNS AND/OR THREATENED ELECTED OFFICIALS | ⇨ | INCREASED INVOLVEMENT IN DESIGN DEBATES | ⇨ | PI: WEAK AND INEFFECTIVE |

PARTICIPATORY BUDGET

| ELECTED OFFICIALS NOT THREATENED | ⇨ | DECREASED INVOLVEMENT IN DESIGN DEBATES | ⇨ | PI: DESIGN INTACT, EFFECTIVE PARTICIPATION EMERGES |

Figure 4.1. Comparing causal processes

When reflecting on the congressional debate and the final CCR legal framework, Congressman Walter Alejos Calderón (2005, 166) writes: "We did not achieve our initial objectives of having a high level of citizen participation in the CCR so it would become a true space for negotiation and coordination." The data show that in the absence of substantive changes, his fear will, in all likelihood, become reality. The participatory budget, by contrast, is considered a valuable space for governmental oversight and consensus building.

Thus, as previous studies have shown, we are reminded that design debates do affect outcomes. Political interests can intervene to create designs that then constrain participation as institutions are implemented. Although this national-level comparison sheds light on how design can constrain PI implementation, it does not allow us to understand the diversity and richness of experiences that are taking place around the country since the reform was passed. A closer look shows that in some regions, the institutions are unfolding in very successful ways in spite of these constraints. This suggests that in some cases, local factors can overcome design constraints. Turning to an analysis of the regional processes in the next part of the book allows us to begin to uncover some of the intricacies of regional politics and participation. It will also unlock the secrets behind the more successful experiences that are taking place.

REGIONAL EXPERIENCES

Part 3

5 SIX EXPERIENCES WITH THE PARTICIPATORY INSTITUTIONS

HOW ARE THE newly created participatory institutions unfolding in Peru's new regions (illustrated in Figure 5.1)? Once the legal framework was complete, the regional governments went about setting up their governments and implementing the new institutions. Yet it soon became clear that regional governments were implementing the participatory institutions—that is, the Regional Coordination Councils and participatory budgets—in very different ways.[1] In some regions, experiences with these institutions were much more successful than others. Yet because of the difficulty in gathering data around the country, experts could not explain why this was happening. To explore this issue, I visited six regions with very different experiences with the participatory institutions. I set out to determine why some regions had more successful experiences than others.

DEFINING SUCCESS

In the Peru case, what constitutes a "successful experience"? Because this is a relatively new issue in the literature, there are no existing definitions or measurements. Rather, I have developed indicators—based on the data that are available for all of the cases—that capture how well the institutions are being implemented. The indicators rely on both quantitative and qualitative data gathered in governmental and independent documents and through my interviews.

With regard to the Regional Coordination Councils, I measure success in light of the following criteria:

1. At least two official meetings—the legal minimum—were held per year in 2004, 2005, and 2006;[2]

Figure 5.1. Administrative map of Peru

2. Civil society members attended and participated in meetings and/or called meetings when there was a regional issue to discuss from 2003 through 2006.

3. The CCR gained additional powers, thereby going above and beyond the letter of the law.

These indicators primarily capture the *process*—the act of holding meetings and that civil society is, in fact, playing an active role in the meetings, defined as attending and participating in meetings or calling them. Because the institution is so weak in most cases, it is not possible to gauge actual outcomes from CCRs.

With regard to the participatory budget, I measure success in light of the following criteria:

1. The regional government followed at least the first seven steps of the MEF methodology in 2004, 2005, and 2006;[3]
2. Civil society participation in the process demonstrably improved over time;[4]
3. The technical team had members from civil society organizations in 2004 and 2005;[5]
4. The resulting budget is linked to the regional development plan.[6]

These indicators capture the process (following the participatory budget methodology), the quality of participation during the process, and the impact of the participation (developing a budget that falls in line with the regional development plan, which should reflect regional development priorities).

Using the data, I develop a typology of the six cases that classifies them as more or less successful experiences with the Regional Coordination Councils and participatory budgets. Successful cases will meet all of these criteria; unsuccessful cases are those that do not have any of the above characteristics; and a moderately successful case will have some but not all of the characteristics. For the purposes of this discussion, then, a successful experience with the participatory institutions is one that is meeting or going beyond the minimum legal requirements and having an impact on regional politics.

Several caveats apply to this analysis. I am not arguing that the successful experiences reflect societal understanding of or approval of the processes. Many average citizens, especially in the first years after the reform, were not aware of the CCRs, the budget process, or, in some cases, that a regional government even existed.[7] These processes generally involve a small subset of regional actors. For example, in Cajamarca, a local survey reports that only 3 percent of the population attended a participatory budget meeting or workshop in 2005 (Moffett 2006). However, data from the cases should help us better understand the factors that lead to more and less successful experiences with participatory institutions early in a reform process.

Second, even in successful cases, as noted in Chapter 3, there are many problems with the processes, especially with the CCRs. No institution is considered extremely successful or a paradigmatic case of participation. Many point to the frustration that occurs if a regional president changes the budget after the participatory process is followed (PRODES 2009). There are almost always problems with at least one civil society representative on a CCR who does not show up to meetings or actively participate. In Cusco, for example, in 2003 and 2004 a representative from the church failed to show up for all but one meeting, much like one of the university representatives in Cajamarca. In both Ayacucho and Loreto, elected representatives from the Chamber of Commerce showed no interest in the CCRs. However, in some cases, it is possible to see dynamism and activism in a very short amount of time. This chapter documents these varied regional experiences.

REGIONAL DATA

Each case discussion provides background information about the region and describes how the participatory processes unfolded during the first term of the newly elected regional presidents (2003 through 2006). The section also provides overall economic and demographic information, general characteristics of civil society in each region,[8] and a description of the regional government in place during these years. In terms of the CCRs, data on meetings, the 2003 and 2005 elections, and the CCR's impact on regional politics are included. Data on the participatory budget process—how many participating agents registered for the process, the way funding was discussed, and the evolution of the process over time—are provided for each region as well. This information helps identify causal mechanisms that explain variation in regional experiences in the next chapter.[9]

THE COAST

Lambayeque

Typical of the northern coast in Peru, Lambayeque is a dry and dusty region populated by people who greet their visitors with great enthusiasm.[10] With a population of about 1.1 million,[11] it is made up of three provinces, all easy to reach by well-maintained roads from its capital city, Chiclayo. Agriculture, primarily sugarcane and rice, is the main source of the region's economy (MCLCP 2002). Seventy-eight percent of the population lives in urban areas and 46.7 percent live in poverty.[12]

Civil Society   When the decentralization reform began, civil society organizations in Lambayeque were generally weak and unorganized. Interviewees called civil society before the reform "passive," "broken," and "apathetic." The activism that had taken place around the country in the 1980s had largely died down in Lambayeque by the 1990s.[13] Unlike other regions during the Fujimori regime, no regional organization emerged in Lambayeque to actively pressure for democracy. Few civil society consortia existed. Existing organizations—such as neighborhood groups, women's organizations, labor organizations, professional organizations, and NGOs—had little experience interacting with the state.

Since the transition to democracy, this has begun to change. As one interviewee noted, since the reform, "civil society has become more dynamic in Lambayeque . . . organizations are now free to act." In 2001, the regional Mesa de Concertación para la Lucha Contra la Pobreza began to take an active role in organizing civil society to become members. Once set up, the MCLCP worked with the regional government on the development plan and the budget process. Since the decentralization reform, civil society is increasingly starting to work together and form coalitions to create change. Many interviewees noted that slowly more organizational networks are emerging—such as a network of youth organizations—and examples of citizen activism are increasing over time. One NGO activist argued that civil society organizations are mobilizing around concrete issues more since the reform. Thus, although hard to measure, interviewees consistently argued that civil society showed improved levels of organization and mobilization since the reform.

Regional Government Lambayeque—historically an APRA stronghold—surprised national observers with the election of Yehude Simon in 2002.[14] The very close race (the APRA candidate garnered 29.44 percent of the vote; Simon won with 32.05 percent of the vote) illustrates two national trends in the 2002 election: the growth of regional movements and very slim margins of victory. In the case of Simon, this translated into constant opposition from the APRA party, such as public name calling, refusal by APRA mayors to work with his government, and calls for impeachment from *apristas* on his regional council.[15] This also led to the need for Simon (and most regional presidents) to constantly seek public support during his first administration.

As a result, Simon openly sought support from civil society organizations in the region. Interviewees cited his personality, leadership skills, and ideology as partly explaining this decision. Simon's leftist background, with alleged ties to an armed insurgency, the Movimiento Revolucionario Túpac Amaru (MRTA),[16] and time representing the IU in Congress in the late 1980s, is consistent with his embracing civil society participation and the participatory institutions. He professes to present an alternative to traditional politics in Peru.[17]

Although interviewees repeatedly cited Simon as an important supporter of participatory politics, both supporters and detractors mentioned his tendency to use participation to garner votes, calling many of his appearances "photo-ops." When interviewed, Simon himself recognized the grains of truth in the criticism. He noted that several constraints prevented him from opening his government as much as he would like, such as the small budgets, central government meddling, and the inherent distrust people have in government. He also used his position as a stepping-stone for entering national politics. For example, he ran a failed national presidential campaign in the 2005 elections and served as prime minister of Peru from October 2008 to July 2009. As testament to Simon's popularity and effectiveness as a regional leader, however, he was one of two regional presidents reelected in 2006.

Simon's regional team, including Vice President Nery Saldarriaga de Kroll and the government's team in charge of the CCR and participatory budget, shared his commitment to citizen participation. For example, officials in charge of registering organizations for the 2003 CCR elections were extremely flexible with the rules in order to encourage broader participation in the elections. Thus, an open attitude to civil society's participation existed in most levels of the regional government structure from 2003 through 2006.

Regional Coordination Council   The CCR during the period under study functioned successfully and was very involved in regional politics. Data on meetings, elections, and impact clearly illustrate that it was a dynamic space for civil society participation. According to NGO reports and interviews with CCR members, the CCR met twice in 2003 (Centro de Estudios Sociales Solidaridad 2004) and three times in 2004. In 2005, the CCR met four times, and in 2006, the group met six times (Gobierno Regional Lambayeque 2007a; Pinglo 2007).

Data on the registration of CSOs for the CCR election clearly reflect its success over time.[18] In 2003, thirty-four organizations registered to participate in the 2003 CCR elections (see Table 5.1). Approximately ninety-nine organizations registered in 2005 (Gobierno Regional Lambayeque 2005).[19] Analysts were glad that more grassroots organizations participated that year, demonstrated, for example, by the sharp rise in the number of neighborhood organizations and the addition of youth as a category in 2005. A sign of the CCR's continued success was the registration numbers in the 2007 CCR election. By 2007, the number of registered groups had increased to 236 (Gobierno Regional Lambayeque 2007b).

Table 5.1. CSO registration list: Lambayeque

Type of organization	2003	2005
Producers	2	4
Business organizations	1	5
Labor unions	5	8
Professional associations	2	8
Agricultural organizations	1	3
Neighborhood groups	1	14
Campesino and Afro-Peruvian organizations	2	3
Women's groups	4	6
Youth groups[1]	0	2
Universities[1]	0	1
Others (including NGOs)	16	45
Total	**34[2]**	**99**

SOURCE: Gobierno Regional Lambayeque 2003a, 2005.
[1] Youth and universities were not categories for the 2003 registration process.
[2] After the elections, ten additional organizations showed interest in participating in the regional Civil Society Assembly (explained below); thus, the actual number of registered organizations increased to forty-four.

According to interviewees, the elections for civil society representatives of the CCR took place in a timely and organized fashion in both 2003 and 2005. Because the regional government did not mandate a gender quota, which exists in many electoral processes in Peru,[20] the organizations themselves agreed on the need to have at least one woman as a representative. Thus, registered organizations elected two representatives—one female and one male—to the CCR. As discussed in earlier chapters, the law states that the provincial mayors make up 60 percent of the CCR and the civil society organizations make up 40 percent. However, in this region with only three provinces, only two representatives from civil society were elected to avoid exceeding 40 percent. An early complication arose when the male civil society representative failed to participate in the CCR actively (although he did appear periodically in meetings) and quit the organization that he represented.[21] To address this problem, the regional government agreed to call another election and open up the CCR to two more members with voice but no vote. To ensure the 40 / 60 proportion, the regional government also opened up membership to district mayors. Lambayeque maintained this structure for the 2005–2006 CCR. Thus, during the period under study a total of four members from civil society and six mayors participated on the CCR.

Several aspects regarding Lambayeque's CCR stand out as exceptional. The most important achievement is the organization of the Civil Society

Assembly. The civil society organizations that registered for the 2003 elections, led by the most active representatives of the CCR, set up an assembly made up of all registered organizations. When the CCR's civil society representatives are called on to participate in a regional government decision, they first consult the assembly. This is not dictated by the law, and Lambayeque is one of the few regions to set up a mechanism like this that allows civil society to meet and discuss initiatives. The assembly's main objective is to improve the participatory budget process. In 2005 interviews, members expressed the desire to develop a civil society agenda for investment projects and present proposals during the budget process.

In meetings, CCR civil society representatives played an active role and had a discernible impact on the task at hand. For example, when asked to approve the development plan in 2003, the civil society representatives consulted other CSOs and presented formal recommendations to address four additional issues in the plan: gender, youth, marginalized populations, and institutionalizing spaces of civil society participation (Centro de Estudios Sociales Solidaridad 2004). The government accepted these recommendations. In 2005, the civil society representatives proposed the regulations for the participatory budget to the regional government. Again, the regional council approved this document with few modifications.

Another important achievement is that civil society members lobbied for space in the regional government and were given an office. This implies that the regional government is willing to dedicate at least some resources to this institution. Further, the CCR itself elects its own president. By law, the president of the CCR is the regional president (in this case, Simon). However, the CCR asked for and received permission to elect a new president to lead the CCR in Lambayeque. Thus, the CCR presidency is a rotating position among the civil society representatives.

During fieldwork I observed fluid relations between members of the CCR, the Civil Society Assembly, and the government's team. There is also a high level of coordination between the CCR and other entities that promote civil society participation at the regional level, specifically the MCLCP. This coordination is evident in membership—members of the CCR are also members of the regional MCLCP.

Of course, the CCR does face problems. In addition to the problem with one representative from civil society who did not participate from 2003 to 2004, two provincial mayors did not attend meetings regularly. In 2006, the mayor of the capital city did not attend any of the meetings and the mayor of Chiclayo (the largest city) did not attend 33 percent of the 2006 meetings (Gobierno Regional Lambayeque 2007a). CCR members also mentioned the challenge of representing such a diverse set of actors in the regional government. There is often no one "civil society position" with regard to the issues that they discuss. Finally, according to some interviewees, the CCR meetings during the first few years were formalistic. In other words, the government used them primarily to pass recommendations and/or approve documents. However, even given these challenges, the CCR in Lambayeque emerges as the most successful studied.

Participatory Budget   The participatory budget process in Lambayeque has also been successful. Although the first year was rushed and not extremely open to civil society participation, the government rectified this problem in later years. After hiring a professional evaluator in late 2003, the regional government, led by the regional vice president, changed the process in 2004 to make it more participatory. They began the 2004 process earlier and increased the size of the technical team to include more members of civil society. During the each of the subsequent yearly processes, the government undertook almost all steps of the MEF's methodology, and interviewees mentioned great satisfaction with the process. The government organized projects and voting around sectors, such as education and health. Sectoral specialists were assigned to teams as they debated projects to ensure that the debates were grounded in an understanding of the issues.

Several indicators demonstrate the important role that civil society actors have played. First, during the time under study civil society played an active role on the technical team. In 2003, the regional MCLCP coordinated the process, and eleven of its members represented civil society on the team. In 2004, seven members from civil society participated, and in 2005, eight representatives participated on the technical team.[22] This active participation continued in 2006 as well. The number of participating agents increased over time as well. According to MEF records, seventy-seven PAs registered in 2005, and this number increased to 121 in 2006.

In terms of the quality of participation, while observing the 2004 process, it became clear to me that the participating agents, including the active members of the CCR, underwent a learning process. They participated in debate and scored activities with careful thought and concern for regional priorities. A certain degree of flexibility with the scoring became common practice in the small groups. Also, there was an atmosphere of compromise that bodes well for the future. In the end, politicians left with their projects, and the technical team had viable proposals. The national MCLCP conducted a nationwide survey of the 2004 budget process and found that Lambayeque's budget was, in fact, linked to the development plan in a satisfactory manner (Del Aguila Peralta 2004).

Of course, problems also exist in the participatory budget process. First, there was a sense of rushing throughout the 2004 workshop. Participants had to debate and score more than 150 projects in two days. Second, problems with the scoring criteria became apparent early in the process. The participants used the MEF scoring cards, which privileged infrastructure programs like highways over those with more "social" development goals like schools and hospitals. Finally, forming an active oversight committee was difficult to achieve, especially in the early years. However, these problems are shared in all regions, and despite these shortcomings, interviewees repeatedly mentioned satisfaction with the process.

Moquegua

Moquegua—an isolated region in the dry foothills of the Andes—lies on the southern coast of Peru with a population of slightly more than 150,000 sprinkled over three provinces. Moquegua's economy is based on mining and fishing, and Ilo, a port town, is the largest city in the region (Gobierno Regional Moquegua 2003a). The capital, however, is Moquegua City. Approximately 37.2 percent of the region's population lives in poverty, and 84 percent lives in urban areas.

Civil Society It is hard to describe the nature of civil society at the regional level in Moquegua. Although there is a relatively long history of participatory politics and organizational initiatives in one province (Ilo), CSOs are unevenly distributed and fragile in the other two provinces. According to one government document, Moquegua's civil society is primarily made up of *frentes de defensa* (defense fronts); territory-based organizations (neighborhood or housing groups); women's organizations; agricultural groups concerned with water and land issues, called *usuarios de riego*; and NGOs (Gobierno Regional Moquegua 2003a).

As noted in Chapter 2, Ilo hosts one of Peru's most successful experiences with participatory budgets. Starting in the 1980s, community actors began to organize to improve and protect the city from uncontrolled development.[23] In

1980, a leftist government began to discuss planning options in open town hall meetings. After learning about the Villa El Salvador experience in participatory planning, the community decided to put together a strategic plan using the same methodology in the mid-1990s. To further expand this participatory planning process, in 1999 Mayor Ernesto Herrera Becerra decided to adapt the Porto Alegre process and implement a participatory budget process in Ilo. The town was organized by neighborhood, and representatives from each neighborhood attended meetings to discuss projects and lobby for their geographic area. The process continues today, and national and local reports note that it has been highly successful over time.[24]

Things changed in 2002 when Jorge Mendoza Pérez, an independent who did not support this process, was elected as Ilo's mayor. Interviewees noted that he attempted to stall the process, but did not completely succeed. The neighborhood organizations continued to push the process forward, and the legal framework of the decentralization reform, especially the participatory budget law, backed them up. But interviewees consistently noted that the future of the participatory budget is much more fragile under an uncommitted leadership. Ironically, the new mandated process is not as participatory as the original Ilo experience. As one former mayor of this city noted when interviewed, "The problem with the process now is that it is like riding a bicycle after driving a Ferrari."

Ilo's dynamism and high level of organization has not spread to neighboring areas. According to an NGO report on civil society in the province to the east of Ilo, Mariscal Nieto, social organizations, especially labor groups, were weakened during the 1980s and 1990s due to economic crisis and Fujimori's neoliberal policies (CEOP-ILO 2004). The Andean province in Moquegua—Sánchez Cerro—is even less organized. Interviewees mentioned that only the *campesino* sector is organized in this province, and even those groups are poorly organized. Thus, although some areas of this region are relatively organized, the region as a whole is not characterized as highly organized.

Regional Government María Constantinides, the regional president from 2003 to 2006, ran on the right-leaning Somos Perú party list and won with 23.48 percent of the vote (Meléndez Guerrero 2003). She enjoyed a majority on the regional council with five of the seven members hailing from the same party and the remaining two members independent. Interestingly, like the president of Lambayeque, she was active in the left during the 1980s and participated in Ilo's participatory processes. She was a forceful critic of the regional mining sector and is a former member of the Socialist Party (Meléndez Guerrero 2003). Thus, she brought experience as a regional activist and some familiarity with the Ilo process to the government. However, her regional government supported some, but not all of the participatory institutions.

It is not entirely clear how committed the Constantinides government was to the PIs. Some mentioned that in principle, she was open to participation, primarily due to Constantinides's personal conviction and leftist past. However, this attitude did not translate into practice. On the one hand, both the high-level leadership and the budget team had an open and collaborative attitude toward the participatory budgeting process. On the other, the government did not actively support the CCR, citing a lack of time. One high-level government official stated that she supports civil society participation but not in "excess." She went on to say that her "work is very difficult and there is not much time to focus on these mechanisms." Another indicator of the internal contradictions in her government is the fact that the regional government used strict criteria to register organizations for the 2003 CCR elections and turned several organizations away.[25] Yet the government did show a degree of flexibility in terms of encouraging participation in the budget exercise. Electoral calculations might explain this inconsistency. Some argued that the president believed that the budget process has more political payoffs than the CCR.

Regional Coordination Council   Moquegua's CCR during this period was very weak. In 2003, the CCR met twice to approve the regional development plan and the budget. In 2004, it participated in the budgetary process and met to approve the budget. It is not possible to discern how many meetings were held in 2005 and 2006.[26] Another indicator of the overall weakness of the CCR is that although elections were held on time in 2003, the government failed to call the 2005 elections. When asked why, government officials stated that they did not have time to call elections. Constantinides's critics accused her of not wanting to lose her supporters in the first CCR. According to government documents, elections were held in April 2006 (Gobierno Regional Moquegua 2007). Although the entire registration list is not available, interviewees who work in the region confirmed that only thirteen organizations registered in 2006, a slight decline from the 2003 election.

In the 2003 election of the civil society representatives, a total of eighteen organizations registered (see Table 5.2), which by all estimates is a small num-

Table 5.2. CSO registration list: Moquegua

Type of organization	2003	2005
Labor unions	3	3
Small and medium businesses	4	2
Business (Chamber of Commerce)	2	0
Professional associations	1	1
Frentes de defensa	3	3
Users' groups (juntas de usuarios)	2	2
Neighborhood groups	1	0
Women's groups	1	1
Youth groups	1	0
MCLCP	0	1
Total	**18**	**13**

SOURCE: Gobierno Regional Moquegua 2003b, 2006.

ber of regional organizations. Like the other regions, the organizations that participated are hardly representative of the region's civil society. For example, as noted earlier, organizations from Sánchez Cerro, the poorer Andean province, are absent from the entire registration process. Unlike Lambayeque, NGOs are absent from the list as well.[27]

The 2003 CCR electoral process demonstrated problems. The government decided to organize the candidates by lists and then each CSO representative voted for one list. One list was made up of labor organizations and frentes, and the other list was made up of small and medium business groups. The makeup of the two lists split the vote between two historically competing sectors (labor and business). The labor/frente list won the election. The group that lost then sued the government for mishandling the election.[28]

The 2003–2004 elected CSO members captured some geographic diversity—the two provinces that participated were equally represented— and, because one representative was a woman, conformed to the regional government's mandated gender quota. Yet the three civil society CCR members interviewed in 2004 for this study demonstrated passive interest in participating in the CCR. When faced with the regional government's lack of time to dedicate to the CCR, for example, they did not pressure for more involvement or for more meetings. Nor were CCR members coordinating with other entities in the region. In interviews, members of the regional MCLCP, for example, mentioned a lack of coordination with the CCR. Thus, as a whole, the CCR failed to emerge as an important regional institution.

Participatory Budget   The budget experience, by contrast, met with more success. Each year the government divides the budget evenly by province, and projects are debated in an open regional forum. Although interviewees said it got off to a rocky start, the process ran much more smoothly by 2006. Moquegua is the only region represented in this study that participated in the 2002 pilot program described in Chapter 3. According to interviewees, in 2002 the regional government (led by the CTAR) encountered problems getting their projects accepted by the national government because they did not meet SNIP requirements. As a result, the region lost money that would have been transferred for projects. Perhaps because of this failure, the newly elected regional government approached the 2003 process in a very technically aggressive way. The regional government came with profiles ready to meet SNIP requirements. They did not lose projects this time, but did go to the other extreme, and civil society agents viewed the government as too controlling.

According to interviewees, by 2004 the government had found an effective balance between technical quality and participation. The MEF methodology ran smoothly, although no functioning oversight committee existed from 2002 to 2006. The budget itself speaks to the success of the process—the MCLCP found that the regional budget developed in 2004 (to be spent in 2005) did reflect the regional development plan in a satisfactory way (Del Aguila Peralta 2004).

The 2005 process improved even more. Agents involved in the process signaled that the government evaluated the 2004 process in an effort to learn from past mistakes. Evaluators recommended working with mayors to ensure that the district, provincial, and regional processes were coordinated to avoid confusion.[29] The process was also less centralized—the government decided to hold the regional workshop in Sánchez Cerro. To demonstrate its commitment to participation, the government paid for the PAs' transportation to that province for the workshops. According to MEF statistics, approximately sixty-two PAs arrived, and that number increased almost twofold, to 108 PAs, in 2006. According to those involved, the agents are learning over time how the process works as well as about governmental investment in general.

Has past experience influenced the process? One might imagine that the successful experience in Ilo would improve regional processes. Several interviewees mentioned, however, that the regional budget process is not tapping into human and social capital generated in Ilo.

To what extent is civil society participating in the process? No local CSOs participated on the technical team in 2003 or 2004. A Lima-based NGO, Centro de Estudios para el Desarrollo y la Participación (CEDEP), working closely with the MCLCP, was active in all phases of the process by 2004.[30] CEDEP was specifically tasked with ensuring that the regional budget and development plan take gender concerns into account, but it provided more general technical assistance as well. However, as mentioned before, the CCR did not participate actively as an agent and generally provided rubber-stamp approval. Nor did civil society agents present their own projects for funding. Thus, there is still room for improvement in terms of civil society's participation in the budget process.

THE ANDES (NORTH, SOUTH, AND CENTRAL)

Cajamarca

Cajamarca, with its rolling hills and green valleys in the northern Andes, has a population of approximately 1.36 million living in thirteen provinces, Cajamarca City being the largest and the capital. Seventy-two percent of the population is rural, and 74.2 percent live in poverty. The economy is primarily based on agriculture—potatoes, rice, and dairy production—and mining (Gobierno Regional Cajamarca 2003c).

Civil Society   According to interviewees, Cajamarca's society has been organizing for decades. Historically, rural society has been especially active in this region. APRA began to organize peasants to demand land rights and road construction in the late 1940s—earlier than in other parts of the country—and throughout the 1960s. Today the strongest regional organizations bring together labor and peasants. There is also a strong environmental movement, spearheaded by some progressive leaders from the Catholic Church. Several development NGOs are also active in the region.

Like Moquegua, organizational activity varies around the region, which is generally divided into three zones: north, south, and center. Because the Shining Path was active in the southern part of Cajamarca, organizational life suffered in that area. The center is mainly rural and has a well-organized *campesino* sector. And *rondas campesinas* (peasant vigilante committees) were born in the northern areas of Cajamarca.[31]

Contemporary Cajamarcan civil society is marked by two contrasting characteristics: high levels of conflict around mining issues and a strong history of consensus building in the form of district and provincial roundtables, or *mesas*. First, the world's largest gold mine—Yanacocha[32]—has been both a blessing and a curse for the region. It has brought employment, roads, and growth in general to the region—especially in and around the capital city. However, the region has also struggled with environmental and land conflicts. In effect, the mine has polarized civil society in the region. Several *campesino*, church, environment, and labor organizations are adamantly against its activities in the region. Other organizations have more moderate positions, especially some NGOs. And many business associations see the mine as beneficial to the economy. There is very little dialogue between the sides, and the mining sector is generally absent from the institutions that bring state and civil society together, such as the CCR and the MCLCP.[33] Moderates and "pro-mine" organizations are accused of "selling out" and anti-mine organizations are called inflexible and unrealistic. Violent protest is frequent. For example, according to *El Comercio*, on September 8, 2004 a group of *campesinos* took over the mine's local office in protest of the mine's exploration in a nearby community. Eleven police and journalists were wounded. In May 2005, the issue exploded again as strikes and protests were organized around the mine's decision to expand its activities (CEDEPAS and GPC 2005). The issue has divided civil society organizations at the regional level. In a 2007 interview, the president of the MCLCP in Cajamarca stated that Cajamarca continues to experience "a period of conflict and social polarization resulting from this conflict" (Navarro Sarmiento 2007).

Second, the region is well known around the country for having extensive experience with *concertación* politics since the 1980s. In 1993, for example, one of the first roundtables in Peru was set up by the local leftist leadership in the city of Cajamarca.[34] Over the six years during which it was most active, it designed a provincial development plan using a participatory methodology. The mayor shared the experience with members of the national mayor's association, which spurred similar programs in other parts of the country (Portocarrero et al. 2002). However, because of personality problems and conflict among key actors, this particular *mesa* stopped functioning in 2000 (Díez Hurtado 2003). In 2004, the new *aprista* mayor, Emilio Horna Pereira, revived the *mesa*. Thus, Cajamarca is unique in the sense that there is a regional MCLCP structure *and* a provincial roundtable that works in the capital city.

Regional Government   From 2003 to 2006, the regional government in Cajamarca was firmly *aprista*, with the president and eight of the thirteen regional council members hailing from this party. However, even in this region, which is also a traditional APRA stronghold, the president did not win with a strong majority. Luis Felipe Gastelumendi won with 23.67 percent of the vote (Meléndez Guerrero 2003). One peculiarity of this government is that the president was often inexplicably absent, and Vice President Alejandro Rebaza Martell tended to be considered the de facto highest regional authority.

The government's support for the participatory institutions was often described by interviewees as lukewarm, especially at the beginning of its tenure. Although high-level officials complied with many of the legal requirements, they did not actively promote the PIs, especially the CCR. In interviews, government officials noted that the CCR did not work and that they planned to use other ways to directly reach the people, such as town hall meetings that are open to the public.

By contrast, the government put more time and effort into the participatory budget process. Interviewees attributed this to the presence of a strong budget team working in the government whose support increased over time. Early in the process, the regional-government officials did not actively support the participatory budget process. In 2003, they received offers of help from other actors, such as the MCLCP, but did not accept them. However, this attitude changed over time, in part when the president's office realized the political payoffs of the process. According to interviewees, the vice president viewed the participatory budget as a way to get political support, often to the detriment of technical standards. For example, as one participant noted, during the 2004 workshop to debate regional projects, if one participating agent voiced a concern about points for a project, instead of following common voting protocol, the vice president would call a revote on those points. This was seen as an effort to please the agents, not to stick to a technical process. As a result of this change of attitude, most interviewees noted that in 2004 and 2005, the government, especially the budget team, was open to assistance by the MCLCP and local NGOs.

Regional Coordination Council   The CCR in Cajamarca does function, primarily to fulfill its role in the participatory budget process.[35] According to CEDEPAS (2007), a local NGO that works with the GPC to monitor participation in the new regions, a total of ten meetings were held from 2003 to 2006. Only two of these meetings, both in 2005, included 100 percent of its members (CEDEPAS 2007). In 2003, the CCR met five times (GPC 2003c). One meeting was actually part of the budget process and another was called to debate the CCR's internal regulations.[36] In 2004, three meetings were called but two were suspended due to lack of quorum (GPC 2005b). In 2005, two meetings (one official and one extraordinary) were held in one day to install the new representatives and discuss the participatory budget process (CEDEPAS 2005b). A third meeting was held later that year. Only one meeting was held in 2006 (CEDEPAS 2007).

A total of fifty-two organizations registered to participate in the 2003 elections (see Table 5.3). That number increased slightly, to fifty-five, in 2005 (see Table 5.4).

As in the other regions, the list of CSOs that registered to participate in the region does not represent the diversity of the organizations in the region, illustrated in the fact that organizations came from only six of the thirteen provinces. The *rondas* did not fully participate (only two organizations registered in 2003 and three in 2005). There is no gender quota, but there is an indigenous quota (mandated by the regional government).

The CCR in Cajamarca faced two problems. First, the regional government decided that certain *types* of organizations must be elected. They also man-

Table 5.3. CSO registration and election lists: Cajamarca 2003

Type of organization	Number registered	Number mandated	Number elected
Church	0	0	0
Universities	0	2	2, neither registered for the elections
Business organizations and producers	7	4, one invited	4, one of which was not registered for the elections
Labor unions, agriculture and neighborhood groups	16	1	1
Professional associations	11	1	1
Native organizations	0	1	0
Women's and youth groups, *mesas*	2	1	1 (really an NGO)
NGOs	8	1 invited	1 invited and not registered for the election
Transportation	0	1 invited	1 invited
Rondas campesinas	2	1 invited	1 invited
Campesino communities	6	1invited	2, one of which was not registered for the elections
Other	0	–	–
Total	**52**	**14**	**14**

SOURCES: Gobierno Regional Cajamarca 2003a, 2003b, 2005; CEDEPAS 2005b.

Table 5.4. CSO registration and election lists: Cajamarca 2005

Type of organization	Number registered	Number mandated	Number elected 2005
Church	1	0	0
Universities	2	2	2
Business organizations and producers	4	4, one invited	3
Labor unions, agriculture and neighborhood groups	23	1	2, one invited
Professional associations	4	1	2, one invited
Women's groups and *mesas*	5	1	1 (same NGO)
NGOs	7	1	1 invited
Transportation	0	1 invited	1 invited
Rondas campesinas	3	1 invited	1 invited
Campesino communities and native organizations[1]	2	1 invited	0
Youth groups[2]	1	1	1
Other	3	0	0
Total	**55**	**14**	**14**

SOURCES: Gobierno Regional Cajamarca 2003a, 2003b, 2005; CEDEPAS 2005b.
[1] In 2005, the government combined native organizations and *campesino* communities into one category.
[2] In 2005, the government listed this as a separate category instead of combining it with women's organizations and *mesas*.

dated the number of organizations that would represent each type of organization (noted in Tables 5.3 and 5.4). During the 2003 elections, this led to irregularities because there were some types of organizations that did not register to participate. For example, the regional government dictated that universities must be on the CCR, yet no university registered to participate in the election, As a result, participants nominated some organizations that were not present. Two university representatives were elected in absentia.

Second, the government decided to expand the number of CCR representatives, purportedly to allow for increased civil society participation. According to the law, Cajamarca's CCR should have nine civil society members and thirteen provincial mayors. The regional government decided to include "invited" representatives: eight additional mayors and five additional civil society members—all from the poorest districts and areas that are farther away from the capital, called "border areas" (Gobierno Regional Cajamarca 2003a). Yet it is unclear how the regional government chose the civil society invitees; the registered civil society organizations were not consulted and most invited organizations had not registered to participate in the 2003 election. Interviewees suspected that political motives were at work, indicating that the regional government wanted to make sure that more historically *aprista* organizations were represented on the CCR. In sum, in 2003 it was unclear how decisions were made regarding who to elect and who to invite, and the registration list appears, to some extent, irrelevant.

The 2003 electoral process was best described to me as "informal." During the election, there was no formal vote taken; rather, groups agreed informally who would represent different types of organizations. According to observers, the 2005 process was more organized. However, only three more organizations registered to participate, indicating a lack of increased interest on behalf of regional civil society in participating in this mechanism.

The CCR is not active and has achieved little in terms of results. Its role has centered on approving the participatory budget, and it has never presented a project to the regional government (CEDEPAS 2007). Those who were elected in absentia (such as the university representative) were especially uninterested in participating. In the case of one university, when contacted by phone, it was not even clear who their representative was, since the original person had left the university. I was told that two different people were the new representative yet both denied this. In a 2004 interview, another civil society representative indicated that she was no longer interested in participating, although she continued to be the formal representative of her organization. Only representatives from the NGOs seemed to take an interest in strengthening the CCR.

Attendance is also low in this case. In the first CCR (2003–2004), an average of 34.5 percent of the mayors attended the meetings and 51.5 percent of the civil society representatives attended (CEDEPAS 2007). Attendance rates improved during the 2005–2006 CCR, with 72.5 percent of the mayors attending sessions and 64 percent of the civil society representatives attending (CEDEPAS 2007). Many cited time and distance as explaining problems with attendance. Cajamarca is typical of the Andean regions in that transportation and communication within the region are very difficult because of poor infrastructure. According to the government, for example, a mere 30.7 percent of all the districts are easily accessible by road (Gobierno Regional Cajamarca 2003c). In more practical terms, traveling from one end of the Andean region to the capital city by bus can often take more than a day. Hard rains during the rainy season often destroy or block the roads that do exist. However, members who live and work in the capital city are also among those who do not attend, thus this factor clearly does not account for the entire problem.

According to participants and government officials, mayors had even poorer attendance rates than civil society members. Both *aprista* and other mayors did not show up, citing the fact that it takes too much time and the meetings are not important. In this case, time and distance are not excuses either. Mayors are paid for the time and the municipality can pay for their travel. Instead, interviewees attributed low attendance rates to other factors, such as not wanting to support the president (even when they are from his own party) and their frustration with the urban bias in all development efforts.[37]

Other regional civil society actors, such as the provincial *mesa* and the MCLCP, were not particularly involved in the CCR process during the period under study. Several interviewees mentioned a general confusion about the difference between the roundtables and the CCR. A MCLCP representative stated that they had not clearly defined the different roles and responsibilities for the two entities. Thus, overall the 2003–2004 and 2005–2006 CCRs in Cajamarca were relatively weak.

Participatory Budget   According to observers, the budget process in Cajamarca evolved in an "organized and consensual manner" (CEDEPAS 2005b, 23). In terms of the methodology, the 2003 process was rushed and generally unsatisfactory (O'Brien 2004; López Ricci and Wiener 2004). In the end, the regional council changed the budget after the participatory prioritization workshop. Why did the council make these changes? Interviewees argued that both political bargaining and the fact that several projects did not meet SNIP requirements explain the outcome. All interviewees agreed that the process was more successful in 2004, primarily because there was more time to develop it correctly. Also, there were more regional workshops and an expanded technical team. However, the regional council decided to change the budget again after it left the regional workshop.

In all years, the government decided to divide the investment funds by territory. Seventy percent of the funds was distributed by province (weighted by population), and 30 percent was set aside for projects of a regional nature. During decentralized workshops, the mayors presented proposals for their province's portion. At the regional workshop, PAs discussed the remaining 30 percent. In terms of proposals, in 2004 the government let participants bring "ideas" (not necessarily developed project proposals) to the workshops and the technical team then filled out one-page summaries. Although this can be useful to generate ideas for future projects, it is not always clear that the participants understand that only more developed project proposals can make it into SNIP for funding. Interviewees worried that this could generate false expectations for PAs whose projects may be approved in the workshop but then do not make it into the final budget.

The number of PAs from civil society (eighty-two) in 2004 and 2005 did not change in terms of number or types of organizations (CEDEPAS 2007). In addition to government officials, the technical team in 2004 comprised nine representatives from NGOs and two from the MCLCP (Gobierno Regional Cajamarca 2004a). This number is expanded from the 2003 process when there were two representatives from NGOs, one from a university, and two from the MCLCP (López Ricci and Wiener 2004). According to interviewees, this continued in 2005 and 2006. NGOs provided other forms of technical assistance as well. For example, CEDEPAS helped a consortium of small producers to write a proposal to submit for consideration. Although the CCR was not actively involved as a PA, the regional MCLCP did play an important role in the process. Of course, problems exist here as well. Like most regions, a functioning oversight committee did not form during the period under study. And the 2004 final product did not necessarily reflect regional priorities. According to the MCLCP, the budget that eventually emerged from the 2004 process was not satisfactory in terms of its adherence to the regional development plan (Del Aguila Peralta 2004).

Ayacucho

Ayacucho lies in the central Andean highlands with approximately 620,000 inhabitants living in eleven provinces. An estimated 57 percent of the population lives in the urban area surrounding the capital—known as both Huamanga and Ayacucho City. Visiting Ayacucho is like stepping back in time. It is one of the poorest regions in Peru—64.9 percent of its population lives in poverty. An estimated 50 percent of the population lives without access to water, 87 percent without access to sewage systems, and more than 70 percent without electricity (Gobierno Regional Ayacucho n.d). Livestock and agriculture are the principal sources of income in this region, and 99 percent of those who work in this sector are small to medium farmers (Gobierno Regional Ayacucho n.d.).

Civil Society   Organizational initiatives are extremely fragile in this region primarily because of the armed conflict between the Peruvian state, *campesinos*, and Sendero Luminoso (Sendero), or the Shining Path, that went on for twenty years.[38] According to the Peruvian Truth and Reconciliation Commission's report, an estimated 69,280 people died during the conflict, most of whom were *campesinos* and 40 percent of whom lived in Ayacucho (CVR 2003). In addition to severe economic consequences, the region's social structure suffered as *campesinos* fled to urban areas of the region and/or Lima. Many civil society professionals and activists fled the region or ceased activities to avoid attack. Others were killed because Sendero saw them as perpetrating an inherently unjust system.

Today, although Sendero still exists, it is no longer a serious threat to the state and is mainly linked to narcotics trafficking in the coca-growing regions of Peru.[39] Although several factors are widely cited for the fall of Sendero, one factor was the emergence of the *comités de autodefensa civil* (CDCs), another form of self-defense committee or *ronda* that emerged in this area during the early 1990s. These committees, which are often confused with the *rondas* in Cajamarca,[40] emerged in alliance with the Peruvian armed forces to fight against terrorism in the region. Although this reaction to the terror was based on organizing to fight back, the committees never expanded their functions or served to rebuild the organizational fabric after the conflict died down.

Civil society in the region has never fully recovered from this violence. Huber et al. (2003, 52) characterize civil society in Ayacucho as one of

> extreme division, where distrust, accusations, and gossip reign. The common denominator that sometimes unites the different social sectors is being from Ayacucho. However, when alliances are formed, they are generally against something or someone . . . and rarely based in proposals.[41]

Although the civil society sector as a whole is weak, the region does boast a relatively active labor and *campesino* sector, highly influenced by the radical leftist discourse that was popular in the region for decades. In their studies of Ayacuchan society, Huber et al. (2003) and Díez Hurtado (2003) document the role and history of three additional regional grassroots organizations, the Frente de Defensa del Pueblo de Ayacucho (Defense Front for the Ayacuchan People);[42] Federación Agraria Departamental de Ayacucho (Ayacucho's Departmental Agricultural Federation);[43] and the Federación de Clubes de Madres de Ayacucho (Federation of Mothers' Clubs in Ayacucho).[44] Another important regional social movement is the coca leaf producers, known as *cocaleros*.[45] NGOs are also present in the region and work in a variety of sectors, such as agriculture, micro-credit, and human rights (Díez Hurtado 2003). Yet, as Díez

Hurtado (2003, 111) notes, "they suffer periodic and episodic critical accusations by some political sectors and the media." These attacks vary from accusations of supporting the Fujimori mafia to being controlled by Yankee imperialists. And there is no regional consortium that brings these different groups together.

Historically, the region has very little experience with participatory institutions. One exception is a provincial-level experience that took place in Huanta where the mayor set up a successful roundtable and implemented participatory planning techniques during the 1990s.[46] This experience began to fail in 1998 when personal conflicts impeded its progress (Panfichi and Pineda 2007). Apart from this experience, the regional movements and organizations that do exist are not particularly focused on participatory methods.

Regional Government   The 2003–2006 regional government in Ayacucho was also *aprista*, with the president and seven of the eleven regional council members representing this party. Werner Omar Quezada Martínez won with only 22.97 percent of the popular vote (Meléndez Guerrero 2003). Two aspects characterize the regional president. First, he was often accused of criminal behavior. For example, according to a September 16, 2004, report in Peru's national newspaper, *La República*, the president was formally accused of abusing his authority and covering up illegal acts. As a result, the media frequently and vociferously criticized him.[47] Second, his constituents often called him a populist. His regional team did not support the reform's participatory institutions, stating, for example, that the CCR "is not really an effective mechanism to channel participation." Like the regional government in Cajamarca, this government preferred to hold town hall meetings to reach the people directly.

Regional Coordination Council   Ayacucho's CCR during the period under study was inactive and weak. In both 2003 and 2004, it met only once each year to approve the participatory budget (GPC 2004c, GPC 2005b). It did not participate actively in the budget process, however. Two meetings were held in 2005 (Asociación SER 2005). According to one CCR member, there were two CCR meetings in 2006, both linked to the participatory budget process. The regional CSO registration list for the 2003 and 2005 elections demonstrates that over time, *fewer* CSOs were interested in participating in the CCR (see Table 5.5). In 2003, a total of nineteen organizations registered to participate in the CCR. In 2005, according to records sent from the regional government to the Defensoría del Pueblo, fifteen CSOs registered.[48] According to one CCR

Table 5.5. CSO registration list: Ayacucho

Type of organization	2003	2005
Producers and labor unions	3	1
Business	2	2
Professional associations	6	2
Agricultural organizations	1	2
Campesino community	1	0
Women's groups	2	1
Human rights (children, disabled, displaced families)	3	3
NGO and others	1	3
Youth	0	1
Total	**19**	**15**

SOURCE: Gobierno Regional Ayacucho 2003, 2005.

member, to compensate for the underrepresentation of youth and sectors who were affected by the violence, the regional government mandated that the 2005–2006 CCR include representatives from these sectors. Thus, in 2005, five seats were up for open election, instead of the seven that had been elected in 2003.

The list of organizations that registered is hardly inclusive of the regional CSOs that do exist. On the one hand, in contrast to the other regions, some grassroots organizations did come out to participate.[49] On the other hand, in 2003, organizations from only three of eight provinces participated and several sectors were underrepresented, such as *rondas*, universities, labor unions, and agricultural producers (Defensoría del Pueblo 2005b). None of the regional grassroots actors documented by Huber et al. (2003) and Díez Hurtado (2003) participated in the 2003 and 2005 elections nor did the *cocaleros* register. Most elected members from civil society reside in the capital city. Independent monitors have expressed concern that no female or indigenous representative participated in the CCR from 2003 to 2006 (Asociación SER 2005). Furthermore, two of the civil society representatives in the 2005–2006 CCR did not participate actively, described by one interviewee as having "deserted" the CCR.

Civil society actors such as NGOs and the regional MCLCP opted not to participate in the CCR elections, attributing this decision in interviews to the fact that the law was not originally designed for NGO participation. They decided instead to put their efforts into strengthening the MCLCP, which they believed to be a more effective space to dialogue with the state. However, by

2005 it was clear that their participation was needed to make the CCR more active in regional dialogue. Thus, they coordinated among themselves informally and asked one NGO, Agenda Sur, to participate. This NGO was elected to the 2004–2005 CCR and actively pressured the government to work more closely with the CCR.

In interviews, civil society members of the 2003–2004 CCR mentioned frustration with the experience and a general level of discontent. One member noted that she was "tired of pressuring for change." Another member had resigned from his organization in 2003, and the organization did not appoint another representative in 2004. These problems continued to plague the 2005–2006 CCR. Solari (2005) notes that of the seven civil society members who were elected in 2005, only two are active. Independent reports call the entire institution "passive," noting that "while it meets the legally mandated number of times, it has not been able to become an active space that brings together the regional government, local governments, and representatives from society" (Asociación SER 2005, 40). Nor does the CCR have a collaborative relationship with other organizations, such as the MCLCP. Representatives of the MCLCP reported in interviews that they analyzed the institution and decided that because it was purely consultative, it was not worth the effort.[50] Thus, the CCR during the period under study was, as one interview stated, "null and void."

Participatory Budget   The participatory budget process has also been extremely problematic in this region. In all of the years under study, the government divided the investment funds on a territorial basis. The provincial workshops took the same form: the government announced how much each province would receive and then mayors decided how to spend the money.

In contrast to the other regions under study, the process actually *worsened* from 2003 to 2004 and remained weak during the tenure of President Quezada. In 2003, the process was relatively open, and a pro-participation team in the government, working with the MCLCP, developed a timeline of activities and defined roles and responsibilities early in the process. The MCLCP formed a technical team of professionals who could assist in the process. Then the government held workshops in the provinces to gather proposals and a final regional workshop to approve them. In the end, however, the regional council did not fund the projects that came out of the process and changed the final budget. Early in the 2004 process, the government changed teams and broke the alliance with the MCLCP and decided to control the process directly with the assistance of an international organization. In interviews, regional government officials blasted the role that NGOs had played in the process, saying that from now on the government plans to have complete control over budgetary processes. In 2004, when interviewed about the process, one official stated that "this year the government will run the process. We have said 'enough!' to the NGOs." After this year, local CSOs in general were less involved, for example, not being invited to participate in the technical team.

Interviewees described the 2004 regional workshop as a failure. The government basically presented the budget and did not allow real debate or discussion about the projects. According to interviewees, several PAs withdrew from the 2004 regional workshop—especially activists from grassroots organizations—because of their disagreement with how it was evolving. At least 50 percent of the CCR members did not participate in the process, and the CCR as a body did not sign the final minutes. The MCLCP's analysis shows that the 2004 budget, in the end, did not reflect regional priorities in a satisfactory manner.

Participants noted that the 2005 process was poorly organized and not participatory. The process was similarly controlled by the government and participation suffered. Although PAs came to the regional workshop, interviewees noted that decisions were driven by political officials, not PAs. However, participants noted that the methodology was smoother and the government allowed agents to participate a bit more. But no oversight committee was formed and mostly government projects were considered. Again, the regional council changed the final budget after it left the workshop. The process continued in the same vein in 2006 as well. According to an interviewee, the 2006 workshop was the worst of President Quezada's tenure as he knew he would be leaving office and would not be held accountable for budget. Another interviewee noted that regional government officials never embraced the process and, instead, viewed it as a threat to their power.

The Ayacucho case provides an interesting glimpse into how government officials can manipulate these processes. As we recall from Chapter 2, the government must send proof of the regional workshop—in the form of a memo or minutes signed by participating agents—to the MEF to receive its funds. To receive their 2005 annual budget funds, the regional government still sent its 2004 report to the MEF with the final minutes signed by participants and a list of organizations that participated in the process. And the MEF did send the region its funds. Yet several interviewees reported having left the workshop in disgust. When I obtained a copy of the minutes from the MEF, I realized that the signatures were all initials, thus it was impossible to verify PA attendance. MEF statistics about the number of PAs do not reflect any of these problems, however. According to their database, fifty-eight PAs attended the workshop in 2004, and 127 attended in 2005.

Cusco

Cusco—located in the southern part of Peru's highlands and home to the famous Inca site Machu Picchu—has a population of slightly less than 1.2 million. Livestock agriculture, tourism, and mining are the principal economic activities in this region. According to Peruvian government statistics, 48 percent of Cusco's population is rural, and 59.2 percent live in poverty.

Civil Society   Cusco's civil society is one of the most organized in the country. As in Cajamarca, the organizational dynamic was especially active during the 1980s and throughout the 1990s. Several leftist mayors set up participatory programs, such as Limatambo, where the mayor used participatory methods to develop the municipal government's budget in the 1990s.[51] There were also some municipal experiences with *mesas* sprinkled around the region (Grompone 2004).

The presence of a Regional Assembly, formed in 1998, partially explains the high level of organization during the period under study. This coalition of CSOs formed in reaction to Fujimori's attempt to privatize a hydroelectric plant near the area around Machu Picchu. A variety of sectors, including labor activists, *campesino* organizations, NGOs, and business associations, all agreed that privatizing the plant would go against regional interests. The coalition rallied around the banner of "democratization, decentralization, and anti-privatization." In the end, the groups succeeded and the plant remained in the state's hands. As a result, alliances emerged that continue to exist today.

Regional Government   Cusco's 2003–2006 regional president, Carlos Cuaresma, also won with a slim margin, garnering 19.95 percent of the vote (Meléndez Guerrero 2003). His government was extremely divided—his regional council consisted of pure opposition parties. Cuaresma represented the Independent Moralizing Front party (on the right of the Peruvian political spectrum), although his roots—like Simon in Lambayeque and Constantinides in Moquegua—were in the left. Unlike Simon and Constantinides, however, he is not personally committed to participatory processes. Rather, interviewees note, he slowly became convinced that the new institutions served his political goals. One interviewee noted that Cuaresma "seemed to be getting legitimacy from civil society" through these institutions.

This change of attitude took place during the process of putting together the regional development plan in 2002 and early 2003.[52] Because the president was not aware that a plan already existed—developed with high levels of participation in 2001 and 2002 by the MCLCP—once elected, he began a new process. Civil society actors complained, and as a result, he decided to modify the plan that already existed for quick CCR approval. When faced with the need for a mid-term plan, again Cuaresma put something together quickly without consulting the population. The civil society organizations complained, and this time the CCR—led by the civil society representatives—refused to approve it.

Eventually the CCR and the president struck a compromise. The CCR would approve the plan if he agreed to make the process more participatory. The president agreed and held several regional workshops to update and modify the regional development plan. During these workshops, according to interviewees, Cuaresma realized that the process served his political interests. It helped him legitimize his government (which at the time had very low approval levels), justify his decisions, and allow him to politick for future votes.

The regional government's technical team was also very open to the PIs and committed to improving them over time. When interviewed, representatives from the budget office repeatedly mentioned the need to base the budget in the regional development plan and not change it according to political interests. Nongovernmental representatives lauded their work as well. Thus, the regional government can be described as committed to implementing the participatory institutions for mostly strategic purposes.

Regional Coordination Council   The CCR is organized and meets regularly. NGO reports document that the CCR met four times in 2003, twice in 2004, and three times in 2005 and 2006 (Asociación Arariwa 2007). According to governmental and civil society interviewees, Cusco did not call a 2005 election in a timely fashion. This was because civil society members of the 2003–2004 CCR wanted to further institutionalize some of their projects and requested that they extend their tenure until 2005. They also wanted to make sure the elections were held in a way that captured the diversity of regional civil society. For example, they wanted to ensure that more women's groups and groups that advocate for the disabled participated (Asociación Arariwa and Centro Bartolomé de las Casas 2006).

Table 5.6. CSO registration list: Cusco

Type of organization	2003	2005
Mesas, NGOs, development councils	34	N/A
Church	1	N/A
Labor unions	1	N/A
Professional associations	11	N/A
Business associations	3	N/A
Agriculture, *campesino*, and native organizations	3	N/A
Universities	1	N/A
Producer and small business organizations	3	N/A
Women, neighborhood, and youth groups	8	N/A
Total	**65**	**110**

SOURCES: Gobierno Regional Cusco 2003b; Asociación Arariwa and Centro Bartolomé de las Casas 2006.

The government spent the first half of 2006 consulting the regional MCLCP and other civil society actors to develop a regional ordinance that expanded the powers of the CCR. According to NGO monitors, the ordinance (039-2006-CRC-GRC) defines the role of the new CCR, expanding its power to emit a formal opinion about the regional annual plan and the annual participatory budget, the regional development plan, and the general vision and the strategic objectives of the programs that make up the regional development plan, as well as other issues as determined by the Regional Council (Asociación Arariwa and Centro Bartolomé de las Casas 2006).

In 2003, sixty-five organizations registered for the election of civil society representatives (see Table 5.6), and the elections were reportedly smooth. During the election, CSOs were grouped by categories and a representative from each category was elected.[53] Two problems immediately emerged after the 2003 election, and the responses speak to the success of Cusco's CCR. First, the representative from the Catholic Church never attended a meeting. Second, placing women, youth, and neighborhood organizations in the same category proved problematic. The women's organizations split their vote and a male representative from the Lion's Club emerged as the representative (even though the government had mandated a gender quota). However, the CCR was able to move along without the active participation of the Church representative.[54] And to address the gender issue, the Lion's Club representative and the women's organizations decided to appoint a co-representative from the women's organizations to attend meetings. The flexibility in front of these problems illustrates the resilience of the institution in Cusco.

Another indicator of success is the fact that almost twice as many organizations registered in 2006. Because the entire 2006 list of organizations is not available, only the total number of registered CSOs, it is impossible to see what kinds of organizations participated over time. Regional experts noted in interviews that there is an urban bias in the 2003 list as the organizations that registered tended to be located in the city of Cusco, and organizations from only three of the thirteen provinces registered. These same experts noted that NGOs were overrepresented and that several types of organizations, including youth, religious, labor, indigenous and/or *campesino*, university, and producer groups were underrepresented in the CCR registration lists.

The civil society CCR representatives interviewed for this study were well organized and called their own meetings when they felt that an issue needed to be discussed. A good level of communication among the CCR representatives from civil society existed. In addition, these same people were actively involved in regional politics. In 2004, for example, the CCR participated in the design of a mid-term development plan, which goes beyond their legal mandate (see Gobierno Regional Cusco 2003a). When consulted about the mid-term regional development plan, the CCR suggested adding another strategic objective environment, which was accepted and included in the final plan (Gobierno Regional Cusco 2004).

In many ways, the success of the 2003–2004 CCR lay in its civil society membership. With the exception of the church representative, they were active members of the community and committed to dedicating time and resources to the CCR. Furthermore, several interviewees mentioned the important role that NGOs played in consolidating the CCR. "They have the funds and time for research, organize meetings, and even provide the simple things like a cup of coffee and some cookies for meetings." Yet the downside of this role is that NGOs generally have more tenuous links to the population and do not really represent a particular constituency. Although their participation strengthens the CCR, the benefits are generally enjoyed by a relatively elite set of actors.

The CCR is actively supported by other regional civil society actors. In Cusco, the MCLCP made a conscious decision to support this entity. The coordinator of the MCLCP was also a member of the 2003–2004 CCR, which allowed for fluid relations and communication channels between the two groups. The Regional Assembly is not formally present, because it does not meet the legal requirements to register, but many of its members are on the CCR and it is supportive of the CCR in general.

Of course, the CCR has problems as well. Absenteeism among mayors is a problem. For example, in the third meeting of 2003, no mayors attended (Asociación Arariwa and Centro Bartolomé de las Casas 2003). As one interviewee noted, this is because they feel that they should deal directly with the president, not through this consultative, nonbinding space. However, according to interviewee accounts, the president personally talked to them and pressured them to attend. Although the attendance rate never reached 100 percent, enough members attended most meetings to achieve a quorum.

Participatory Budget   The participatory budgeting experience in Cusco during this period was one of the most successful in the country. As in other regions, the 2003 process did not go well. The government held participatory workshops at both provincial and regional levels to discuss and prioritize projects. Group work took place and decisions were made based on territorial criteria (that is, money was divided by province). However, in the end, the government did not fund the list of projects that came out of the final workshop (O'Brien 2004). Instead, the regional council and president decided to renovate the soccer stadium, a populist move that they assumed would increase their popularity (López Ricci and Wiener 2004).

Civil society representatives, especially from the CCR and the MCLCP, actively pressured the government not to make the same mistake in 2004 and to instead focus on linking regional projects to the regional development plan in order to ensure regional impact. As a result, in 2004, participants organized their working groups in the regional workshop around the nine strategic objectives of the regional development plan. The MCLCP found that the resulting budget was successfully linked to the objectives of the plan (Del Aguila Peralta 2004).

After the rough start, the process is widely considered to have improved over time. Independent monitors argue that it has served to "democratize" public spending (Asociación Arariwa 2007). The number of participants over the years reflects this success. According to independent monitors, sixty-five PAs registered in 2004, ninety-one in 2005, and 107 in 2006 (Asociación Arariwa and Centro Bartolomé de las Casas 2006). The process has led to more projects that reflect the regional development plan (Asociación Arariwa 2007), and it was recently singled out as one of the most successful experiences in the country (Colectivo Institucional de Presupuesto Participativo 2006).

CCR members and civil society have pressured for more social projects, especially in the area of education. Members of the CCR mentioned with pride the fact that Cusco's 2005 regional budget dedicated 15 percent to education programs. They also pushed the government to separate money for "democracy promotion" projects, that is, the costs associated with promoting the region's participatory institutions. Another important result of civil society participation is that they fought to include the funds generated from Camisea[55] in the participatory process, thereby going well beyond the legal requirements. Starting in 2005, the funds from this pool of money were included in the process.

The composition of the technical team reflects the active role of civil society as well. The technical team in 2003 was limited to three members representing civil society organizations: one NGO, one university, and the MCLCP. In 2004, the team was increased to include four NGOs, the MCLCP, and the Association of Economists (Asociación Arariwa and Centro Bartolomé de las Casas 2005). Civil society continued to play an active role in 2005, and interviewees reported that the team included the MCLCP, three NGOs, and one *campesino* organization. And the role of NGOs has gone beyond participating on the technical team—several NGOs are participating in the training of agents and have organized fora to discuss the regional priorities for the additional money from the Camisea project.

The CCR was active in the 2004 and 2005 budget processes, participating as agents and making comments when the budget was presented for its approval in 2004. Since 2004, an oversight committee has been elected, but it is unclear if the committee is actively monitoring government spending. It is safe to say that the budget process has been successful in Cusco. As one analysis states, "[T]he participatory budget in Cusco has gone beyond a management instrument, it has become a space to institutionalize regional efforts to bring together the roles and responsibilities of both the state and civil society" (Colectivo Interinstitucional de Presupuesto Participativo 2006, 33).

THE AMAZON JUNGLE

Loreto

Loreto, with its lush landscapes and tropical climate, is located in the far northeast of the country, bordering Ecuador in the north. The population of a little less than 900,000 is spread over six provinces. More than 63 percent of the population lives in the urban province of Maynas, which is home to the capital city of Iquitos, and 62.7 percent of the population lives in poverty. Most of the jobs and economic growth stem from the fishing and lumber industries. The region suffers from severe transportation and communication problems due to its geography. The thick jungle forests that cover 80 percent of its area prove almost impossible to clear for building roads, and most transportation takes place on canoes or speedboats along the tributaries of the Amazon (Gobierno Regional Loreto 2004a).

Because of its proximity to Ecuador, the region has historically suffered from territorial conflicts with its neighbor. The most recent flare-up took place in 1995 when both sides began to redeploy troops to the border area and eventually fighting broke out. Peacekeeping efforts began almost immediately and high-level international and domestic officials began a two-year process to resolve the territorial dispute.[56]

Civil Society Loreto's civil society has historically been unorganized and fragile due to the region's marginal economic, political, and geographical status.[57] The most organized sectors are business, *campesinos*, indigenous, and the urban poor.[58] One relatively organized regional actor is the Frente de Defensa de Loreto (Loreto's Defense Front), which formed in the 1970s and has been especially active in regional politics since the most recent conflict with Ecuador.[59] The Frente de Defensa (Frente) quickly organized during the 1995 conflict to pressure for a resolution that favored the region. After the peace process finished, the Frente was disappointed with Fujimori's concessions and began to publicly criticize his leadership. It mobilized its members for a democratization and decentralization campaign in the late 1990s and has even expressed a desire for the region's complete administrative autonomy.

Although the Frente has created a certain degree of cohesiveness among grassroots organizations and political parties, it demonstrates a highly confrontational attitude and an unwillingness to work with the regional government. In interviews, Frente leaders noted that they did not want to support this regional government because it was trying to "neutralize the power of the people." One interviewee argued that "the government can do very little for the population," thus why should they participate in regional participatory institutions? It is also plagued by internal conflicts and leadership problems. Thus, while it sometimes emerges to play an important role, it does not effectively unite the diverse civil society sector in the region.

Regional Government President Robinson Rivadeneyra Reátegu, Loreto's president from 2003 to 2006, exemplifies the emerging political clout of regional movements. His movement, Unidos por Loreto (UNIPOL), or United for Loreto, won the presidency with 36.51 percent of the vote and captured five

of the seven regional council seats (Meléndez Guerrero 2003). Like his counterparts in Cusco and Moquegua, Rivadeneyra Reátegu is also an ex-leftist
who has moved closer to the right over time. Yet even with these roots, he
never fully supported the participatory institutions. Instead, he was often described as having an authoritarian and anti-participatory personal style.

For example, during his administration he stated publicly that the participatory budget would never improve democracy. According to him, it merely
raises false expectations that because of budgetary constraints, the regional
government cannot meet. His regional budget team followed his lead. When
interviewed in 2004, government officials demonstrated a resigned attitude
about the CCR, suggesting that their own efforts would be better spent promoting other mechanisms, such as town hall meetings.

Regional Coordination Council   As in Ayacucho, Loreto's CCR hardly functioned during the years under study. Because no national organization is actively monitoring the CCR in Loreto, reliable data are scarce. Interviewees who
participate in the CCR or monitor it locally (such as the MCLCP and the Ombudsman) reported two meetings in 2003, but none in 2004 or 2005. The regional government reported one meeting in 2006 (Gobierno Regional Loreto
2007). The quality of civil society participation was not high; for example, when
it met to formally approve the regional development plan in 2003, the CCR did
not recommend changes.

Even though the registration list indicates that interest in the CCR increased over time—thirty-seven organizations registered for the elections in
2003 and eighty-eight registered in 2005 (see Table 5.7)—it hardly functioned,
partly because of problems with distance and transportation. Interviewees
from the MCLCP, regional CSOs, and the government noted that mayors did
not participate and the representatives from the provinces could not travel to
the capital for meetings.[60] The government did not dedicate time or resources
to the CCR. For example, in 2003 the CCR asked for space to meet and the
government denied this request. Members of the CCR have asked for the government to fund their travel to meetings, and again, this request has been
denied.

Other actors did not support the CCR either. Although the MCLCP is active in regional politics, it did not actively support the CCR during the period
under study. The MCLCP did not register to participate in the election, and the
CCR never emerged as a priority for this regional organization. NGOs could

Table 5.7. CSO registration list: Loreto

Type of organization	2003	2005
Producers and agriculture	10	9
Business	2	5
Labor unions	2	14
Professional associations	6	4
Small business associations	1	4
Frentes/juntas de defense	2	16
Campesino and native groups, rondas	6	7
Women's groups	3	4
University	1	0
Church	3	5
NGO	1	2
Other	0	18
Total	**37**	**88**[1]

SOURCE: Gobierno Regional Loreto 2003, 2005.

[1] This list includes only organizations from the province of Maynas, where the capital city is (Defensoría del Pueblo 2007). There are no national or regional government records of the organizations that registered in the other provinces.

not provide time and resources to make it work either. In fact, there were very few NGOs working on topics such as democracy promotion or local governance—that is, the NGOs that would normally support this process—because of the extremely high operating costs involved in working in the Amazon basin.

Participatory Budget   Like Ayacucho, interviewees referred to the budget process as formalistic. In terms of civil society participation, the process worsened from 2003 to 2004 and remained problematic in 2005.[61] Every year the government held workshops in several provinces to explain the process and collect proposals. As in Ayacucho, the government divided the regional budget evenly by province (taking into account population). First, provincial meetings were held to gather proposals followed by a regional workshop to validate and prioritize them. However, interviewees noted that the regional, provincial, and district processes tend to overlap, which caused confusion among PAs and even government officials.

In 2003, the first year of the process, the regional government came in resistant to the participation of civil society. MCLCP representatives noted that before 2003, they had developed positive relations with the CTAR, that is, the regional government appointed by Fujimori, after coordinating the regional development plan. As a result, they went into the 2003 budget process eager to help. However, the regional government refused assistance and undertook the process alone. This continued throughout the following years.

Government officials expressed discontent with the 2003 process in terms of the quantity and quality of participation of the participating agents. Apparently, there were too many agents present and they were "difficult to handle." Thus, for the 2004 process, the government asked the MCLCP to take over the task of registering PAs. They passed an ordinance stating that only twenty-five representatives from civil society could participate in the regional workshop in order to ensure more "orderly" participation (Gobierno Regional Loreto 2004b). The MCLCP registered organizations and trained the twenty-five elected representatives on the budget process. After the election, the government proceeded to carry out the rest of the process alone, with no technical assistance from civil society.

In 2005, regional CSOs effectively pressured the government to open up the process to more agents. However, participation was restricted in another sense. The government held the final regional workshop in Mariscal Ramón Castilla, a province to the east of the capital. Although the regional government's intention—to decentralize the process—was laudable, this prohibited many organizations from participating.[62]

What impact did civil society have in the process? The CCR did not participate in the process at any point during 2003 and 2004 (Del Aguila Peralta 2004). Nor did civil society participate on the technical team in those early years. Although oversight committees had been elected in both 2004 and 2005, efforts are hard to coordinate because the members hail from several provinces. The problems with the process are reflected in the fact that the MCLCP found that the budget that was sent to the MEF for approval in 2004 was not satisfactorily linked to the regional development plan (Del Aguila Peralta 2004).

CONCLUSION

The regional discussions highlight that in terms of the CCRs and the budget processes, regional variation exists around the country. Although no region is implementing the CCR or the participatory budget process in a completely perfect manner, some regions are undoubtedly emerging as more successful than others. By delving more carefully into regional processes, we can begin to examine the local forces that are overcoming the design problems discussed in Part 2.

Table 5.8. Categorizing regions

Region	CCR			Participatory budget			
	Two meetings (2004–2006)	Representatives from civil society attend and participate	CCR gains additional powers	Steps 1–7 of MEF method	Improved over time	Civil society on technical team	Linked to regional development plan (2004)
Successful							
Lambayeque	✓	✓	✓	✓	✓	✓	✓
Cusco	✓	✓	✓	✓	✓	✓	✓
Moderately successful							
Moquegua				✓	✓		
Cajamarca				✓	✓	✓	✓
Unsuccessful							
Ayacucho							
Loreto							

As shown in Table 5.8, when we compare these indicators, the regions clearly fall into three distinct categories. Two regions—Lambayeque and Cusco—demonstrate high levels of success with the participatory institutions. Moquegua and Cajamarca are examples of moderately successful cases. The final two regions—Ayacucho and Loreto—reflect severe problems with the PIs.

In Lambayeque during the years studied, at least two, and often more, CCR meetings were held (four in 2005 and six in 2006). Almost every representative from civil society attended meetings regularly and participated actively, even calling their own meetings and convening the Civil Society Assembly when deemed necessary. The CCR has more civil society members than the law mandates, and the government has given them an office. Thus, the CCR has expanded its role beyond the legal minimum. In terms of the participatory budget, the regional government consistently followed the MEF's methodology and interviewees were satisfied with the process, noting that it improved every year. Civil society has participated on the technical team in almost every year and is actively involved in setting up the schedule as well as all meetings and discussions. And the budget itself is linked to the region's development priorities, as demonstrated by the MCLCP's 2004 analysis, which rated the budget successful, and by the fact that debate is organized around sectoral criteria, which work toward development goals.

Cusco emerges as another successful case. Again, the CCR met more than two times in almost every year from 2003 to 2006 (four in 2003, three in both 2005 and 2006), and civil society members attended and participated, sometimes calling meetings among themselves to discuss issues. They participated in more activities than the legal mandate requires (for example, the mid-term development plan). When civil society made recommendations to the government, such as suggesting changes to the 2004 mid-term development plan, the recommendations were often respected. The budget process was similarly successful during these years. Civil society played an active role on the technical team and in the budget workshops, and generally, interviewees noted that their participation was active and important. For example, one governmental official called civil society participation in 2004 "dynamic." The budget itself funds many projects in the education and social sectors that are stressed in the regional development plan.

Moquegua and Cajamarca represent moderately successful cases of participatory institutions. According to available information, we cannot state that either region met the legally required number of meetings every year. In Moquegua, the CCR met two times in both 2003 and 2004, but data are not available about 2005 and 2006. In Cajamarca, the CCR failed to meet twice in 2004 (when two of three meetings were cancelled) and in 2006 (when it met only once). The CCRs suffered from the lack of participation by civil society representatives. Some had been elected without their knowledge (such as the university members in Cajamarca), and others did not fully know what they were elected to do (such as one CCR member interviewed in Moquegua). Both CCRs play a minimal role in regional politics. Some call the CCRs "rubber stamps," indicating that either the members did not recommend changes to the development plans and/or budgets or that the government did not take the members' comments seriously. The budget processes were slightly more successful, in both cases. In Cajamarca, civil society participated on the technical team, and in Moquegua, at least in 2004, the budget reflected regional development priorities. Interviewees often mentioned that the budget process improved with time. As one interviewee in Moquegua stated in 2004, "The process is slowly getting better; people are trained and understand the process."

Ayacucho and Loreto are clear examples of unsuccessful cases in terms of the participatory institutions. In Ayacucho, the CCR failed to meet the legally mandated two times per year during the period under study (holding one meeting in 2003 and one in 2004), and civil society members rarely participated. One CCR representative in Ayacucho called the experience "frustrating." Another interviewee called it a "null and void" institution in the region. In Loreto, the CCR did not meet at all in 2004 or 2005 and met only once in 2006. Thus, it played no role in regional politics.

Ayacucho's and Loreto's participatory budget experiences were also problematic. In both cases, regional government officials restricted participation. In Ayacucho in 2004, the government did not follow the MEF's instructions for process and several PAs left early. Interviewees noted that the 2006 process was even worse. The government carefully controlled funding for projects. In both cases, civil society never played an active role on the technical team. According to the MCCLP, neither region's 2004 process produced a budget that conformed to the regional development plan. Interviewees noted that the budgets in the following years were mainly dictated by the government and chosen by political officials, not PAs.

In sum, even though the legal framework—with all its strengths and weaknesses—is the same across the nation, the six regions implemented

Table 5.9. Summarizing socio-demographic characteristics and PI experiences

Region	Population	Percent total poverty	Percent literacy (aged 15 years and older)	Percent secondary education	Percent GDP	PI experience
Ayacucho	619,338	64.9	71.84	75.53	0.9	Unsuccessful
Cajamarca	1,359,023	74.2	77.81	56.58	2.4	Moderately successful
Cusco	1,171,503	59.2	83.74	68.11	2.4	Successful
Lambayeque	1,091,535	46.7	90.2	81.33	2.5	Successful
Loreto	884,144	62.7	92.01	64.83	1.8	Unsuccessful
Moquegua	159,306	37.2	93.09	93.28	1.3	Moderately successful
Lima Met.	6,954,583	N/A	96.93	95.68	47.0	N/A
National	26,152,265	51.6	89.7	80.42	100.0	Varied

SOURCES: All data, excluding percent poverty and GDP, are available at http://www.mesadeconcertacion.org.pe/indicadores.php (accessed June 18, 2008); percent GDP is taken from "INEI: Cuentas Nacionales del Perú: Producto Bruto Interno por Departamentos 2001–2007," http://www1.inei.gob.pe/biblioineipub/bancopub/Est/Lib0784/index.htm, p. 20 (accessed September 8, 2009).

the participatory institutions in different ways from 2003 to 2006. This cannot be explained by socioeconomic variables, since the case selection holds these constant to the extent possible (see Table 5.9). If these variables do not explain this outcome, what does? The next chapter delves into this question.

6 FACTORS THAT FACILITATE SUCCESSFUL PARTICIPATORY INSTITUTIONS

THE REGIONAL STORIES documented in the previous chapter illustrate both the successes and the failures of Peru's efforts to codify participatory democracy as part of its decentralization reform. They point to the challenges inherent in attempting to mix direct and representative democratic models in order to improve democratic governance. The regional experiences also highlight a variety of local processes at work, many of which facilitate or impede civil society participation in the new governments. They demonstrate that these processes can either overcome or exacerbate the constraints set by the institutions' design.

The purpose of this chapter is to better understand the factors that explain the regional variation through a structured, focused comparison of the participatory institutions. Specifically this chapter asks: What factors contribute to the successful implementation of participatory institutions in Peru? As noted in Chapter 1, the structured, focused comparison proves especially useful, as it allows us to seek causal mechanisms in complex situations. Within geographic regions, such as the coast and the Andean region, several factors are constant, such as the legal framework and some socioeconomic variables. This allows us to discard these factors as having explanatory power. Instead we can explore factors that vary across cases. What variables, then, might help us understand the conditions that facilitate participatory institutions in newly formed subnational governments?

EXPLAINING VARIATION

Chapter 1 outlined five factors that emerge from the existing literature on similar institutions in other countries. The purpose of this section is to systematically review each of these variables in light of the cases and identify plausible causal mechanisms.

Regional Resources

First, do economic factors explain variation? This variable emerges as important in studies of participatory institutions in other areas of Latin America (see Goldfrank 2007b). And several Peruvian experts pointed out in conversations and interviews that perhaps large regional budgets, that is, "richer regional governments," have more successful experiences with participatory institutions. They might have extra resources to pay for meetings and travel. They could pay attention to PAs' votes because there is enough money to go around. We can explore this in light of two indicators: the overall amount of the regional investment budget and the per capita regional investment budget.

As annual data on investment spending[1] from 2004 to 2006[2] on the modified regional budgets (*presupuestos institucionales modificados*, or PIMs[3]) shows, richer regions are not necessarily more participatory. Table 6.1 demonstrates that a larger regional budget does not lead to more successful experiences. Both one of the most successful cases—Lambayeque—and one of the least successful cases—Ayacucho—have the smallest investment budgets almost every year. Cajamarca and Loreto, moderately successful and unsuccessful cases, respectively, have some of the largest budgets in 2004 and 2005.

What about per capita spending? Maybe some regions have more to spend on each inhabitant. When we calculate per capita spending on an annual level (see Table 6.2), we do not find that this indicator is a better predictor of successful experiences. In 2004, there is almost a clear reverse trend toward higher

Table 6.1. Annual regional investment budgets (in millions of Peruvian soles)

Region	2004	2005	2006
Successful			
Lambayeque	22.8	21.5	136.9
Cusco	40.5	85.7	213.4
Moderately successful			
Moquegua	27.6	68.5	151
Cajamarca	57.7	133.2	233.3
Unsuccessful			
Ayacucho	34.2	44.4	79.6
Loreto	94.6	116.8	172.3

SOURCE: GPC 2007a.

Table 6.2. Regional per capita investment spending
(in Peruvian soles, based on 2005 census)

Region	2004	2005	2006
Successful			
Lambayeque	20.9	19.7	125.4
Cusco	34.6	73.2	182.2
Moderately successful			
Moquegua	173.3	430	947.9
Cajamarca	42.5	98	171.7
Unsuccessful			
Ayacucho	55.2	71.7	128.5
Loreto	107	132.1	194.9

SOURCE: Author's calculations based on data from Tables 5.2 and 6.1.

per capita spending and decreased success rates with the participatory institutions. In 2005 and 2006, Ayacucho and Lambayeque have the least amount to spend per capita and Moquegua and Loreto have the most. Thus, the regional budget data do not suggest that richer regions are more participatory in Peru.

Institutional Capacity of Regional Government

If the amount of money that a region spends does not explain variation, does the government's capacity to spend its money shed light on this puzzle? There are several ways of measuring a government's institutional capacity. In *Making Democracy Work: Civic Traditions in Modern Italy*, Robert Putnam (1993) developed an index for measuring government effectiveness using twelve indicators: cabinet stability; budget promptness; statistical and information services; reform legislation; legislative innovation; day care centers; family clinics; industrial policy instruments; agricultural spending capacity; local health unit expenditures; housing and urban development; and bureaucratic responsiveness. This has spurred a large body of literature on government effectiveness, some of which has tackled countries in Latin America. For example, Merilee Grindle (2007) asks what makes municipal governments more effective in Mexico. She measures governmental performance in light of efficiency, effectiveness, responsiveness, development orientation, and change initiatives. Using eighteen indicators—including the existence of operational laws and regulations and a development plan; a government's reputation for corruption; signage; regular meetings; a Web presence; the use of public money for development projects; and initiatives to change—she ranks six municipalities as more or less effective.

Unfortunately, extensive and comprehensive data on these indicators do not exist for the Peru cases during the years under study for this book. Because the reforms were relatively new and regional governments were just starting to be formed, analysts tended to focus on different issues.[4] Data are, however, available regarding one very common measure of regional government capacity in Peru: the percentage of the annual investment budget that is actually executed, or used, in a given year. Regional governments—because they are new, often poorly staffed, and lack resources—often have a hard time spending their money. Thus, data on the percentage of their budget that they can spend is an indicator of the government's ability to function effectively. Perhaps governments with higher capacity, that is, those that spend more effectively, are also more participatory?

Table 6.3 demonstrates that no clear trend emerges in terms of a region's capacity to spend its budget. In 2004, the second year of the new regional governments' administrations, our successful cases, Lambayeque (87 percent) and Cusco (91 percent) *did* spend more of their investment budget. However, one unsuccessful case, Loreto also spent a healthy portion of its investment budget (82 percent). In 2005 and 2006, however, the spending evened out, and the least successful cases executed a higher percentage of the budget, on average, than the successful cases.

Some might be struck by these low numbers. However, this is not unique to these regions. Most governments in Latin America have trouble spending their budgets. Peru's central government also has problems executing its entire budget, even more so than some regions. For example, in 2004, the central government spent 76 percent of its PIM; in 2005, it spent 77 percent; and in 2006, it

Table 6.3. Percentage of investment budget executed (2004–2006)

Region	2004	2005	2006
Successful			
Lambayeque	87%	88%	61%
Cusco	91%	59%	48%
Moderately successful			
Moquegua	79%	51%	45%
Cajamarca	62%	37%	55%
Unsuccessful			
Ayacucho	75%	81%	73%
Loreto	82%	89%	52%

SOURCE: GPC 2007a.

spent only 66 percent (GPC 2007a). It is unclear why some governments (both national and regional) spend more effectively, but spending capacity, an indicator of institutional capacity, does not explain successful experiences with participatory institutions at the regional level.

Party Politics

As noted in Chapter 1, many studies point to the importance of political parties, especially those that are on the left, in explaining the successful functioning of a participatory institution (Bruce 2004; Heller 2001; Wampler 2007a). Does the regional government's political party influence the success of the participatory institutions in Peru?

Interestingly, as Table 6.4 demonstrates, the political party of the regional government does not have a relationship to success rates. This finding probably reflects the weak political party system and general ideological confusion that typifies party politics today in Peru. Several of the regional presidents discussed in Chapter 5 have switched parties and have not consistently belonged to the parties they represent. Therefore, no one party is consistently antiparticipatory in practice. Presidents who ran on the list of a regional movement oversee examples of both the most and the least successful processes. Politicians representing right-leaning parties, such as Somos Perú and the FIM, emerge as more participatory than APRA, the so-called party of the people.

Related to this, does support or nonsupport for the institutions align with the partisan affiliations of those fiercely opposed to including the CCR in the regional government structure during the congressional debate in 2002? During the debate, APRA and the right joined forces to purportedly

Table 6.4. Regional government political party affiliation (2003–2006)

Region	Party
Successful	
Lambayeque	Regional Movement
Cusco	FIM
Moderately successful	
Moquegua	Somos Perú
Cajamarca	APRA
Unsuccessful	
Ayacucho	APRA
Loreto	Regional Movement

salvage representative democracy in Peruvian politics and prevent the CCRs from having binding political power. Do these partisan positions translate to the implementation of the CCRs and participatory budgets in the regions?

Interestingly, in Congress, FIM representatives wanted to restrict civil society's participation in the CCRs, yet FIM's regional president in Cusco expanded the CCR's powers in 2006. Further, even given its vocal opposition in Congress to the CCRs, APRA does not emerge as nonparticipatory across the board. Although it did not implement particularly successful PIs, APRA is not consistently unsuccessful either. Instead, the case studies point to two tendencies within the APRA party, one that is open to civil society participation for utilitarian purposes (such as the leadership in Cajamarca) and another that is anti–civil society because of its belief that civil society is "red" (for example, the leadership in Ayacucho). These differences are evident even in the same regional office, illustrated in the case of Ayacucho in 2003, when a team open to participation worked under leadership that was not. Thus, there seem to be distinct positions *within* the APRA party with regard to civil society participation that did not appear during congressional design debates.

Regional Government Leadership

When assessing why some PIs work better than others, several Peruvian analysts and political scientists point to the important role that leaders play (Abers 1998, 2003; Avritzer 2007; Conterno n.d.; Fung and Wright 2003; Grindle 2007; Malena 2009; Van Cott 2008; Wampler 2007a, 2008). This variable can be broken down to two levels: at the higher level, leadership of the regional presidency; and at the lower level, nonelected regional officials' support for the participatory institutions.

Regional Presidents' Leadership   Two dimensions are worth exploring in terms of the 2003–2006 regional presidents' leadership and its effect on the success of a participatory institution. First, does the president support the process through concrete actions? Does he or she spend time in CCR meetings, meet with civil society, and listen to actual recommendations? The regional presidents studied fall into three categories: supportive (spending time on the CCR and listening to its recommendations); neutral (neither pushing the CCR ahead or blocking it); and what many interviewees called "antiparticipatory" (finding ways to suppress civil society participation in these institutions). When we compare this dimension of the variable, a very clear pattern emerges.

Table 6.5. Level of regional president support for PIs

Region	Support
Successful	
Lambayeque	Supportive
Cusco	Supportive
Moderately successful	
Moquegua	Neutral, some support for participatory budget
Cajamarca	Neutral, some support for participatory budget
Unsuccessful	
Ayacucho	Antiparticipatory
Loreto	Antiparticipatory

Table 6.5 clearly shows that success increases as levels of support for the participatory institutions increase.

In successful cases, the regional presidents spent time in the meetings and accepted recommendations. In Cusco, the president frequently consulted the CCR. In Lambayeque, the president and the Regional Council accepted changes to the development plans. The president also attended the 2004 participatory budget process that I attended. In moderately successful cases, the president did not actively block participation in both institutions, but did nothing to actively support them, especially the CCRs. In Cajamarca, the regional government purported to expand the CCR membership, but this was done on an ad hoc basis that interviewees suspected was an attempt to grant positions to political allies. Regional government officials, when interviewed, stated that they "do not support the CCR" since it is not supported by the population and was "dictated by Congress." Another official called civil society "a distraction; they ask for too much information." Moderate cases tended to support the participatory budget process more. In Ayacucho and Loreto, the regional presidents did not support the PIs. For example, the president in Ayacucho, when interviewed, called the participatory budget a "cruel form of participation" because it is "an invitation to the unattainable."

Why do some presidents support the CCR and participatory budget more than others? Are they participatory democrats? Do they inherently value civil society input more than others? Or is there something else at work in some areas of Peru? When we explore this question in light of the regional presidents analyzed in this book, three motivations emerge in the cases under study: ideology, electoral calculations, and populist tendencies.[5] Those motivated by ideological factors are personally committed to participatory democracy, and their political experience supports that belief. Electoral calculations might also lead one to support the processes, but for different reasons—mainly the belief that the institutions will increase his or her level of support by the population, which could pay off at the polls. Finally, those whom I call "populists" prefer to circumvent the legally mandated institutions (especially the CCRs), which are more corporate in nature, and create or utilize other means to directly reach a higher number of people (for example, town hall meetings). Populists tend to distrust civil society organizations and prefer to interact with individual citizens.

Again, the data, presented in Table 6.6, lend themselves to some interesting findings. In Lambayeque, a highly successful case, the president was both personally committed to participatory democracy and, as his supporters and critics often mentioned in interviews, convinced that these processes would further his political goals. Thus, he was motivated by both ideological and electoral factors. In Cusco, the president (an ex-leftist) was less committed on an ideological level, but because of his hope that supporting both the CCR and the participatory budget would boost his ratings in the polls, he supported them.

In Moquegua, a moderately successful case, a representative of the president noted the president's distrust of having civil society representatives make government decisions. In Cajamarca, the president found the CCR lacking, calling it a way for the national government to control regional governments. Rather, he planned to "open up participation" to all through town hall meetings. Yet both supported the budget process—interviewees attributed this

Table 6.6. Motivations behind levels of support

	President's motivations		
Region	Ideology	Electoral calculations	Populism
Successful			
Lambayeque	√	√	
Cusco		√	
Moderately successful			
Moquegua		√	
Cajamarca		√	√
Unsuccessful			
Ayacucho			√
Loreto			√

SOURCE: Interview data.

support to the fact that they saw this as an opportunity to garner votes. Finally, the least successful cases—Ayacucho and Loreto—point to the problems that emerge when pure populists are in charge. These two presidents restricted participation in these institutions.

Do electoral calculations about PIs reflect actual electoral outcomes? One way to explore this is to compare levels of support with electoral margins. Perhaps the margin of victory tells us something about these calculations. When we look at the results of the elections that brought each of these regional presidents into power, as reported by the National Office of Electoral Processes (Oficina Nacional de Procesos Electorales),[6] electoral calculations do not correlate to a president's margin of victory. Populists *tend* to have come in with a larger majority than nonpopulists. In Loreto, Rivadeneyra Reátegu won with a 4.6 percent margin over the second-place candidate, and Quezada, in Ayacucho, won with a 7.6 percent margin. Those who reportedly supported the participatory institutions in part because of electoral calculations tend to have lower margins of victory. In Lambayeque, Simon won with only 2.6 percent more votes than the APRA candidate in 2002, and Cuaresma, in Cusco, won with 2.2 percent more votes than the second-place candidate. However, the two presidents from our moderately successful cases, both relatively neutral in their support, had a very slim margin (1.1 percent for Gastelumendi in Cajamarca) and a relatively wide margin (5.5 percent for Constantinides in Moquegua). Thus, further research on more cases would be needed to definitely link electoral strategies to concrete electoral support.

Did the strategies pay off? Interestingly, in no case except Lambayeque was the regional president reelected for the 2007 to 2010 term. However, this outcome probably reflects complex regional political realities and the electoral system, which allows for multiple candidates and lends itself to split votes, rather than mere levels of support of participatory institutions. Simon's margin of victory did increase greatly—he won with almost 20 percent more votes than the second-place APRA party. However, Cuaresma landed in sixth place (out of eight presidential candidates), with a mere 6.7 percent of the vote. Thus, support for participatory institutions probably had no impact on the eventual electoral outcome in the 2006 elections.[7] More research is needed on this relationship as well.

The analysis clearly shows that supportive regional leadership is a necessary factor for success. The cases show that one route to success is when a leader has an ideological commitment to participatory ideas, backed by strategic calculations. The case studies also demonstrate that a politician who promotes these institutions to further his or her personal ambitions but is not ideologically committed can support an equally effective experience. The worst cases, however, are those that are led by presidents with strong populist tendencies. These officials prefer to go directly to individual citizens to garner support and avoid consulting elected representatives from civil society, in the case of the CCRs, and agents from civil society organizations, in the case of the participatory budgets.

Nonelected Regional Government Officials The second aspect of leadership that we can explore is nonelected regional officials' support for these processes. These officials make up the teams that support the daily operations of the PIs. In general, the regional officials whom I interviewed are professionals with experience in local government management. Some of these officials were local supporters who were appointed or hired when the president assumed power, and others were employed as regional government officials under the CTARs. Since these are the officials who implement the day-to-day aspects of the CCRs and the participatory budgets, their support is not trivial.

The analysis of this aspect shows that the attitude of lower-level officials toward the processes also helps us understand more or less successful outcomes. As noted in Chapter 1, regional governments have some flexibility in terms of the registration process. This flexibility is sometimes codified in regional ordinances regulating the process. But more often, when interviewed, some regional nonelected officials mentioned that they would "bend rules" when registering CSOs to participate in the CCR elections. For example, some allowed registration later than the closing date and allowed organizations to register that did not have all the required paperwork. Others, however, insisted that all organizations meet the strict legal requirements. It may not have even occurred to these officials to make it easier for civil society organizations to participate. In some cases, regional officials restricted participation once it came down to the technical processes of the CCR elections and/or the budget workshops. Similar to my analysis of regional presidents' support of PIs, I categorize the more flexible nonelected officials as supportive, those who strictly follow the law as neutral, and those who reject participation as antiparticipatory.

As shown in Table 6.7, in the most successful cases, there is a clear pattern of support by nonelected officials of both institutions. For example, the Office of Citizen Participation in Lambayeque tried to be flexible in terms of legal requirements for registration during the 2003 CCR election, sometimes "bending the rules." And Cusco interviewees often mentioned the important role

Table 6.7. Nonelected regional officials' support for PIs

Case	CCR	Budget
Successful		
Lambayeque	Supportive	Supportive
Cusco	Supportive	Supportive
Moderately successful		
Moquegua	Neutral	Supportive
Cajamarca	Neutral	Supportive
Unsuccessful		
Ayacucho	Antiparticipatory	Antiparticipatory
Loreto	Neutral	Antiparticipatory

SOURCE: Interview data.

that Cusco's regional teams were playing in pushing the budget process along in terms of the day-to-day operations. They organized a complex consultation process, supported by the president, to extend the CCR's powers for the 2006 CCR election.

In moderate cases, such as Cajamarca and Moquegua, the nonelected officials were more supportive of budget processes than of the CCRs. And in the least successful cases, the government refused to be flexible about registration requirements and openly demonstrated negative attitudes toward civil society participation in both the CCR and the budget process. For example, nonelected officials in Loreto's government argued that civil society participation in the budget process in 2003 was "uncontrollable," so they instituted a regulation that specified the maximum number (twenty-five) of organizations that could participate. In Ayacucho, government officials lamented the role of NGOs and restricted their participation, for example, by not including them on the technical teams. Thus, the data suggest that the support of both elected and nonelected leaders in the regional government plays an important role in the successful cases. However, no case suggests that the support of the lower-level officials can overcome the lack of support by a regional president.

Civil Society

As noted in Chapter 1, scholars often argue that the nature of civil society will determine the success of a PI. This section explores two aspects of civil society in turn.

History of Organization and Participation   Some literature on civil society and social capital points to the importance of historical experience with organization and participation as explaining variation in government performance. The most important study supporting this finding is Robert Putnam's (1993) study on efficacy of government in Italy. He argues that the historical tendency to form civic organizations in the north of Italy led to higher levels of social capital, which then explains variation in government effectiveness. Do his findings translate to the Peruvian experience with participatory institutions? More specifically, do historical experiences with organizational initiatives or participatory planning—one potential indicator of historical presence of social capital—explain variation in Peru?

It is important to note that, unlike Putnam, I do not purport to undertake an extensive historical analysis of organizational initiatives in each region. Rather, the universe of experiences is limited to those that have taken place since the 1980 transition to democracy and up to the 2002 reform. I use 1980 as a cutoff point because that marks a moment of increased organizational activity around the country. I do not include cases of regional experiences *after* the reform to avoid conflating historical experiences with the effects of the actual reform. Specifically, I document the absence or presence of two types of initiatives from 1980 to 2001: (1) the presence of regional organizations and/or social movements; and (2) a history of participatory planning in at least one province in the region.

Interestingly, no trends emerge in light of these variables either. As Table 6.8 shows, all cases except Lambayeque had regional organizations and/or social movements that were active in regional politics before the reform. Nor does the presence or absence of local participatory planning processes before

Table 6.8. Historical organizational factors (1980–2001)

Region	Regional organizational initiatives	Pre-reform experience with participatory planning?
Successful		
Lambayeque	None	No
Cusco	Regional Assembly (1998)	Yes
Moderately successful		
Moquegua	Defense fronts (mainly at provincial level)	Yes
Cajamarca	*Rondas,* environment coalition	Yes
Unsuccessful		
Ayacucho	*Rondas, cocaleros*	Yes
Loreto	Regional Defense Front	No

the reform affect success rates. The most successful case, Lambayeque, did not have any such experiences. Both Cusco and Ayacucho had experimented with participatory planning in at least one province. And Cajamarca and Moquegua, our moderately successful cases, had extensive experience in this area. Therefore, this research contradicts scholarly expectations that a history of organizational initiatives would improve the functioning of governmental institutions such as the Peruvian participatory institutions.

Nature of Post-Reform Regional Civil Society   We cannot discount, however, the role of civil society in these processes. As noted in Chapter 1, several studies point to the important role that the nature of civil society has played in ensuring these institutions' success. For example, in his comparative study of participatory decentralization reforms and the institutions that are set up in Kerela (India), Porto Alegre (Brazil), and South Africa, Heller (2001) finds that civil society is "critical" to the process. Wampler (2007a) argues that the CSO (and citizen) response to participatory institutions partly explains variation in experiences in Brazil. Thus, maybe different aspects of a regional civil society sector matter. Perhaps the nature of present-day civil society in each of the regions helps us understand outcomes.

Measuring the nature of civil society at the regional level is quite difficult. There are no official databases or lists that can help us understand the number of kinds of organizations in each region. Thus, I rely on my fieldwork and interview data to operationalize this variable in light of two factors: (1) levels of organization as a sector; and (2) levels of collaboration within the sector.

Post-Reform Levels of Organization   If civil society has not been organizing for centuries at the regional level, or for decades in this case, can it still play an important role in successful experiences? For the purposes of this study, an organized regional civil society is one that is united by one regional organization (for example, a regional consortia or assembly) after the reform.[8] Table 6.9 shows that cases that are more successful have regional organizations that bring civil society actors together at the regional level. In the case of Lambayeque, born *after* and *as a result of* the decentralization reform, the Civil Society Assembly brings groups together to discuss both institutions. In the case of Cusco, the Regional Assembly has brought diverse actors together to participate in regional political activities since 1998.

The remaining regions do not have high levels of organization in the regional civil society sector. Civil society does not work together because of

Table 6.9. Post-reform levels of organization in the regional civil society sector

Region	Organized?
Successful	
Lambayeque	Yes
Cusco	Yes
Moderately successful	
Moquegua	No
Cajamarca	No
Unsuccessful	
Ayacucho	No
Loreto	No

SOURCE: Interview data.

historical conflicts such as war (Ayacucho), active conflicts with other organizations (Cajamarca), or geographical limitations and conflicts with the government (Loreto). The Loreto case is interesting because it does have the Regional Front, but this consortium is very loosely organized and interviewees referred to high levels of conflict within the group.

Another interesting factor emerges when we explore the *types* of organization that participate. The cases studies present data on whether grassroots organizations and/or regional NGOs were participating in the institutions. The cases illustrate the important role that NGOs are playing—as opposed to grassroots organizations—in the successful regions. In three of the four most successful cases, NGOs did participate in the CCR election and were active members of the council. In all of these cases, the momentum that did exist behind the CCRs was attributed partly to the time and resources that these NGOs brought to the experience. As one interviewee in Cusco noted, "Because NGOs are paid to do this type of work, they have the time and resources to dedicate to the CCR. Their role has been invaluable." Thus, although NGOs are often distrusted and declared to be nonrepresentative, they are playing an important role in bringing time and resources to the process in our more successful cases.

Unlike our other variables, there is a clear pattern in terms of the less successful cases here as well. High levels of conflict in Cajamarca, Ayacucho, and Loreto seemingly *prevent* CSO organization. Could this explain failed cases? The regions have such different and unique sources of conflict (war in Ayacucho, regional conflicts and distrust of the regional government in Loreto, mining in Cajamarca) that a conclusion about this is impossible. Further research into a larger number of cases with more similar conflicts is needed before we can point with certainty to a causal mechanism at work in the failed cases.

Post-reform Levels of Collaboration   In addition to the presence of regional organizations that bring together actors, we can also explore the extent to which different regional civil society actors work well together. Two measurements lend insight into this variable. First, does the CCR collaborate with other regional civil society actors? This is gauged by civil society organizations' level of collaboration with another regional actor, the Mesa de Concertación para la Lucha Contra la Pobreza. And second, are the internal dynamics among civil society organizations collaborative, according to interviewees? This indicator is measured in terms of the presence of diverse groups working together toward common goals. Interviewees often spoke about divisions and conflicts within the civil society sector or the surprising fact that in some cases, diverse organizations were working well together to promote regional development.

As Table 6.10 shows, in the more successful cases, civil society organizations collaborate with each other and the MCLCP. For example, the successful cases demonstrate higher levels of collaboration between the CCR and the regional MCLCP. In both Cusco and Lambayeque, the MCLCP and the CCR have fluid and collaborative relations. CCR members are often members of the MCLCP, and the MCLCP consciously made a decision to support the institution in both cases. In Moquegua, Cajamarca, and Loreto, the MCLCP had a more benign relationship with the CCR. Although not active supporters, they

Table 6.10. Post-reform levels of collaboration in the regional civil society sector

Region	Level of CCR collaboration with MCLCP	Do diverse actors in civil society collaborate?
Successful		
Lambayeque	High	Yes
Cusco	High	Yes
Moderately successful		
Moquegua	Medium	No
Cajamarca	Medium	No
Unsuccessful		
Ayacucho	Low	No
Loreto	Medium	No

SOURCE: Interview data.

did not work against the CCR. Only in Ayacucho, where the MCLCP is very active, did the members make a conscious decision not to support the CCR.

Our successful cases also demonstrate collaboration among diverse actors in the civil society sector. In the case of Cusco, the Regional Assembly has brought diverse actors together to participate in regional political activities since 1998. In Lambayeque, several grassroots organizations, labor unions, and NGOs are represented in the assembly. Both cases are particularly impressive because they bring key actors with a diversity of viewpoints and perspectives together to work toward regional development. In contrast, distrust among civil society organizations prevails in Cajamarca and Ayacucho.

Thus, the data show that high levels of organization and collaboration in the civil society sector tend to facilitate the effectiveness of participatory institutions. By contrast, low levels can frustrate these same processes. One question that demands further research is why some of these sectors have been able to come together more effectively than others. We do not know what underlying processes are in place to allow for this organization and collaboration in our successful cases.

Table 6.11 sums up the main variables explored in this section, how they are measured, and the central findings with regard to their role in explaining variation in the success of participatory institutions at the regional level in Peru.

Table 6.11. Summary of findings

Variable	Measurements	Findings
Economic factors: Amount of regional budgets	• Annual regional investment budget • Per capita investment spending	No explanatory power
Regional government's institutional capacity	• Percentage of investment budgets executed annually	No explanatory power
Political party	• Political party of the president and vice president	No explanatory power
Leadership		Explanatory power
Regional president	• Level of support for PIs • Motivation behind support	Explanatory power
Nonelected officials	• Level of support for PIs	Explanatory power
Civil society Historic organizational factors (1980–2001)	• Existence of regional organizational initiatives before the reform? • Experience with participatory planning at the provincial level?	No explanatory power
Nature of post-reform civil society	• Organized? • Collaborative?	Explanatory power

Table 6.12. Summary of variables

Region	PI experience	Regional per capita spending (in Peruvian soles)			Regional government capacity: Percentage of budget executed			Political party	Leadership	Civil society organized and experienced with PIs before reform?	Civil society organized and collaborative after reform?
		2004	2005	2006	2004	2005	2006				
Ayacucho	Unsuccessful	55.2	71.7	128.5	75%	81%	73%	APRA	Antiparticipatory	Yes	No
Cajamarca	Moderately successful	42.5	98	171.7	62%	37%	55%	APRA	Neutral	Yes	No
Cusco	Successful	34.6	73.2	182.2	91%	59%	48%	FIM	Supportive	Yes	Yes
Lambayeque	Successful	20.9	19.7	125.4	87%	88%	61%	Regional Movement	Supportive	No	Yes
Loreto	Unsuccessful	107	132.1	194.9	82%	89%	52%	Regional Movement	Antiparticipatory	No	No
Moquegua	Moderately successful	173.3	430	947.9	79%	51%	45%	Somos Perú	Neutral	Yes	No
National	Varied	N/A	N/A	N/A	76%	77%	66%	N/A	N/A	N/A	N/A

CONCLUSIONS

Table 6.12 summarizes the data presented in this chapter. When reviewed, we see that leadership and civil society are the two factors that help us understand why PIs succeed in some cases, in spite of constraints put in place by the national legal framework.

These findings support a growing body of literature that points to the importance of both leadership and civil society in PI experiences. As Goldfrank (2007a, 148) notes, this study confirms what most studies on democracy and participation find, "that successful participation programs require a partnership between state and civil society actors." Avritzer's (2009) comparative study of several kinds of participatory institutions in four Brazilian cities puts forward a similar conclusion. When moving toward what he calls "a theory of participatory institutions in Brazil," Avritzer (2009, 165) writes that "the relevant analytical element is how civil and political society interact." This growing consensus suggests that we may be closer to an explanatory theory regarding why some PIs work better than others.

It is surprising that this finding rings true even when the reform is mandated from above. Most of the studies to date point to these variables in PIs that emerged from bottom-up experiences, not those that were mandated in a top-down PDR. Reformers hoped for less room for variation in the implementation, given the top-down nature of the PI design. They may not have expected other factors emerging to enhance or impede success.

In other ways, these findings go against several scholarly findings regarding what *should* matter in these processes. It is easy to imagine that larger budgets and governments with the capacity to spend them would give a region more flexibility to be participatory. However, the data do not support this finding. The data also contradict popular arguments about the importance of extensive historical experience with organization, which, according to some, should foster high levels of social capital and improve governmental effectiveness. Finally, the data show that politicians from a broad political spectrum, rather than only the left, will support these processes in cases like Peru where political parties are weak. Thus, the Peruvian experience challenges us to rethink our expectations in many ways.

The Virtuous Cycle

The regional experiences suggest that when participatory institutions are being implemented through mandatory, state-led reforms, two central factors

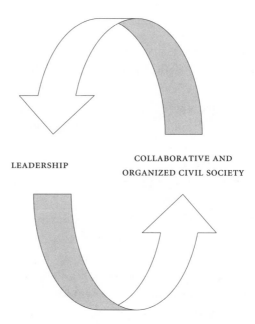

LEADERSHIP

COLLABORATIVE AND
ORGANIZED CIVIL SOCIETY

Figure 6.1. Participation's virtuous cycle

contribute to higher rates of success: leadership and the nature of regional civil society. It is important to note that these two factors do not work independently. In our most successful cases, we see them working together to create a virtuous cycle of participatory democracy (see Figure 6.1). A collaborative and organized civil society works with regional leadership, and vice versa, to facilitate participatory institutions' success.

The Peru case demonstrates the interactive nature of both the structural aspects (civil society) and the agents (leaders) in terms of PI success. Leadership, by itself, does not explain the emergence of a successful PI, for example. We cannot imagine the Lambayeque experience taking on such a dynamic nature without both the energy of the civil society sector and the leadership of its president, Yehude Simon, and his vice president. And merely organizing civil society better in Loreto will not lead to improved implementation of the participatory budget or improved functioning of the CCR. The regional leadership would need to open up the processes and dedicate resources to the CCR to allow civil society members to participate. Neither structural factors nor agents can fully explain outcomes; rather they have an interactive relationship as demonstrated in the virtuous cycle.

Further, the case studies demonstrate that national reform process and design, although important, are not determinate. Structural constraints, such as weaknesses in the legal framework governing the CCRs (that is, civil society participation is restricted to 40 percent and the decisions are not binding), can be overcome when the right set of circumstances exist at the local level. Regional leadership and civil society sectors can surmount challenges that national political actors put in place. These committed agents of change can push institutional change forward in a context of poor and weak states and governments. This finding has important implications for the quality of democratic governance at the subnational level in Latin America. The next chapter discusses these implications in more depth.

CONCLUSIONS

Part 4

7   CONCLUDING NOTES AND LOOKING AHEAD

OVERALL, THE 2002 decentralization reform has met with mixed results. Macro-regions have not been formed. The transfer of powers is taking place at a slow pace, and regions lack adequate budgets to meet the rising demands of their populations. The average Peruvian does not fully understand the reform. Yet Peruvians support the reform and want it to move forward. According to a 2006 survey commissioned by the (then existing) National Decentralization Commission (Comisión Nacional de Descentralización), 73.8 percent of the respondents "agree with the process of decentralization," and 55.3 percent considered it to be advancing (PRODES 2007a).

Most Peruvians feel that the reform has achieved one important result—it has increased citizen participation. In another 2006 survey, when asked what the most successful aspect of the reform has been, more than 30 percent of the respondents argued that increased participation is its crowning achievement (Carrión, Zárate, and Seligson 2006). Participation has become a part of everyday discourse around the country (Azpur 2006). Some scholars also argue that Peruvians participate in local political processes in greater numbers when compared with other Latin American countries (Carrión, Zárate, and Seligson 2006, 2010). They attribute this, in part, to the participatory institutions—that is, the Regional Coordination Councils and the participatory budgets—discussed in this book. What does this book tell us about these efforts?

SUMMARY OF FINDINGS

The analysis offers some interesting findings for scholars of decentralization and participation. It both tests old arguments and generates new hypotheses to test in future research.

First, what explains national policy-makers' decision to devolve power to regional governmental and societal actors? Peru's recent reform offers a chance to test prevailing arguments about why countries decentralize. The case largely confirms much of the scholarly literature that explores similar questions and points to domestic political factors as holding explanatory power. The transition to democracy provided an important opportunity structure for the reform. By itself, however, it does not explain the decision to design and pass a participatory decentralization reform in Peru. Political variables, specifically electoral strategies of national political elites, provide explanatory leverage when we are trying to understand how this reform came to pass.

In many of the previously documented cases, scholars find that negotiations between political party elites at the national and regional levels tend to play an important role in explaining the outcome. In countries like Peru, with weak political parties and few subnational elites, the case points to the importance of *national* political elites and their strategies. In Peru, subnational elites did not actively pressure for the reform. Instead, national elites wanted to strengthen their power bases at the regional level. This confirms Eaton's work (2004a), which argues that in countries with weak regional actors (for example, political parties, political elites), decision-making will take place at the national level.

The case study also allows us to delve into an underanalyzed issue, that is, why national politicians would grant voice and vote to civil society actors in regional decision-making. Again, the transition to democracy after Fujimori's regime partly explains this outcome, specifically the fact that several pro-participation actors held top elected and appointed positions in the newly elected government. An explanation for this outcome also lies in additional factors. The reform represents the culmination of several historical processes in Peru that stress civil society organizations and their participation in local politics. The Velasco regime set up corporate structures around the country as part of his development efforts. Mayors in cities like Ilo, Cajamarca, and Villa El Salvador had experimented with these institutions in the 1990s. Further, in the case of the participatory budgets, institutional factors intervened to set up a nationwide process that allows civil society organizations to participate with voice and vote in regional and local budget decisions. Specifically, the Ministry of Economy and Finance, a powerful and respected institution, spearheaded the design process in order to control spending and prevent clientelism and corruption.

Since there is very little literature on this topic, this finding generates a hypothesis that can be tested in future research. We would expect PDRs, as opposed to less participatory reforms, to emerge in the context of democratization processes, perhaps especially when there are high levels of public dissatisfaction with the representative democratic institutions. Ultimately, political strategizing will prove most determinate, however, in explaining the decision to design and legislate a PDR.

Finally, the study expands our understanding of the implementation of participatory institutions. These institutions are appearing around the world, sometimes as a part of a decentralization reform (for example, Bolivia and the Philippines) and sometimes not (for example, Brazil and Mexico). The Peru case points to the importance of the design process. It illustrates the role of electoral strategies and ideology in constraining some PIs. And, it points to the important role that national institutions with political and technical clout, like the MEF in Peru, can play in designing effective institutions. Finally, the case shows that the design of PIs conditions their implementation once newly elected subnational officials begin to put them in place.

Figure 4.1 on page 79 captures the processes at work. In Peru, as subnational elections approached, national politicians' interests—motivated by ideology and strategic calculations—intervened in the debates about the CCR to design an institution that had purely consultative, nonbinding power in decision-making processes. As a result, in most regions in the country CCRs are, as one analyst of participatory processes noted, "irrelevant." By contrast, politicians stepped back and let the MEF—a powerful and respected actor— take the lead on the design of a mandatory participatory budget process in the new subnational governments. Elections had passed, and these members of Congress were focused on other issues. This meant that the MEF's proposed process, including incentives for compliance, stayed intact during the design process, and as a result, the participatory budget has emerged as a space with great potential to restructure state-society relations at the subnational level.

The book asks: How are the newly created participatory institutions unfolding in six of Peru's new regional governments? Interestingly, the six regional case studies demonstrate that some regions have overcome the design constraints put in place by national politicians, and others have ignored mandated processes. Regional presidents expanded the CCR's membership (in Lambayeque) and powers (in Cusco). They consulted the CCRs frequently about regional policies. Other regional governments ignored the legally mandated forms of participation and/or manipulated them to serve their ends. In Loreto, the regional government restricted the participation of civil society in the participatory budget process, calling civil society's unrestricted participation unruly and hard to manage. In Ayacucho, regional government officials ignored civil society actors, who then left the participatory budget meeting in disgust in 2004. Thus, the cases suggest that regional factors can overcome constraints on participation. They can also allow for the disregard of the legal framework.

What factors contribute to the successful implementation of participatory institutions? Table 6.12 on page 140 restates the data that are provided for the six regional experiences. The analysis allows us to uncover the causal mechanisms that explain variation in outcome. First, the cases demonstrate that several variables do *not* explain this outcome. The amount of the budget and the government's capacity to spend its budget do not explain variation. Thus, a region with access to more money, and/or the capacity to spend that money, does not guarantee success. Nor does the political party of the regional president influence the implementation of the PIs. Contradicting popular arguments regarding the importance of social capital in government functioning, the studies also demonstrate that historical experience with organizing and/or participatory planning at the subnational level does not explain higher success rates. One successful case, Cusco, has only a few isolated cases of implementing similar experiences before the reform. And, regional organization in Lambayeque began to take place since (and as a direct result of) the reform. Thus, these factors can be discarded when we look for explanations for more successful participation.

The case studies suggest that two factors facilitate the successful implementation of PIs and overcome design constraints: the regional government's leadership and the nature of regional civil society since the reform (see Figure 6.1 on page 142). These findings confirm an emerging hypothesis regarding the conditions that facilitate the success of PIs (see Avritzer 2009; Wampler 2007a; Goldfrank 2007a, 2007b). This consensus suggests that we are closer to an explanatory theory regarding PI success.

In terms of leadership, the cases show that it is not necessary to have left-leaning or even ideologically committed regional leadership in charge of the processes. In Peru, we see that when politicians are convinced that these institutions serve their political interests, as is the case of the president in Cusco, then the processes can be effective. This confirms scholarship that documents PIs emerging in different ideological scenarios. For example, Peruzzotti and Selee's (2009, 10) comparative work on innovative institutions in Latin America finds that "In many cases, politicians pursued participatory innovation out of short-term strategic considerations." This is important because participatory reforms are generally associated with leftist sectors. This finding suggests that advocates of these reforms can achieve similar results across partisan lines if they convince politicians of the potential political payoffs associated with these processes.

By contrast, the opposite outcome emerges when politicians with populist tendencies are in charge. They tend to overlook these institutions and create new ones, like town hall meetings, that allow them to reach a greater number of citizens. Although reaching out to a larger number of citizens is not inherently bad, these leaders are avoiding the law, and there is no evidence to suggest that they actually respond to citizen demands in these different fora.

Combined, the two explanatory factors—leadership and an organized and collaborative civil society sector—create a virtuous cycle of participation that improves the implementation of participatory institutions. One factor without the other will not lead to the same result. A highly organized civil society will pressure for change, but without receptive leadership, these efforts will be frustrated. This can lead to a civil society sector that may take on more violent or conflictive tactics over time. And without a civil society to push the processes ahead, leadership will rarely take on this role.

The presence of the virtuous cycle may prevent the tendency for these experiences to be fleeting and unsustainable over time. Scholars often note that PIs often suffer from challenges to their sustainability. One element of Lambayeque's success lies in the fact that civil society has become more cohesive and organized since the reform and could remain so. This seems to be the case in Cusco, where civil society gained the chance to institutionalize participation over four years and government officials are committed to the processes. Even though a president who was less supportive of the processes had been elected to office in 2006, interviewees continue to report that the participatory budget remains one of the most successful in the country.

Beyond the issue of decentralization, the case also contributes to the development of future theories about participatory institutions, especially when mandated by the central government. The first lesson that emerges is the importance of a thoughtful, flexible design. Second, and more important to theory development, the analysis points to several variables for scholars to explore when trying to understand what factors facilitate successful implementation at the regional level once PIs are mandated by law.

This finding begs some related questions that are beyond the scope of this book, but merit additional analysis in future research. What conditions facilitate the emergence of the particular kind of civil society sector that promotes the successful implementation of these institutions? Why did organizations organize more successfully in Cusco and Lambayeque and not in Cajamarca, Moquegua, Ayacucho, and Loreto? Future research might look at the causal processes that explain the emergence of an organized and collaborative civil society sector at the regional level.

We also see that less successful experiences with PIs also tend to occur in regions that experience conflicts. Ayacucho was the center of the conflict with the Shining Path; Cajamarca's society is divided around the mining issue and conflicts erupt regularly; and Loreto has been negatively affected by the war with Ecuador. This suggests that there may be a relationship between conflict and the nature of regional civil society; however, the roots and nature of the conflicts in the cases studied in this book are too different to allow for generalizations. Additional research is needed to fully understand the conditions that explain the emergence of an organized and collaborative civil society or the lack thereof.

Additional research on the nature of leadership is also warranted. Although there is a relatively small, but interesting body of literature on the role of leaders in the development process (for example, Malian 2009; Rondinelli and Heffron 2009; Van Cott 2008), there is still much work to be done in theorizing this variable.

Two potential criticisms may emerge from this analysis. First, critics might suggest that where the cycle exists, the reform therefore becomes unnecessary. In other words, if these factors are in place, should reformers bother to devolve power to civil society formally? Won't participation increase without a reform? Should governments mandate participation? The Peru case confirms that state crafting, in fact, does play an important role in this outcome. Before the reform, we do see some spontaneous local experiences with participatory mechanisms, such as Ilo, Villa El Salvador, and Limatambo. However, these experiences were generally short-lived and linked to the specific mayor that was in charge. In no case did they become sustainable beyond the leadership's tenure.

Second, what if these two factors do not exist? Are participatory decentralization reforms efforts futile? No. In fact, these findings merely suggest that if these conditions do not exist at the subnational level, reformers and advocates would do well to design a series of complementary programs that would facilitate the eventual emergence of a virtuous cycle. For example, advocates could work to educate leaders about how these institutions serve their political goals. A leader who is convinced of the political payoffs can become an important agent during the process. Further, efforts that organize civil society and work toward solving conflicts among organizations will also push the process closer to the ideal. Civil society organizations need to get used to working together and toward a common regional agenda in order to facilitate efforts described in these pages.

Finally, it is important to stress that I am not advocating the adoption of these institutions nor am I a naïve supporter of participatory democracy. I am merely evaluating the reform based on its own stated objectives and the reformers' own stated goals. By exploring several questions—such as, why do national politicians decide to mix participation and decentralization? When this happens, what is the result?—I am shedding light on this experience as it evolves in one country. I am not arguing that all countries should adopt this reform or that these reforms are inherently positive.

PROSPECTS FOR DECENTRALIZATION *AND* PARTICIPATION IN PERU

What does the future hold for these efforts in Peru? By most counts, Alan García, the president who succeeded Toledo, remained committed to decentralization. From the beginning of his administration, he made decentralization a priority. It was a key part of APRA's political platform during the presidential campaign in 2006 (see Partido Aprista Peruano 2006). Just four months after taking office, he announced the Decentralization Shock, which includes twenty steps to push the decentralization efforts ahead. The policies include transferring several powers to regional and local governments, strengthening the new governments, forming a pilot macro-region (following the problems with the 2005 referendum), and further decentralizing the use of funds.[1] García also stressed the issue in his political discourse. In his 2007 Independence Day address to Congress, he stated:

> In 2007, two governmental decisions stand out. First, a great increase in the money destined to social investment, and second, how that money will be distributed in the country. . . . The state has changed; it has decentralized its

spending. This is a silent revolution, without adjectives or shouting, but very profound.[2]

In this speech, he highlighted his government's achievements in funding regional and local projects and reinforced his plans to transfer social spending to the subnational level.

Although the rhetoric is that of a decentralizer, critics charge that he did not follow through in practice. Upon taking office, he immediately deactivated the CND, a highly controversial decision.[3] Most analysts argue that his twenty-point plan was not based on a coherent vision, rather that it put forth an ad hoc set of ideas. Although his government transferred additional powers to subnational governments, critics charge that these were not backed with additional funds (PRODES 2007c; Defensoría del Pueblo 2006b).

Although García might be considered a "decentralizing" president, he does not promote participatory institutions. In his campaign platform he stated his plans to "strengthen representative democracy" and he later promised to give regional presidents more discretionary power in the participatory budget process. Interviewees referred to him as "antiparticipatory," which is not surprising. García has never pretended to be a fan of participatory democracy, considering it a project of his greatest enemies on the left. However, interviewees also noted that he is not actively trying to weaken or prevent participation from occurring as it is legally mandated in the regions.

García's contradictory position on decentralization has led to very tense relations with regional and local officials. Most subnational officials are intent on exercising their powers and promoting the growth of their regions. Early in the García government, after he immediately deactivated the CND, the regional presidents formed the National Assembly of Regional Governments (ANGR), with the goal of promoting and defending decentralization. This group has emerged as a relatively important player on the national political scene (Ballón 2008).

The emerging role of regional presidents is a double-edged sword. On the one hand, it is a clear indicator that decentralization is moving forward and subnational governments are gaining strength. On the other hand, as the regions and the ANGR gain strength, they clash more frequently with an executive who is not always committed to empowering these actors.

Thus, to a large extent the PIs continue along the same path. The CCRs barely exist in most regions and by 2010 were mostly considered "irrelevant." The participatory budget, by contrast, continues to be successful. Interviewees noted that the process is relatively institutionalized and continues to improve. Analysts agree that, "there is a general recognition that the participatory budget is the most valid mechanism in the decentralization framework" (World Bank 2010, 38–39).

From 2007 through 2010, the regions demonstrated a surprising level of continuity in experience, even given the changes in the regional government in early 2007. Variation in the actual implementation of PIs continues to exist. In Lambayeque, the institutions continued to be strong. By 2007, the number of registered groups to elect civil society representatives to the CCR had increased to 236 (Gobierno Regional Lambayeque 2007b). Ayacucho and Loreto were still struggling to institutionalize their PIs. One interviewee noted that the regional government in Loreto continued to "fear participation." In Ayacucho, the next regional president did not make regional spending numbers available to PAs as they debated projects, leading one interviewee to call the 2008 process "illegal and unethical."

The future of this reform is in the electorate's hands. Commitment on behalf of future presidents will bode well for decentralization in the long-term. It is up to Peruvians to determine the future of this particular experiment in participation and decentralization.

PROSPECTS FOR DEMOCRACY

Although the effect of the reform is not a central research question driving this book, some might wonder if the reform is, in fact, strengthening democracy. Is this reform helping Peru overcome the problems facing the country after Fujimori fled? Is democracy getting stronger? Are politicians being held accountable by their constituencies? Are people participating? Has decentralization helped improve democracy in Peru? These questions deserve much more analysis in future research.

Of course, no one reform can solve the deep-rooted and multifaceted crisis facing Peru after the Fujimori regime. And the reform is still very new. Peru's problems in 2000 had roots in centuries of social, economic, and political problems. A very brief analysis suggests that given these constraints, the nature of democracy has not changed at the national level since the reform. By contrast, modest changes at the subnational are taking place just a few years after the reform was passed.

At the national level, indicators of strengthened democracy are mixed and ambiguous. Four years after the reform, voter turnout had increased slightly at the national level. In 2001, 83.71 percent of the voters turned out for the first round of the presidential election, and this increased to 88.71 percent in the first round in 2006.[4] However, the percentage of Peruvians who support democracy over other political systems had declined slightly since the reform. According to the Latin American Public Opinion Project, 65 percent supported democracy in 1998, and that number had gone down to 62.3 percent in 2006 (see Carrión, Zárate, and Tanaka 1999; Carrión, Zárate, and Seligson 2006). Finally, Peru ranks very low in "political participation," according to the Latinobarómetro survey of participation around the region (Corporación Latinobarómetro 2008). The mixed nature of these changes probably reflects the fact that democracy is complex and strengthening it takes time. Further, as noted above, one reform cannot solve the democratic ills of a country.

More tangible results of the decentralization reform are more evident at the subnational level, in regions, towns, and cities where citizens feel that the state is at least present and that they have a voice in decision-making. One indicator of this change is the emerging role that regional governments are starting to play in the mind of citizens and in national politics. The ANGR is active and present in national debates. Regional officials note the constant presence of protestors in front of regional governments' offices. When visiting regions in 2004, government officials would often point outside to protesters and note that people are starting to organize and demand change from their regional officials.

Since the decentralization reform, there also has been a notable increase in the number of fora that bring together state and societal actors to discuss regional development issues. This increase indicates a tendency toward the rapprochement of the state and civil society actors at the regional level. The Grupo Propuesta Ciudadana has documented this increase in its analyses of fifteen regions. In 2003, it documented seventeen examples of state/society collaboration in the fifteen regions that they track (GPC 2004c). By the end of 2004, this number had increased to at least forty-nine, all of which had been recognized formally by the regional governments (GPC 2005b). In the first three months of 2005, it documented an additional fifteen examples in the regions that it tracks (GPC 2005c). Thus, by April 2005, there were at least fifty-one more spaces for collaboration than in 2003 in these fifteen regions (not including those mandated in the reform).

Important to keep in mind is that a PDR is not meant to replace representative democracy; rather, it is meant to reform or strengthen democracy by instituting new means of participation. According to Peruvian analyst Martin Tanaka (2007, 2), "In spite of the intense reform process, the problems of political representation persist." He blames this in part on the fact that reformers failed to strengthen representative institutions (such as political parties and the regional councils), focusing instead on increasing civil society's participation. He correctly argues that more efforts should be put into strengthening these institutions and not solely on expanding participatory processes. Working on both forms of democratic institutions will be more effective in the long run.

RECOMMENDATIONS: IMPROVING FUTURE EFFORTS

How can future reformers ensure success if they decide to undertake a similar project? Several Peruvian groups and analysts follow the CCRs and the participatory budget processes and think about how to improve them.[5] Although the following recommendations are not comprehensive, they provide some important insight for future efforts.

The Importance of Design

- When a PI is perceived as threatening politicians' power, such as the CCR, it might be weakened during the legislative debate process. Politicians who do not support participatory democracy will hesitate to share power with new societal actors. Electoral strategies also intervene when the debate takes place close to elections. Reformers can avoid this by finalizing design processes before calling subnational elections. This should reduce the effect of political strategizing on the design. Enlisting the support by a powerful ally, such as the Ministry of Economy and Finance in Peru, should help empower societal actors.
- PI design should include a clear and binding incentive structure. In Peru, the fact that the participatory budget is tied to tangible incentives and has a more defined legal framework has led to more effective implementation in most regions. A region cannot receive its budget without demonstrating some degree of compliance with the process. By contrast, there are no concrete incentives for governments to hold CCR meetings and no sanctions for regions that do not hold meetings.
- Be flexible and allow for changes as the reform evolves. Part of the legal framework for the participatory budget includes annual instructions that are published by the MEF. Every year these instructions

improve, in part because the MEF evaluates the processes on a regular basis and solicits feedback from both regional government officials and civil society actors. The CCR legislation, by contrast, can only be changed by congress.

Foster the Virtuous Cycle

Reformers would do well to try to foster both factors in the virtuous cycle when trying to implement a reform of this nature.

- Work with leaders from all political backgrounds to convince them that increased civil society participation can promote their interests. Participatory budgets offer a chance to meet new constituencies and respond to their demands. A council like the CCR could provide an important forum to gather information on new policies and learn about citizen preferences. If used well and strategically, these institutions can help politicians achieve their objectives.
- Work with lower-level regional government officials when implementing the PIs. The Peru case demonstrates that, although their support is not determinate in the process, they will prove to be important allies in the implementation process.
- Strengthen civil society by promoting regional organization and collaboration. Where conflict exists, such as in Cajamarca and Loreto, conflict resolution techniques may provide useful means for bringing actors together more effectively.

Regional Coordination Council

- To be effective, the civil society representatives of an institution like the CCR need voice *and* vote in regional decision-making. Grant binding decision-making power to CCRs (or similar councils). This facet should be included in the original legal framework.
- The success of this kind of institution lies in its members' ability to truly represent an inherently diverse civil society. Lower the barriers for participation by making registration less difficult and more flexible. Publicize meetings and elections widely in all regional languages using a variety of media (print, radio, and Internet).
- In a country like Peru, travel is time consuming and costly. Find a way to offset the costs of council members' travel to the capital city for meetings. This is the only way to ensure attendance and participation.

- Convince mayors to attend meetings as well. Ensuring well-attended meetings is the only way to make this council an effective institution.

Participatory Budgets

- To make participation meaningful, those involved need to feel like the debate is worth their time. Be creative. Increase the amount that a region can debate in its participatory budget process by either increasing regional investment budgets or adding some aspect of fixed costs to the debate.
- Encourage projects that have a regional impact in regional fora. Clarify the different nature of regional and municipal investment projects. PAs might confuse regional investment projects (a highway that connects several cities) with local projects (a city park). Create incentives for projects that benefit / affect larger areas of a region and not just the capital city.
- Strengthen oversight committees. In Peru, most regions are meeting the first seven steps of the MEF methodology. However, few oversight committees exist and function. Yet this is one of the keys to transparent and accountable spending. Spend time forming and strengthening oversight committees. Educate members about their oversight roles. Local NGOs should convene quarterly meetings to help the members oversee spending. Provide templates for press releases by members to educate citizens about spending to date.

FINAL NOTES

The book documents the way that Peruvians attacked the crisis of democracy facing them after the Fujimori regime. Peruvians designed a participatory decentralization reform to complement and strengthen the institutions that no longer met citizens' needs. This kind of crisis is not unique to Peru. Citizens find themselves frustrated with elected leaders around Latin America and the world. They feel cheated and ignored by representative institutions such as their congress, executives, and the judiciary. In some ways, the future of democracy in countries struggling to meet citizens' demands rests on incorporating new actors into the public sphere and keeping politicians accountable to these new constituents.

Several scholars argue that creating new channels of participation may be the key to strengthening democracy in these countries (for example, Avritzer

2002; Drake and Hershberg 2006; Fung and Wright 2003). This book suggests that these channels could very well improve democracy and participation in a short amount of time at the local and regional level. Merely mandating a reform is not enough. To succeed, the reforms need to be implemented by committed leaders who are sold on their effectiveness. Civil society organizations have to decide to overcome their differences and work together for a common project. Where this does happen, the possibilities for democracy and governance are endless.

REFERENCE MATTER

NOTES

Chapter 1

1. See Faiola 2001; Krauss 2001.

2. There are several working definitions of decentralization in the literature (see, for example, Manor 1999; Rondinelli 1981; Rondinelli and Cheema 1983; Shah and Thompson 2004). For the purposes of this book I employ the World Bank's definition, which states that decentralization is "the transfer of authority and responsibility for public functions from the central government to intermediate and local governments or quasi-independent government organizations and/or the private sector" (World Bank "Decentralization Topics").

3. This aspect of the reform is discussed further in Chapter Two. Civil society is a concept that has undergone a recent boom in the social sciences. In its most general usage, the terms refers to "the space of uncoerced human association and also the set of relational networks—formed for the sake of family, faith, interest, and ideology—that fill this space" (Walzer 1991, 296). This definition can be operationalized as several forms of associational activities, both formal and informal, such as religious groups, grassroots organizations, professional associations, social movements, nonprofit or nongovernmental organizations, and the media. It is to be distinguished, however, from market-related actors, such as corporations and businesses, and the state. It is important to note that the Peruvian reform is set up to increase civil society's participation, not individual citizen's participation.

4. Brian Wampler (2007a, 1; italics in original) defines participatory institutions as institutions that "provide citizens with the opportunity to work directly with government officials and their fellow citizens in formal, state-sanctioned public venues, allowing them to exercise *voice* and *vote* in decision-making processes to produce public policy solutions that may resolve intense social problems." Also, see Avritzer 2009 for a discussion of participatory institutions.

5. Participatory budgeting is an increasingly popular means of making budgetary decisions at the municipal and regional levels around the world. According to the website participatorybudgeting.org (accessed August 6, 2009):

> Participatory budgeting consists of a process of democratic deliberation and decision-making in which ordinary city residents decide how to allocate part of a public budget through a series of local assemblies and meetings. It is generally characterized by several basic features: community members identify spending priorities and elect budget delegates to represent their neighborhoods, budget delegates transform community priorities into concrete project proposals, public employees facilitate and provide technical assistance, community members vote on which projects to fund, and the public authority implements the projects. . . . The municipality of Porto Alegre, Brazil, developed the best-known participatory budgeting process, starting in 1989. Since its emergence in Porto Alegre, participatory budgeting has spread to hundreds of Latin American cities and dozens of cities in Europe, Asia, Africa, and North America.

For more, see Avritzer 2009; Cabannes 2004; Shah 2007; Wampler 2007c.

6. Some scholars discuss citizen participation as part of the "political" aspects of decentralization reforms, which can be considered conceptually different from administrative and fiscal aspects (see, for example, Cameron 2010; Cheema and Rondinelli 2007; Kauzya 2007). I prefer the term "participatory decentralization reform" because it separates electoral participation from the participatory institutions that are created to encourage more direct participation.

7. For more on the Bolivian experience, see Grindle 2000; O'Neill 2004; Van Cott 2008; Zas Friz Burga 2001.

8. For a discussion of the participatory aspects of decentralization in these countries, see Shah 2007; United Cities and Local Governance and the World Bank 2008.

9. An excellent example of this distinction is the Brazil case. In this case, decentralization opened up the opportunity for PIs such as participatory budgets to emerge once power was devolved to new governments, but the reform itself did not mandate societal participation. For more on similar innovations, see Tulchin and Selee 2004; Campbell and Fuhr 2004; and Peruzzotti and Selee 2009.

10. For a sample of democratic theory from this perspective, see Avritzer 2002; Barber 1984; Cohen and Arato 1992; Habermas 1975a, 1975b; Mansbridge 1983; Mouffe and Laclau 1985. For more extensive discussions of participatory democratic theory, see Van Cott 2008; Moehler 2008.

11. There is, of course, an extensive body of literature on decentralization reforms, which have been increasingly common around the world since the 1980s. This interdisciplinary body of work focuses on several questions, most of which do not directly relate to this study. For example, excellent studies discuss how subnational govern-

ments function (Borja et al. 1989; Cohen and Peterson 1999; Nickson 1995; Prud'homme 1995), economic management (Fox and Aranda 1996; Tendler and Freedheim 1994), and different patterns of decentralization (Escobar-Lemmon 2001; Manor 1999; Shah and Thompson 2004). For more on decentralization policy in general, see Cohen and Peterson 1999; Montero and Samuels 2004; Selee 2004; Willis, Garman, and Haggard 1999.

12. See, for example, Campbell 2003; Eaton 2004a; Eaton and Dickovick 2004; Escobar-Lemmon 2002; Falleti 2010; Grindle 2000; Montero and Samuels 2004; O'Neill 2003, 2004; Sabatini 2003; Selee 2004; Willis, Garman, and Haggard 1999.

13. See Eaton 2006 for a discussion of military regimes' decentralization efforts in Brazil and Argentina.

14. For more on this school, see Oates 1972, 1999.

15. Another variable, design, emerges as explanatory in several cases where the participatory institution is not mandated at the national level (see, for example, Cameron 2010; Falleti 2010; Olowu and Wunsch 2004; Wampler 2007a). Although I discuss design issues more extensively in Chapter 4, I do not develop it as a potential explanatory variable for variation in outcome because the PI designs are mostly fixed.

16. For more on the Villa El Salvador experience, see Bracamonte, Millán, and Vich 2005; Burt and Espejo 1995; Grey Figueroa, Hinojosa, and Ventura 2003; Llona 2002; Portocarrero et al. 2002; Remy 2005; Zapata Velasco 1996; Zolezzi 2004.

17. See Heller 2001; Isaac and Heller 2003.

18. See Van Cott 2008 for more on Ecuador.

19. Grindle (2007, 11) discusses these leaders as "agents in public positions of authority who develop ideas, mobilize coalitions, and make strategic choices about how to advance new organizational or policy agendas. . . . Ideas, leadership skills, and the strategic choices made to promote a reform agenda and acquire resources play a central role in such an approach."

20. Brian Wampler (2007a), Leonardo Avritzer (2007), and William Nylen (2003) argue that the rule structure of the budget process explains outcomes in Brazil. However, this is less salient in the case of Peru because the PIs are part of a top-down PDR. Thus, there is less room for rules to vary.

21. For more on this concept, see, for example, Coleman 1988; Farr 2004; Portes 2000, 1998.

22. See Burt 2007 for an excellent overview of the evolution of state-society relations in Peru.

23. For more on APRA, see Contreras and Cueto 2004; Graham 1990; Kenney 2004. See also APRA's political writings in García 1982; Haya de la Torre 1936.

24. For more on political parties on the left, see Kenney 2004; Roberts 1998.

25. For more on the agrarian reform, see, for example, Arce Espinoza 2004; Contreras and Cueto 2004; Gitlitz 1971; McClintock 1981.

26. See Schmitter 1974 for a discussion of this model.

27. For more on the cooperatives, see Gitlitz 1971; McClintock 1981.

28. See Mauceri 1997 for more on the transition.

29. For more on this presidency, see Kenney 2004, 17–29.

30. For example, the official number of registered NGOs, one kind of civil society organization for which data are available, increased from eighteen in 1970 to 738 in 1995 (Beaumont n.d.). For more on Peruvian NGOs, see Beaumont n.d; Burt 1996; McNulty 1996, 1999; Schonwalder 1998.

31. The proliferation of organizations occurred for several reasons: including the increasingly active and organized leftist sector that encouraged grassroots organizational initiatives; an ensuing economic crisis, which forced people to form service organizations to survive (such as *commodores populares*); an increase in donor funding to civil society organizations (particularly NGOs); and a high unemployment rate among middle-class professionals, who then formed nongovernmental organizations.

32. As Cynthia McClintock writes, "By the end of the García administration, real per capita GDP was estimated to be less than in 1960, and accumulated inflation over the five years was more than 2 million percent" (1999, 329). See Wise 2003 for a discussion of this period and an overview of Peru's economic policies in general.

33. Shining Path activity increased throughout the 1980s. According to Cynthia McClintock, "[By] 1989, the Shining Path numbered approximately 10,000 combatants, had the support of roughly 15 percent of Peru's citizens, and controlled about 28 percent of the country's municipalities" (1999, 329). For more comprehensive analyses of the Shining Path, see Burt 2007; Contreras and Cueto 2004; Degregori 1996, 1990, 1989; Gorriti 1990; McClintock 1984, 1998, 1999; Palmer 1994; Stern 1998.

34. For more on the party system in general, see Cotler 1994; Planas 2000; Tanaka 1998. For more on the Peruvian party system before and after the Fujimori regime, see Carrión 1992; Grompone and Mejía 1995; Kenney 2004; Levitsky and Cameron 2003; Mainwaring 1998; Planas 1996, 2000; Roberts 2002; Tanaka 1998, 2002b, 2005.

35. For more on the 1990 elections, see Bowen 2000; Degregori 2003; Degregori and Grompone 1991.

36. There are several excellent accounts of the Fujimori years in Peru, such as Burt 2007; Conaghan 2005; Kenney 2004.

37. Regarding Fujimori's economic reforms, see Stokes 1997; Mauceri 2000; Wise 2003.

38. See Kenney 2004 for an in-depth analysis of the coup.

39. Palmer (2000) and McClintock (1999) argue that this constitution paved the way for more authoritarian rule.

40. See Tanaka and Trivelli 2002 for more on his social programs and his direct democracy philosophy.

41. For more on Fujimori's second term, see Bowen 2000; Burt 1997, 2004; Cameron and Mauceri 1997; Conaghan 2001, 2005; Degregori 2003; Tanaka 2001; Youngers 2000. See Schmidt 2000 on the 1995 election and Conaghan 2001 on the reelection project.

42. See McClintock 2001 for more on the OAS mission.

43. Peru's presidential election system consists of two rounds. During the first round, candidates from all the registered parties run. In the event that no candidate receives a majority of the votes, a second round is held for the top two candidates.

44. *Suyos* in this context means "corner in Quechua," a direct reference to the four corners of the Incan empire.

45. There is extensive literature on the Montesinos-Fujimori partnership and their mafia-like hold on the government. See, for example, Bowen 2000; Conaghan 2005; Dammert 2001.

46. See O'Donnell and Schmitter 1986 for the clearest description of this phenomenon. For a discussion of the role of civil society in Peru's transition, see Burt 2000, 2007; Conaghan 2001; McNulty 2003. For the role of one specific actor, the Human Rights Coordinator, see Youngers 2003; Youngers and Peacock 2002.

47. This refers to a network of associates that helped keep Fujimori in power and continued to support him after he left the country.

48. This is an "ethnic nationalist" movement that wants to reestablish indigenous power in Peru and prevent foreign influences.

49. See McClintock 2006 for an analysis of his electoral victory.

50. There is extensive literature on the case study as a method. See, for example, Collier 1993; Eckstein 1975; George and Bennett 2005; Gerring 2004; Lijphart 1971; Mahoney 2007; Ragin 1987; Van Evera 1997; Yin 1994.

51. Interviewees (except Toledo) remain anonymous. To protect their identities, interviewees are identified in very general terms (i.e., where the person resides and his/her occupation).

Chapter 2

1. For discussions of the history of centralization in Peru, see Contreras 2002; Schmidt 1989; Vargas 1989; Zas Friz Burga 1998.

2. For example, Contreras and Cueto (2004) describe fiscal decentralization efforts under Caceres's regime (1886–1890) after an economic crisis led the government to realize the need for an increased tax base from the rural areas of Peru. As a result, *juntas departamentales* (departmental councils) were formed to assist in tax collection. Although they eventually failed and were dismantled, they represent Peru's first attempt to set up administrative structures in the departments.

3. Planas (2000) notes that at least eight of the twelve Peruvian Constitutions reference this concept.

4. See Article 79 of Peru's 1979 Constitution and Articles 79 and 43 of Peru's 1993 Constitution.

5. For more on the 1979 constitutional reform, see Zas Friz Burga 2004. For more on the legal framework of decentralization since 1979, see Adrianzén 2003; Defensoría del Pueblo 2003c; Ojeda Segovia 2003; Planas 1998; Zas Friz Burga 1998, 2004.

6. See Zas Friz Burga 2004.

7. Building on regional committees that had existed since the 1970s, the twelve regions and the departments that made them up were: Grau (Túmbes and Piura); Nor Oriental de Marañon (Cajamarca, Lambayeque, Amazonas); La Libertad (San Martín); Amazonía (Loreto); Cáceres (Junín, Pasco, Huanuco); Libertadores-Wari (Ica, Ayacucho, Huancavelica); Arequipa; Inka (Cusco, Apurímac, Madre de Dios); José Carlos Mariátegui (Puno, Moquegua, Tacna); Ucayali; Chavin (Ancash); and the Lima metropolitan area (Lima and Callao).

8. Jessica Bensa Morales made this point in a personal communication dated July 21, 2005. For more on this ideological position, see Haya de la Torre 1936; García 1982.

9. Although the law allowed them to generate some resources, the tax base was too weak to make this a significant amount.

10. Carlos Contreras, Peruvian historian and expert on decentralization, notes that it was not only the governmental structure that centralized the regions' capitals. He argues that a centralist culture—especially in rural areas—also existed (and probably continues today). In practice, this means that Peruvians prefer to interact with authorities at the national (or in this case regional and not municipal) level because they are convinced that they are the only ones who can address their needs (Contreras, personal communication, July 22, 2005).

11. For example, some regions hesitated to join with the poorest regions, which then generated conflicts (Contreras 2002).

12. During the Fujimori government, CTARs were set up in twenty-three departments. For a more extensive discussion of the CTARs, see Adrianzén 2003; Zas Friz Burga 2001, 2004.

13. In *Neocentralismo y neoliberalismo en el Perú* (2000), Gonzales de Olarte carefully argues that privatization and liberalization of trade have favored the center in terms of economic growth and GDP.

14. As Remy (2005) argues, this law was the first example of a national legal reform that implemented participatory democratic mechanisms.

15. For more on this issue, see Panfichi 2007; Sagasti et al. 2001.

16. The concept of "concertar" in Spanish is difficult to translate. Generally, it means discussing issues and coming to an agreement or a consensus about them. It can be traced to the Hispanic tradition of placing value on oral debate and community. I use terms such as discuss, agree on, debate, coordinate, and dialogue to describe this process.

17. See Monge 2002 for a discussion of what some call the "concertation" model (that is, the processes that promote consensus building and dialogue between state and society). For examples of these and similar experiences, see Panfichi and Pineda 2004, 2007; Portocarrero et al. 2002; Remy 2005.

18. For more on this experience, see Guerrero Figueroa 2002; Díez Hurtado 2003.

19. For more information on the conference, see Remy 2005 and http://www.anc .org.pe. Starting in 1998, the annual conference focused on the need to decentralize.

20. Because the terminology is confusing, I refer to roundtable experiences in general as *mesas* and this particular roundtable as the MCLCP.

21. In 2001, Paniagua's administration passed D.S.01-2001-PROMUDEH, a decree that institutionalized this experience at the national and subnational level. As of mid-2008, the MCLCP had 1,436 roundtables at the local, district, provincial, and regional levels. At least 732 were active (see www.mesadeconcertacion.org.pe). For more on the history and activities of this roundtable, see Remy 2005; Panfichi 2007; Panfichi and Dammert 2005; the MCLCP website (http://www.mesadeconcertacion.org.pe/).

22. Another example is the Organization of American States' roundtable that brought civil society and the state together during the end of Fujimori's regime to address problems during the 2000 elections. See Conaghan 2001; McClintock 2001; Remy 2005.

23. For instance, APRA spokesperson Enrique Cornejo Ramírez published a piece stating the party's platform in *El Comercio*, Peru's leading newspaper, on June 4, 2001. He wrote that APRA "suggests a state reform that includes regionalization, decentralization, the incorporation of civil society, and improved efficiency."

24. For a discussion of the legal framework until July 2010, see PRODES 2009.

25. There are several ways to divide power in a state. In a unitary state, the central government retains ultimate authority and subnational governments remain dependent upon its will. In a federal state, subnational and central governments have independent and separate powers.

26. A region is much like a state in the United States. Each region has a capital city, which is generally its largest city. The regions are based on preexisting departments, therefore the terms "region" and "department" are used interchangeably in Peru. Regions are made up of several provinces, which are comparable to counties in the United States. Each province also has a several other cities (including its capital), which are called districts. The use of the terms "local government" and/or "municipality" generally refer to provincial cities and/or districts.

27. Peruvians refer to these phases as "parallel" because each phase is not necessarily dependent on the previous phase in order for it to proceed. This caveat is especially important as Phase Two falters (see next footnote).

28. Several regions came together to form four potential macro-regions in October 2005. The referendum allowed citizens of these regions to vote "yes" or "no" for the

fusion of the region that s/he lived in. For referendum election results, see www.onpe .gob.pe. In no region did the initiative pass, however, and a new referendum was supposed to take place in 2009. Regional presidents then petitioned the national government to cancel the 2009 referendum and now macro-regions are (and will be) formed if and when a group of regions petitions the national government. The regions have created regional coordination committees (*juntas de coordinación interregionales*, or JCIs) to oversee this process. For more on these groups, see Grupo Propuesta Ciudadana 2007c.

29. For an excellent breakdown of the roles and responsibilities of each level of government, see Gonzales de Olarte 2004.

30. See Comisión de Descentralización, Regionalización, Gobiernos Locales y Modernización de la Gestión del Estado 2008 for more information about the transfer of powers to the regions. The Ministry of the Woman and Social Development also has an online database that tracks transfers at http://www.mimdes.gob.pe/descentralizacion/ presupuesto.html (accessed August 24, 2009).

31. Congress also passed laws to define and regulate the municipal governments in a separate set of laws, not discussed in this book. For a copy of the Organic Municipal Law (Law 27,972), see Defensoría del Pueblo 2003c.

32. Regions do not have the same number of provinces. For example, Lambayeque has three provinces and Cusco has thirteen provinces. The three provincial mayors in Lambayeque make up 60 percent of the body. Thus, two representatives from civil society are elected in Lambayeque to make up 40 percent. The thirteen provincial mayors of Cusco automatically make up 60 percent of the CCR. Cusco then elects nine civil society representatives.

33. Congress added this provision to ensure that economic organizations are involved in the process. Congress also assumed that these actors would bring more ideological diversity to the CCRs, as business sectors are generally more conservative. I am grateful to Martín Tanaka for explaining this aspect of the legislation. As will be shown in later chapters, this sector does not always participate in the actual CCRs.

34. Each regional government puts out an ordinance to govern the CCR election every two years. Thus, the process of CCR elections varies in each region. Several different ways that regions organize the election are described in Chapter 5.

35. There is no comparative information regarding the length of meetings.

36. Despite a legal framework's finally existing, confusion about the roles and responsibilities of the CCRs remained. To clarify, several actors developed guidelines to help regional governments along. The Human Rights Ombudsman's Good Government Program developed guidelines for the elections (Defensoría del Pueblo 2003b). A consortium of civil society actors, including the MCLCP and the Grupo Propuesta Ciudadana, developed guidelines to implement the CCRs as well (MCLCP 2003).

37. For information on the participatory budget in Porto Alegre, see Abers 2000; Avritzer 2002; Baiocchi 2003, 2005; Bruce 2004; Gret and Sintomer 2005; Grey Figueroa, Hinojosa, and Ventura 2003; Peterson 1997; Wainwright 2003; Wampler 2007a, 2007b. For a discussion of the Brazilian and Peruvian participatory budgeting experiences, see O'Brien 2004.

38. For more on Ilo's experience, see García de Chu and Piazza 1998; Grey Figueroa, Hinojosa, and Ventura 2003; O'Brien 2004; and López Follega, Melgar Paz, and Balbín Díaz 1995. See also Chapter 5.

39. For more on the Villa El Salvador experience, see Bracamonte, Millán, and Vich 2005; Burt and Espejo 1995; Grey Figueroa, Hinojosa, and Ventura 2003; Llona 2002; Portocarrero et al. 2002; Remy 2005; Zapata Velasco 1996; Zolezzi 2004.

40. For more on the pilot program, see MEF 2004b; O'Brien 2004; Zas Friz Burga 2004.

41. See www.mef.gob.pe for these documents. While the instructions varied slightly during the years under study, the phases mostly remained the same.

42. The details about who exactly can be considered a participating agent are dictated by regional governments in regional ordinances. Thus, regulations vary by region.

43. This refers to the act of ensuring accountability or transparency.

44. The instructions state that minimally, the proposals should include a description of the project, how it relates to the region's development plan, indicators to measure its completion, and a basic budget (including the community resources that will be brought to the project). Regional governments vary in terms of how developed a proposal must be in order to be considered for funding. Some insist on developed projects that have been reviewed by experts. Others allow "ideas" to be proposed, and the technical team then quickly fills out a form. This variation has led to some problems with the process. To be considered in the regional workshops, little information is needed. However, it must meet stricter criteria (such as a feasibility study) in order to receive MEF approval. This means that "ideas" or new proposals rarely meet MEF criteria and are not funded.

45. The regional council's decision is the only officially binding one. Thus, if a CCR does not approve the budget, but the council does, the budget will still move forward. There are various incentives to include the CCRs in the process and follow their recommendations. In some regions, CCR disapproval can slow down the process. Civil society representatives also can mobilize their members and civil society in the region to protest the budget. In other words, this process purports to add some checks and balances to the process of making regional budgets.

46. During visits to the regions, it became apparent that this is the part of the process that is least followed and understood by agents. The 2007 instructions clarify this step in more detail than previous years' instructions.

47. See Grupo Propuesta Ciudadana 2009 and PRODES 2009 for more on these changes. As the legal framework evolves, two organizations, Grupo Propuesta Ciudadana and PRODES tend to publish reports that explain legal modifications on their websites: http://www.descentralizacion.org.pe/vigilaperu-gobiernosregionales.shtml and http://www.prodescentralizacion.org.pe/.

48. This happened in Cusco in 2003, for example, when the regional president disregarded the budget that left the workshop and funded a regional soccer stadium instead.

49. See http://presupuesto-participativo.mef.gob.pe/app_pp/db_distedit.php.

50. Using a scale from 0 to 20, the MCLCP then grouped the responses into four categories: excellent, good, regular, and bad.

51. The MEF portal reports data by the year of the budget (that is, the year that the budget is spent). Thus, the 2005 data pertain to the *process* that took place in 2004).

52. The additional data points do not account for the increases in PAs from 2007 to 2008 and then from 2008 to 2009. For example, in 2008, Huancavelica (a region that did not report in 2007) reported only fifty-three PAs. In 2009, the three regions that had not reported in the previous year reported 244 PAs.

53. The World Bank 2010 study analyzes these same numbers at the regional, provincial, and district levels of government from 2005 to 2009. This report estimates that 150,000 participate in the nationwide process on an annual basis (World Bank 2010: 6). From 2005 to 2009 the average number of participants, when calculating all levels of government, "has been growing over the past few years" from 41 in 2005 to 82 in 2009 (World Bank 2010: 42–43).

54. A participating agent representing a CSO is defined as any participant that is not representing a regional or municipal government.

55. Of course, this is by no means the extent of the legislation that makes up the decentralization package. Literally hundreds of laws, decrees, ordinances, and resolutions have been passed since this process began in 2003. However, much of this is not pertinent to this study.

Chapter 3

1. Interview, Washington, DC, March 12, 2010.

2. All World Bank data in this and the next paragraph are from World Bank Development Indicators http://data.worldbank.org/data-catalog, accessed June 7, 2010.

3. The reforms, however, conformed with thinking about second-generation reforms as part of the neoliberal model. Thus, it was implemented in a positive climate toward this type of reform. But we cannot consider this a *cause* of the reform, something that Alejandro Toledo confirmed when interviewed. I am grateful to Carlos Monge for clarifying this point.

4. According to the National Statistic Institute, 35.4 percent of Peru's population lived in urban centers in 1940. In 1961, the percent increased to 47.4 percent and by 1972, 59.5 percent of Peruvians lived in urban areas. By 1981, 65.2 percent lived in urban areas. In 1993, 70.1 percent of Peruvians lived in urban areas. By 2007, this had increased slightly to 75 percent. See "Migraciones Internas en el Perú," http://www1.inei.gob.pe/biblioineipub/bancopub/Est/Lib0018/n00.htm and "Perú: Grado de Urbanización," http://www1.inei.gob.pe/biblioineipub/bancopub/Est/Lib0018/n00.htm (Accessed September 15, 2009).

5. For more on the concept of opportunity structure, see McAdam 1982; McAdam, McCarthy, and Zald 1996; Meyer and Minkoff 2004; Tilly 1978; Tarrow 1994.

6. Interview, Washington, DC, March 12, 2010.

7. It is important to note, however, that few regional presidents won by a strong margin. Only one regional president won with more than 50 percent of the vote. The majority of them won with between 20 percent and 30 percent of the popular vote. See Meléndez Guerrero 2003 for an analysis of the election results.

8. Interviewees in the regions consistently lamented the absence of congressional representatives once elected. For further reading on this problem, see Pease García 2008.

9. As one reviewer noted, another international aspect of the process that would be interesting to explore in future work is the issue of policy diffusion. Public policy scholars have started to explore the mechanisms that underlie policy innovations (for more on this literature, see, for example, Berry and Berry 1999; Gray 1994; Weyland 2006). They point to decision-makers' learning processes (Meseguer 2005), rational decision-making (Weyland 2006), and emulation (Berry and Berry 1999) as aspects that help us understand innovation. As Chapter 2 notes, some local Peruvian policy-makers learned about Brazil's experience with participatory budgeting in the late 1980s and early 1990s. Although two interviewees in Peru mentioned the Brazil model as having informed the municipal experiences, especially in Ilo, this did not emerge as a strong causal factor in my interviews. The extent to which the diffusion of Brazil's participatory budgeting policy influenced policy-making in Peru would make an interesting case to add to the burgeoning policy diffusion literature. I am grateful to the reviewer for pointing this out.

Chapter 4

1. The GPC has limited funding and, therefore, can only monitor implementation in a sample of the regions. Because much of its funding comes from USAID, it tends to follow the regions that are of high priority to the U.S. government. Some reports cover thirteen regions and others cover fifteen, depending on the year and funding.

2. See http://presupuesto-participativo.mef.gob.pe/app_pp/db_distedit.php.

3. When I was undertaking research, debate transcripts were available through the office of the Oficial Mayor del Congreso. To obtain transcripts, I sent a formal written request citing the law number and name. Since they were not published at the time, but are public, I cite them by using the date of the debate. Transcripts have, since then, been uploaded to the congressional portal at http://www2.congreso.gob.pe/sicr/diariodebates/Publicad.nsf/SesionesPleno.

4. As noted earlier, the Spanish word *concertar* can mean many things in English (such as debate and discuss, negotiate, and come to agreement), but it implies some decision-making authority.

5. Manuela Ramos and Flora Tristan, named after prominent Peruvian feminists, are two well-known women's organizations in Peru.

6. An article in *El Comercio* titled "No Aprueban Cambios en la Ley de Regiones," published on December 4, 2002, notes this position.

7. Interviewees in the MEF noted that this was never part of the proposal because they knew that Congress would not support this idea.

8. As explained in Chapter 2, depending on the size of the region, the absence of one member affects the CCR differently. In Lambayeque, the smallest region under study, the absence of one member represents 33 percent of the members from civil society. In Cusco, the absence of one member means that only 11 percent of the civil society members are not present.

9. This is not true at the municipal and provincial levels, where governments are struggling to institutionalize the process and less information is available to both citizens and officials.

10. For more on the SNIP and the public investment decision-making process, see MEF 2003; CND 2004.

Chapter 5

1. For documentation of this variation, see O'Brien 2004; GPC 2004c, 2005b; López Ricci and Wiener 2004; Grompone 2005a; Del Aguila Peralta 2004.

2. I do not use data from 2003 because the CCRs had recently formed and confusion existed about their functions.

3. For the same reasons as above, the 2003 process is not included. And because oversight committees do not exist or hardly function in almost every region, I do not consider step eight (setting up an oversight committee) in the analysis.

4. When capturing civil society participation in the PIs, I rely more on qualitative measures than on quantitative. This is due to the fact that quantitative data about the number of participants and meetings are problematic in Peru. Analysts of participatory budgets often track how many people participate. Although this is a useful and interesting measurement, there are several problems with this data in the case of Peru. First, MEF data for the early years of the process (2002 through 2005) often conflict

with regional governmental and independent monitor reports. Furthermore, while all sources clearly document an increase in the number of participants since 2004, this does not tell us much about the quality of participation. As Chapter 4 documents, in some cases the actual participation of PAs is restricted during a meeting. Thus, mere numbers of participants do not shed light on the *quality* of participation. Furthermore, the number of participants in any given year is often subject to exogenous influences such as bad weather, difficult journeys, and/or problems with crops. For this reason, I rely on participant accounts (as provided in interviews with both governmental and civil society attendees) regarding the quality of participation to gauge this indicator. In interviews (and follow-up conversations), I asked participants to describe the budget process and civil society's participation in each year. In some regions, interviewees would talk about how the process improved (for example, civil society participated more actively, civil society presented projects, debate was more open, and/or more people attended). This constitutes an "improved process."

5. These data were gathered during my own fieldwork in 2004 and 2005, thus only these two years are included.

6. I assume that the resulting budget has greater impact on regional development if the projects that are funded work toward goals of the regional development plan. It is hard to analyze this indicator as well because the budgets are complicated and not reported to the national government in a way that can be clearly linked to the region's development goals (outlined in the regional development plan). The only existing national analysis of this aspect of the PI is in a 2004 MCLCP analysis, in which each region's budget was scored using the following categories: satisfactory, less than satisfactory, and unsatisfactory (Del Aguila Peralta 2004). I evaluate the remaining years' impact on the way in which projects were prioritized during the phase seven of the budget process. This is the phase during which projects are prioritized by participating agents and the final list of projects is approved. If a project was debated and then prioritized and/or reported with the regional development plan in mind, it is considered to be working toward the regional development plan.

7. National-level data on citizen understanding of regional governments does not exist; however, in a USAID study of seven coca-producing regions, 36.4 percent did not know the name of their regional president (Zárate and Trivelli 2005).

8. There are no official documents or studies of civil society in all of these regions. Thus, I rely on qualitative analyses of the dynamism and organizational character in each region, as described in interviews by experts. I focus on the dynamics of civil society in each region since the first transition to democracy in 1980.

9. In some cases, data in regional government and NGO reports and my interviews conflict, highlighting one problem in gathering data on regions in Peru. When data in reports conflict with my interview data, I rely on my interview data as they were most often verified several times by interviewees. When data conflict in reports, I tend

to rely on independent monitoring reports provided by NGOs and not the government's reports. If the NGO data conflict, I rely on the most recent publication.

10. Chiclayo, its capital, is popularly known as the "city of friendship."

11. All population statistics in this chapter are reported by Peru's national statistics agency as of 2005. Data are available at www.inei.gob.pe.

12. Poverty statistics are from 2004. Data were accessed on the MCLCP website, from the section on poverty in Peru titled "Evolución de la Pobreza." Retrieved from http://www.mesadeconcertacion.org.pe/contenido.php?pid=121 on June 18, 2008.

13. For example, the peasant-owned sugar cooperatives formed during the military regime proved unviable and, in many cases, had been taken over by private investors by the 1990s (Manrique 1996).

14. The north of Peru is considered APRA territory and is most often referred to as APRA's "solid north."

15. Five of the seven regional council members hailed from Simon's party; two from APRA.

16. As a result of his alleged ties to the MRTA, he served eight and a half years in jail (1992–2000). He often states publically that the time provided him with the opportunity to reevaluate politics in Peru.

17. He openly criticizes many aspects of Peruvian politics, such as clientelism and corruption. For example, in an interview for *CARETAS*, a popular Peruvian newsmagazine, he states that in prison he "confirmed that the practices of the leftist political parties are the same as the parties on the right. I am an enemy of vertical parties . . ." (Hinojosa 2004, 23). He goes on to say: "When one is a politician, he sometimes runs 300 kilometers an hour and doesn't have time to reflect. The eight and a half years in a very tough prison made me see how I was both good and irresponsible in my actions" (Hinojosa 2004, 23–24).

18. It is difficult to systematically compare the regional CCR lists, as each region decides how to organize and/or categorize the different groups. To remain faithful to the regional decisions, I list the organizations as they are documented in official lists provided by the regional government and/or the Defensoría del Pueblo. When they are not grouped into categories by the regional government (which is the case for the Cajamarca's, Ayacucho's, and Loreto's 2005 regional lists), I use the most common categories and group them myself.

19. While the numbers are increasing, experts generally agreed that many organizations are still not participating. In the 2003 elections, grassroots, rural organizations, and business organizations were especially underrepresented, and NGOs and urban organizations were overrepresented. According to the regional government officials, 43 percent of the organizations that registered in 2005 are NGOs. Finally, in both elections the majority of the organizations that registered are from the largest urban area, Chiclayo, and one province is not represented by CSOs at all. Thus, al-

though the CCR has been successful relative to others around the country, it still faces several challenges.

20. As many of the regional case studies show, regional governments can decide to mandate a gender quota in the ordinance that governs the CCR election process. This is relatively common in Peru because gender quotas exist in most national level electoral processes.

21. This issue points to another problem with the CCR. There are no national guidelines regarding what to do if members miss meetings, and the law does not stipulate who exactly is elected—the person or the organization. In Lambayeque, members interpreted the law as electing the person, not the organization. In the other five regions studied, the organization is considered the "member," represented by its legal official.

22. Personal communication with CCR member dated January 26, 2006.

23. Southern Peru Copper Corporation (commonly referred to as "Southern"), the largest mine in the region, had contaminated Ilo's air and water supply. Furthermore, the city suffered from poor urban planning. One problem, consistently referred to in interviews, is the fact that the entire city was growing away from the sea. For many, this symbolized a lack of planning in the sense that the sea is the city's greatest resource.

24. Two indicators speak to the success of this process. First, the amount that the city debated increased from 15 percent of the municipal budget in the first year to 60 percent by 2004 (O'Brien 2004). Another indicator that interviewees used to capture success is the fact that in 2003 and 2004, some wealthier neighborhoods gave up resources to improve poorer neighborhoods, thereby working toward what they considered to be the collective good.

25. According to one regional government official, twenty-four organizations showed up to register and only eighteen qualified.

26. Frequent requests to the government and the regional MCLCP have resulted in conflicting information.

27. The most prominent regional NGOs are those that began the participatory budget process in Ilo. However, these organizations maintained a low regional profile in 2004 and 2005 because, as a result of their protesting the mine, some opponents had waged a publicity war against them. This led to decreased funding and public support and may explain their decision not to register.

28. The suit was eventually dropped.

29. During the period under study, the participatory budgets were developed by all levels of subnational government (region, province, district) during the same general time frame. Thus, there was often confusion among participating agents and even governmental officials with regard to which budget was being discussed. Interviewees noted that ideally, the district budgets should be debated first, then the provincial budgets, and finally, the regional budget.

30. Again, this is primarily due to two factors: the lack of regional NGOs and the "low profile" that the NGOs that do exist in the region were maintaining (see note 27).

31. These committees date back to the 1970s when several communities began to organize to prevent petty theft and cattle rustling (Gitlitz and Rojas 1983). In 2003, it was estimated that more than 100,000 people participate in *rondas* in Cajamarca (Laos Fernández, Paredes, and Rodríguez 2003). They not only monitor crime and theft in the community, but also mediate community issues and penalize thieves for their crimes. Interviewees noted, however, that the *rondas'* regional leadership is currently plagued by internal conflicts and the organizational structure is extremely weak. For a very interesting anthropological study of the *rondas*, see Starn 1999.

32. For more on the Yanacocha mine, see CEDEPAS and GPC 2005; The Economist 2005; Gorriti 2004.

33. As of April 2005, at least nine provincial and local roundtables brought together the mine and community organizations (CEDEPAS and GPC 2005). And, a representative from Yanacocha was elected to the 2005–2006 CCR, which may signal an increased level of interest in dialogue.

34. For more on this *mesa*, see Díez Hurtado 2003; Guerrero Figueroa 2002; Portocarrero et al. 2002.

35. As discussed in Chapter 2, one of the main tasks of the CCR is to approve the regional budget after the participatory process.

36. In an evaluation of the CCRs in 2004, GPC (2005b) notes that it is common for regions to count the CCR's participation in the budget process as an official meeting when in actuality it is not.

37. Many provincial and district mayors believe that too many funds stay in the capital. They demonstrate their discontent by not supporting regional institutions.

38. An extensive literature exists on the causes and consequences of the rise and fall of Sendero. See, for example, Burt 1998, 2007; Contreras and Cueto 2004; Degregori 1989, 1990, 1996; Gorriti 1990; McClintock 1984, 1998, 2005; Palmer 1994; Stern 1998.

39. See Kay 1999 for a discussion of these links.

40. For a discussion of the differences between these two types of organizations, see Laos Fernández, Paredes, and Rodríguez 2003. On *rondas* in general, see Degregori 1996; Starn 1995, 1999.

41. David Scott Palmer (1999) argues that because of the decades of violence, citizens do not have access to more traditional channels of participation in Ayacucho, such as political party structures or a responsive government. As a result, CSOs rely on informal channels when making demands. These channels include protests or going directly to authorities to present their demands. An example lies in a protest organized by the *frente de defensa* in August 2004 regarding teacher salaries. The protest ended in setting fire to the regional government office in downtown Ayacucho City,

causing severe damage to the office building and the records inside. Sadly, education is not an issue that the regional government controls.

42. According to Díez Hurtado (2003), this consortium of labor and business organizations formed in the 1970s to demand better education in the region. It disappeared during the conflict with Sendero, but was reactivated in the late 1990s to unite the labor organizations that still existed.

43. This consortium formed during the agrarian reform to defend *campesinos'* right to land. It is present in five provinces and is relatively representative of the *campesinos* in the region.

44. This organization emerged in the late 1980s to help people meet its families' basic needs. It is a consortium of the *comedores populares* and the *vaso de leche* (glass of milk) committees, both of which receive direct assistance from the state in the form of food and milk (Huber et al. 2003).

45. The original multiregional movement, called the Confederación Nacional de Agropecuarios de las Cuencas Cocaleros del Perú (National Confederation of Farmers in the Coca Basins of Peru) organized their first national conference in 2003. Since then, the farmers in Ayacucho, Cusco, and Huanuco separated from this organization (owing to internal conflicts) and formed the Junta de Productores Agropecuarios de los Valles Cocaleros del Perú (Coalition of Agricultural Producers in the Coca Valleys of Peru). They organize regional strikes to demand an end to the forced eradication of coca and the fumigation of leaves in the valley. They are also allegedly linked to Sendero and drug trafficking (Pariona Arana 2004).

46. For more on this experience, see Panfichi and Pineda 2004, 2007; Ávila 2003; Portocarrero et al. 2002.

47. Excerpts from local media reports illustrate these critiques:

> *The neo-fujimorista Omar Quezada, regional president of Ayacucho, tried to surprise the people from Ayacucho once again by using state resources for a political event.*
>
> **—Regional Impact, August 23–September 6, 2004, front page**

> *What happened to the [money]? . . . He doesn't only offer bread to the mothers, but also wines and dines his "special guests" like Meche Cabanillas and Alan García. This is how government funds are spent.*
>
> **—Linea Roja, August 21, 2004, front page**

48. This number reflects the total number of organizations that registered as reported to the Defensoría del Pueblo. Interviewees from both civil society and the regional government indicated to me that eighteen CSOs registered; however, the regional government's list contains only fifteen. Thus, it would seem that the Defensoría del Pueblo data are truncated. I continue to rely on its data, however, because this is the only

official list that documents the name of individual organizations. This allows for a comparison across categories.

49. It is the only region in which Clubes de Madres (Mother's Clubs) registered, for example, in 2003. In general, these clubs do not meet the legal requirements and exist more informally. However, relying on NGO technical and financial assistance, the regional club put together the paperwork necessary to participate. Of course, not all grassroots groups could benefit from this assistance and several opted out of participating because of their informal nature. And the Mother's Clubs did not participate in the 2005 elections.

50. Unlike the CCR, the MCLCP in the region *is* effectively addressing the demands of societal actors. For example, in 2004 and 2005 it was quite active in regional political issues such as negotiating *cocalero* demands and demanding that the Camisea natural gas line—a pipeline for natural gas that crosses through Ayacucho—benefits regional development.

51. For more on these experiences, see García de Chu and Piazza 1998; Grompone 2005a; Portocarrero et al. 2002; Remy 2005.

52. One of the first tasks for all regional governments was to put together its regional development plan and present it to the National Decentralization Commission.

53. As noted in Chapter 2, the regional government decides how to organize CCR elections.

54. This is partly due to the larger size of this particular CCR—it has nine members from civil society. In Lambayeque, the absence of one voting civil society representative meant a 50 percent absentee rate.

55. In some regions with large extractive projects, such as mining or natural gas, the central government transfers revenue generated from the royalties of these projects to the region and the municipalities that are most affected by the project. These special funds are called *canones*. For more on these transfers, see Zas Friz Burga 2004.

56. For more detailed analyses of the conflict, see Contreras and Cueto 2004; Granero and Barclay 2002; Palmer 1997.

57. For more information on the history of Loreto and the Amazon region, see Contreras and Cueto 2004; Granero and Barclay 2002.

58. Fernando Santos-Granero and Frederica Barclay's (2002) account of Loreto, *The Domesticated Frontier*, offers an explanation for this tendency. While the rest of the country was experiencing organizational changes in the 1960s, these activities did not take place in Loreto. APRA and student movements—two engines of organizational dynamics—did not exist in Loreto and NGOs could not work there due to prohibitive operational costs. Slowly in the 1970s, the groups mentioned here did start to organize around regional development issues.

59. The Frente de Defensa is a regional organization that brings together a large coalition of organizations, such as labor groups, political parties, and grassroots organizations. It began in the 1970s when oil was discovered in Loreto. Their purpose at

the time was to ensure that oil revenues stayed in the region. During the 1980s it was inactive but reemerged as a powerful regional player when the border conflict sparked in 1995. See also Granero and Barclay 2002.

60. This is especially problematic for the 2005–2006 CCR, which was made up of four civil society representatives from the more isolated areas of the regions.

61. Reliable data are not available regarding the 2006 process.

62. Travel to Mariscal Ramón Castilla from the capital city of Iquitos takes three days by boat. A faster boat can make the trip in eight hours, but a round-trip ticket costs more than $100. Thus, the costs of this trip in both time and money are extremely prohibitive to civil society organizations.

Chapter 6

1. Investment spending is the part of the regional budget that is not fixed annually as operational costs, such as salaries and office costs, and is debated in the participatory budget workshops.

2. The large spike in the regional budgets in 2006 reflects an increase in the nations' revenues due to healthy macro-economic growth.

3. In Peru, a region starts with an initial (estimated) budget at the beginning of the fiscal year, which is then modified during each year to account for increases or decreases in state revenues and/or funds left over from the previous year. Thus, the PIM is the most accurate estimate of the region's budget in any given year.

4. This is slowly starting to change. For example, Participa Perú, a watchdog organization, has been reporting on Web transparency for several regional governments since 2007. See http://www.propuestaciudadana.org.pe.

5. Getting at true motivations of politicians is difficult and would require more extensive research. I base this discussion on brief interviews with either the president or vice president in each region, his or her team, and constituents. In all cases, a general consensus in the interviews emerged regarding motivations.

6. See "Resultados Regionales," retrieved from http://www.onpe.gob.pe/infoelec/infoelec03.php on July 16, 2008.

7. For 2006 electoral data, see http://www.onpe.gob.pe/resultadoserm2006/index .onpe.

8. This indicator captures whether civil society is organized into a regional consortium *after* the reform, whereas the earlier indicator (historical organization experiences) captures the absence or presence of an organization *before* the reform.

Chapter 7

1. See GPC 2007b and PRODES 2007a and 2007c for more on the Decentralization Shock.

2. Retrieved from http://aprismo.wordpress.com/2006/07/31/mensaje-presidencial -del-28-de-julio/ on August 15, 2008.

3. To replace the CND, he created a suboffice under the president's ministry to oversee the process. One organization writes of the decision, "as one would expect, modifying the decentralization process brought with it diverse reactions from officials, legislators, and experts. Most agreed that the CND was not functioning in the best way possible. . . . Others expressed that the decision to deactivate the CND was unilateral and not supported by a clear proposal" (PRODES, 2007b).

4. See the International Foundation for Electoral Systems' voter turnout data at http://www.electionguide.org/reports1.php.

5. See, for example, Colectivo Institucional Presupuesto Participativo 2007, which has a list of lessons learned and recommendations put forth by seventeen governmental and nongovernmental organizations that work in this area.

WORKS CITED

Abers, Rebecca. 2003. "Reflections on What Makes Empowered Participatory Governance Happen." In *Deepening Democracy: Institutional Innovations in Empowered Participatory Governance. The Real Utopias Project IV.* Edited by Archon Fung and Erik Olin Wright. London: Verso.

———. 2000. *Inventing Local Democracy: Grassroots Politics in Brazil.* Boulder: Lynne Rienner Publishers.

———. 1998. "From Clientelism to Cooperation: Local Government, Participatory Policy, and Civic Organizing in Porto Alegre, Brazil." *Politics and Society* 26(4): 511–53.

Ackerman, John. 2004. "Co-Governance for Accountability: Beyond 'Exit' and 'Voice.'" *World Development* 32(3): 447–63.

Adrianzén, Alberto. 2003. "La descentralización en el Perú." In *Procesos de descentralización en la comunidad Andina.* Quito: FLACSO.

Agenda Sur Ayacucho. 2007. "No a los retrocesos en la descentralización del Perú." Ayacucho: Agenda Sur Ayacucho.

Agrawal, Arun, and Elinor Ostrom. 2001. "Collective Action, Property Rights, and Decentralization in Resource Use in India and Nepal." *Politics and Society* 29(4): 485–514.

Andersson, Krister, Gustavo Gordillo de Anda, and Frank van Laerhoven. 2009. *Local Governments and Rural Development: Comparing Lessons from Brazil, Chile, Mexico, and Peru.* Tucson: University of Arizona Press.

Angeles, Lorena, and Francisco Magno. 2004. "The Philippines: Decentralization, Local Governments, and Citizen Action." In *Decentralization, Democratic Governance, and Civil Society in Comparative Perspective.* Washington, DC: Woodrow Wilson Center for International Scholars.

Arce Espinoza, Elmer. 2004. *Peru 1969–1976. Movimientos agrarios y campesinos.* Lima: Centro de Estudios para el Desarrollo y la Participación.

Asociación Arariwa. 2007. "Vigila Perú: Sistema de vigilancia ciudadana de la descentralización." Reporte regional Cusco 11. Cusco, Puru: Participa Perú.

Asociación Arariwa and Centro Bartolomé de las Casas (CBC). 2006. "Vigila Perú: Reporte regional Cusco 10." Cusco, Peru: Asociación Arariwa.

———. 2005. "Vigila Perú: Reporte regional Cusco 6." Cusco, Peru: Asociación Arariwa.

———. 2003. "Vigila Perú: Reporte 2." Cusco, Peru: Asociación Arariwa.

Asociación Civil Centro Esperanza. n.d. "Sociedad civil en Lambayeque: Aportes y dificultades." Chiclayo, Peru.

Asociación SER. 2005. "Vigila Perú: Reporte 9: Balance del año 2005." Ayacucho, Peru: SER.

———. 2005. "Vigila Perú: Reporte 4: Balance anual 2004." Ayacucho, Peru: SER.

———. 2002. "Compendio legal sobre descentralización." Lima: SER.

Ávila, Javier. 2003. "¿Descentralización desde abajo?" In *Ayacucho: Centralismo y descentralización.* Lima: Instituto de Estudios Peruanos.

Avritzer, Leonardo. 2009. *Participatory Institutions in Democratic Brazil.* Baltimore: Johns Hopkins University Press.

———. 2007. "Instituições participativas e desenho institucional: Algumas considerações sobre a variação da participação no Brasil democrático." Working Paper. Editora UFMG: Brazil.

———. 2002. *Democracy and the Public Sphere in Latin America.* Princeton, NJ: Princeton University Press.

Azpur, Javier. 2006. "La descentralización y la participación en el proceso de construcción de la democracia." In *Tendencias y desafíos de la democracia Peruana en el nuevo período político.* Cuadernos Descentralistas 20. Lima: Grupo Propuesta Ciudadana.

Bahl, Roy, and Johannes Linn. 1986. "Public Expenditure Decentralization in Developing Countries." *Government Policy* 4: 405–18.

Baiocchi, Gianpaolo. 2005. *Militants and Citizens: The Politics of Participatory Democracy in Porto Alegre.* Stanford, CA: Stanford University Press.

———. 2003. "Emergent Public Spheres: Talking Politics in Participatory Governance." *American Sociological Review* 68(1): 52–75.

Ballón, Eduardo. 2008. "Gobierno y autoridades regionales: Entre tensiones y enfrentamientos." *Revista Quehacer* 169. Lima: DESCO.

———. 2006. "Las Elecciones de noviembre: La competencia de los partidos nacionales y las agrupaciones regionales." *Revista Quehacer* 162. Lima: DESCO.

———. 2003. "Participación ciudadana en espacios locales: Notas para un balance necesario." Lima: Grupo Propuesta Ciudadana.

Ballvé, Teo. 2004. "Peru: Toledo on Shaky Ground." *NACLA Report on the Americas* 38(2): 40–43.

Barber, Benjamin. 1984. *Strong Democracy: Participatory Politics for a New Age*. Berkeley: University of California Press.

Barczak, Monica. 2001. "Representation by Consultation? The Rise of Direct Democracy in Latin America." *Latin American Politics and Society* 43(3): 37–60.

Bardhan, Pranab, and Dilip Mookherjee. 2006. "The Rise of Local Governments: An Overview." In *Decentralization and Local Governance in Developing Countries: A Comparative Perspective*. Cambridge: MIT Press.

———. 2002. "Relative Capture of Local and Central Governments: An Essay in the Political Economy of Decentralization." Paper C99109. Berkeley: Center for International and Development Economics Research, University of California.

———. 1998. "Expenditure Decentralization and the Delivery of Public Services in Developing Countries." Working Paper 90. Berkeley: Center for International and Development Economics Research, University of California.

Beaumont, Martin. n.d. "CIVICUS Country Profile: Peru." Retrieved August 25, 2005, from http://www.civicus.org/content/Peru.htm.

Bensa Morales, Jessica. 2002. "Elecciones regionales en el Perú: Una comparación entre 1989–1990 y el 2002." Lima: Oficina Nacional de Procesos Electorales.

Berry, Francis Stoles, and William D. Berry. 1999. "Innovation and Diffusion Models in Policy Research." In *Theories of the Policy Process*. Edited by Paul Sabatier. Boulder, CO: Westview Press.

Bird, Richard, and Francois Vaillancourt, eds. 1998. *Fiscal Decentralization in Developing Countries*. New York: Cambridge University Press.

Blair, Harry. 2000. "Participation and Accountability at the Periphery: Democratic Local Governance in Six Countries." *World Development* 28(1): 21–39.

Blondet, Cecilia. 1999. "Las mujeres y la política en la década de Fujimori." Documento de Trabajo 109. Lima: Instituto de Estudios Peruanos.

———. 1995. *Hoy: Menú popular: Los comedores en Lima*. Lima: UNICEF.

Borja, Jordi, Teresa Valdés, Hernán Pozo, and Eduardo Morales. 1989. *Descentralización del estado: Movimiento social y gestión local*. Santiago: FLACSO.

Bowen, Sally. 2000. *The Fujimori File: Peru and Its President 1990–2000*. Lima: Peru Monitor.

Bracamonte, Jorge, Armano Millán, and Victor Vich, eds. 2005. *Sumando esfuerzos: Catorce experiencias de participación ciudadana en la gestión local 2004*. Lima: Red para el Desarrollo de las Ciencias Sociales en el Perú.

Bresser Pereira, Luiz Carlos. 1993. "Economic Reforms and Economic Growth: Efficiency and Politics in Latin America." In *Economic Reforms in New Democracies: A Social-Democratic Approach*. Cambridge, MA: Cambridge University Press.

Bruce, Iain, ed. 2004. *The Porto Alegre Alternative: Direct Democracy in Action.* London: Pluto Press.

Bryan, Frank. 2004. *Real Democracy: The New England Town Meeting and How It Works.* Chicago: University of Chicago Press.

Burki, Shahid Javed. 1999. *Beyond the Center: Decentralizing the State.* Washington, DC: World Bank.

Burt, Jo-Marie. 2007. *Political Violence and the Authoritarian State in Peru: Silencing Civil Society.* New York: Palgrave MacMillan.

———. 2004. "State Making Against Democracy: The Case of Fujimori's Peru." In *Politics in the Andes: Identity, Conflict.* Pittsburgh: University of Pittsburgh Press.

———. 2000. "The Reawakening of Civil Society in Peru." *NACLA Report on the Americas* 34(2): 1.

———. 1998. "Shining Path and the Decisive Battle in Lima's Barriadas: The Case of Villa El Salvador." In *Shining and Other Paths.* Durham: Duke University Press.

———. 1997. "Fujimori's Deeper Problems." *NACLA Report on the Americas* 30(4): 5.

———. 1996. "Local NGOs in Peru Devise an Alternative Anti-Poverty Program." *NACLA Report on the Americas* 29(6): 34–36.

———. 1992. "Peru: Façade of Democracy Crumbles." *NACLA Report on the Americas* 26(1): 3.

Burt, Jo-Marie, and Cesar Espejo. 1995. "The Struggles of a Self-Built Community." *NACLA Report on the Americas* 28(4): 19.

Cabannes, Yves. 2004. "Participatory Budgeting: A Significant Contribution to Participatory Democracy." *Environment and Urbanization* 16(1): 27–46.

Calderón, Walter Alejos. 2005. "El consenso alcanzado en la Ley Orgánica de Gobiernos Regionales." In *Concertando la descentralización: Balance del diseño normativo.* Lima: Fondo Editorial del Congreso del Perú.

Calderón, Walter Alejos, and Johnny Zas Friz Burga. 2005. *Concertando la descentralización: Balance del diseño normativo.* Lima: Fondo Editorial del Congreso del Perú.

Cameron, John D. 2010. *Struggles for Local Democracy in the Andes.* Boulder, CO: First Forum Press.

———. 2008. "Participatory Budgeting in the Andes: Between Governmentality and the Infrapolitics of Resistance." Paper presented at the International Studies Association Meeting, San Francisco, CA. March 26–29.

Cameron, Maxwell. 1994. *Democracy and Authoritarianism in Peru: Political Coalitions and Social Change.* New York: Palgrave.

Cameron, Maxwell A., and Philip Mauceri, eds. 1997. *The Peruvian Labyrinth: Politics, Society, and Economy.* University Park: Pennsylvania State University Press.

Campbell, Tim. 2003. *The Quiet Revolution: Decentralization and the Rise of Political Participation in Latin American Cities.* Pittsburgh: University of Pittsburgh Press.

Campbell, Tim, and Harald Fuhr. 2004. *Leadership and Innovation in Subnational Government: Case Studies from Latin America*. Washington, DC: World Bank.

Carrión, Julio. 1992. "Partisan Decline and Presidential Popularity: The Politics and Economics of Representation in Peru." In *Deepening Democracy in Latin America*. Pittsburgh: University of Pittsburgh Press.

Carrión, Julio, Patricia Zárate, and Mitchell Seligson. 2010. "Cultura política de la democracia en Perú." U.S. Agency for International Development (USAID). Retrieved December 14, 2010, from http://www.vanderbilt.edu/lapop/peru.php.

———. 2006. "The Political Culture of Democracy in Peru: 2006." Latin American Public Opinion Project. Retrieved August 1, 2008, from http://sitemason.vander bilt.edu/lapop/PERUBACK.

Carrión, Julio, Patricia Zárate, and Martin Tanaka. 1999. "Democratic Participation in Peru, Final Report." USAID. Lima, Peru. Retrieved August 1, 2008, from http://sitemason.vanderbilt.edu/lapop/PERUBACK.

Castillo R., Oscar. 1996. "NGO and Development in Peru in a Context of Structural Adjustment." *Estudios Sociologicos* 14: 211–26.

CEDEPAS and Grupo Propuesta Ciudadana (GPC). 2005. "Reporte 2. Vigilancia minera Cajamarca: Enero–junio 2005." Cajamarca, Peru: CEDEPAS.

Centro Ecuménico de Promoción y Acción Social (CEDEPAS). 2007. "Vigilancia del proceso de descentralización." Reporte regional 11, Balance 2003–2006. Cajamarca: Participa Perú.

———. 2005a. "Vigila Cajamarca: Reporte 6." Cajamarca, Peru: CEDEPAS.

———. 2005b. "Vigila Cajamarca: Reporte 7." Cajamarca, Peru: CEDEPAS.

———. 2004. "Balance de gestión 2003" Boletín 3. Cajamarca, Peru: CEDEPAS.

Centro de Educación, Organización, y Promoción del Desarollo–Ilo (CEOP-ILO). 2004. *Dinámica de las organizaciones sociales y de la participación ciudadana en la provincia de Mariscal Nieto, Moquegua*. Ilo, Peru: CEOP-ILO.

Centro de Estudios Sociales Solidaridad (Solidaridad). 2004. "Reporte de vigilancia ciudadana al Gobierno Regional de Lambayeque (GRL): Balance anual 2003." Chiclayo, Peru: Solidaridad.

Centro de Investigación de la Universidad del Pacífico. 2001. *Estrategia de descentralización y desarrollo de los gobiernos subnacionales en el Perú*. Lima: Universidad del Pacífico.

Chavez, Daniel, and Benjamin Goldfrank, eds. 2004. *The Left in the City: Participatory Local Governments in Latin America*. London: Latin America Bureau.

Cheema, G. Shabbir. 2007. "Devolution with Accountability: Learning from Good Practices." In *Decentralizing Governance: Emerging Concepts and Practices*. Washington, DC: Brookings Institution Press.

Cheema, G. Shabbir, and Dennis Rondinelli. 2007. "From Decentralization to Decentralized Governance." In *Decentralizing Governance: Emerging Concepts and Practices*. Washington, DC: Brookings Institution Press.

Cohen, Jean, and Andrew Arato. 1992. *Civil Society and Political Theory.* Cambridge: MIT Press.

Cohen, John, and Stephen Peterson. 1999. *Administrative Decentralization: Strategies for Developing Countries.* West Hartford: Kumarian Press.

Colectivo Institucional de Presupuesto Participativo. 2007. "Presupuesto participativo: Agenda pendiente: Balance, lecciones aprendidas, y recomendaciones." Lima: Colectivo Institucional de Presupuesto Participativo.

———. 2006. "Experiencias exitosas de presupuesto participativo en el Perú." Lima: Colectivo Institucional de Presupuesto Participativo.

Coleman, James. 1988. "Social Capital in the Creation of Human Capital." *American Journal of Sociology* 94: S95–S120.

Collier, David. 1993. "The Comparative Method." In *Political Science: The State of the Discipline.* Washington, DC: The American Political Science Association.

Comisión de Descentralización, Regionalización, Gobiernos Locales y Modernización de la Gestión del Estado. 2008. "Evaluación del proceso de descentralización." Período Legislativo 2007–2008. Lima: Congreso de la República del Perú.

Comisión de la Verdad y Reconciliación (CVR). 2003. *Informe final.* Lima: CVR.

Comisión Nacional de Descentralización (CND). 2004. "Los proyectos de inversión publica en los planes de presupuestos locales." Guías para una Planificación Concertada 3. Lima: CND.

Conaghan, Catherine. 2005. *Fujimori's Peru: Deception in the Public Sphere.* Pittsburgh: University of Pittsburgh Press.

———. 2002. "Cashing in on Authoritarianism: Media Collusion in Fujimori's Peru." *Harvard International Journal of Press/Politics* 7(1): 115–25.

———. 2001. "Making and Unmaking Authoritarian Peru." Miami: North South Center.

Conterno, Elena. n.d. "Potenciando la participación ciudadana en el Perú: Presupuesto participativo y Consejos de Coordinación." Monograph. Lima, Peru. Retrieved June 10, 2008, from www.lasociedadcivil.org/uploads/ciberteca/e_conterno.pdf.

Contreras, Carlos. 2002. "El centralismo peruano en su perspectiva histórica." Lima: Instituto de Estudios Peruanos.

Contreras, Carlos, and Marcos Cueto. 2004. *Historia del Perú contemporáneo.* 3rd ed. Lima: Instituto de Estudios Peruanos.

Corporación Latinobarómetro. 2008. "Informe 2008." Retrieved September 18, 2009, from www.latinobarometro.org/ . . . /INFORME_LATINOBAROMETRO_2008 .pdf.

Cotler, Julio. 1994. *Política y sociedad en el Perú.* Lima: Instituto de Estudios Peruanos.

Crook, Richard, and James Manor. 1998. *Democracy and Decentralization in South Asia and West Africa: Participation, Accountability, and Performance.* New York: Cambridge University Press.

Dammert, Manuel. 2003a. "Cambios constitucionales y descentralización en el Perú de hoy." In *Procesos de descentralización en la Comunidad Andina*. Edited by Fernando Carrión. Ecuador: FLACSO.

———. 2003b. *La descentralización en el Perú a inicios del siglo XXI*. Lima: Universidad Nacional de Mayor de San Marcos.

———. 2001. *Fujimori-Montesinos, el estado mafioso: El poder imagocrático en las sociedades globalizadas*. Lima: Ediciones El Virrey.

Defensoría del Pueblo. n.d. "Memoria del taller: Consejos de Coordinación Regional: Balance y perspectivas." Lima: Defensoría del Pueblo.

———. 2007. "Segundo reporte sobre elección de representantes de la sociedad civil ante los Consejos de Coordinación Regional (CCR) para el período 2005–2007." Lima: Defensoría del Pueblo.

———. 2006a. "Rendición de cuentas y buen gobierno: Reporte de audiencias públicas de rendición de cuentas realizadas por los gobiernos regionales durante el año 2005." Lima: Defensoría del Pueblo.

———. 2006b. "Reporte de supervisión de la Defensoría del Pueblo sobre la transferencia de competencias sectoriales a los gobiernos regionales." Lima: Defensoría del Pueblo.

———. 2005a. "Análisis y aportes sobre el presupuesto participativo." Lima: Defensoría del Pueblo.

———. 2005b. "Informe preliminar de elección de Consejos de Coordinación Regional al 30 de septiembre de 2005." Lima: Defensoría del Pueblo.

———. 2005c. "Recomendaciones para la elección de representantes sociales en los Consejos de Coordinación Regional correspondiente al año 2005." Lima: Defensoría del Pueblo.

———. 2003a. "Actores para el buen gobierno: Reporte del proceso de constitución de los Consejos de Coordinación Regional a nivel nacional." Lima: Defensoría del Pueblo.

———. 2003b. "Criterios y recomendaciones para el registro y elección de representantes de organizaciones de sociedad civil ante el Consejo de Coordinación Regional." Lima: Defensoría del Pueblo.

———. 2003c. *Descentralización y buen gobierno: Compendio de normas*. Lima: Defensoría del Pueblo.

Degregori, Carlos Iván. 2003. "Peru: The Vanishing of a Regime and the Challenge of Democratic Rebuilding." In *Constructing Democratic Governance in Latin America*. Baltimore: Johns Hopkins University Press.

———. 1996. *Las rondas campesinas y la derrota de Sendero Luminoso*. Lima: Instituto de Estudios Peruanos.

———. 1990. *Ayacucho 1969–1979: El surgimiento de Sendero Luminoso*. Lima: Instituto de Estudios Peruanos.

————. 1989. *Que difícil es ser dios: Ideología y violencia política en el Sendero Luminoso*. Lima: El Zorro de Abajo.

Degregori, Carlos Iván, and Romeo Grompone. 1991. *Elecciones 1990: Demonios y redentores en el nuevo Perú*. Lima: Instituto de Estudios Peruanos.

Del Aguila Peralta, Irma. 2004. "Procesos de planeamiento concertado y presupuesto participativo 2005." Lima: Mesa de Concertación para la Lucha Contra la Pobreza.

de Mello, Luiz. 2000. "Can Fiscal Decentralization Strengthen Social Capital?" International Monetary Fund (IMF) Working Paper. Washington, DC: IMF.

Díez Hurtado, Alejandro. 2003. *Elites y poderes locales: Sociedades regionales ante la descentralización*. Lima: SER.

Doner, Richard, and Eric Hershberg. 1996. "Flexible Production and Political Decentralization: Elective Affinities in the Pursuit of Competitiveness." Paper presented at the Annual Meeting of the American Political Science Association, San Francisco, CA. August 29–September 1.

Drake, Paul W., and Eric Hershberg. 2006. *State and Society in Conflict: Comparative Perspectives on Andean Crisis*. Pittsburgh: University of Pittsburgh Press.

Eaton, Kent. 2006. "Decentralization's Nondemocratic Roots: Authoritarianism and Subnational Reform in Latin America." *Latin American Politics and Society* 48(1): 1–26.

————. 2004a. *Politics Beyond the Capital: The Design of Subnational Institutions in South America*. Stanford, CA: Stanford University Press.

————. 2004b. "Designing Subnational Institutions: Regional and Municipal Reforms in Post-Authoritarian Chile." *Comparative Political Studies* 37(2): 218–44.

————. 2001. "Decentralization, Democratization, and Liberalization: the History of Revenue Sharing in Argentina 1934–1999." *Journal of Latin American Studies* 33(1): 1–29.

Eaton, Kent, and J. Tyler Dickovick. 2004. "The Politics of Re-Centralization in Argentina and Brazil." *Latin American Research Review* 39(1): 90–122.

Eckstein, Harry. 1975. "Case Studies in Political Science" In *Handbook of Political Science 7*. New York: Addison-Wesley.

Economist, The. 2005. "The Americas: Halting the Rush Against Gold; Mining in Peru." *Economist* 374(8412): 48.

Escobar-Lemmon, Maria. 2003. "Political Support for Decentralization: An Analysis of the Colombian and Venezuelan Legislatures." *American Journal of Political Science* 47(4): 683–97.

————. 2002. "Determinants of Legislative Support for Decentralization." Paper presented at the Decentralization and Federalism Workshop, Texas A&M University, College Station, TX. May 4.

————. 2001. "Fiscal Decentralization and Federalism in Latin America." *Publius* 31(4): 23–43.

Faiola, Anthony. 2001. "Crisis-Ridden Peru Demands Action from New President." *Washington Post* A14. June 5.

Falleti, Tulia. 2010. *Decentralization and Subnational Politics in Latin America.* Cambridge, MA: Cambridge University Press.

Farr, James. 2004. "Social Capital: A Conceptual History." *Political Theory* 32(1): 6–33.

Fox, David. 1992. "Decentralization, Debt, Democracy, and the Amazonian Frontierlands of Bolivia and Brazil." In *Decentralization in Latin America: An Evaluation.* New York: Praeger.

Fox, Jonathan. 2002. "La relación recíproca entre la participación ciudadana y la rendición de cuentas: La experiencia de fondos municipales en el México rural." *Política y Gobierno* 9(1): 95–132.

———. 1994. "Latin America's Emerging Local Politics." *Journal of Democracy* 5(2): 105–16.

Fox, Jonathan, and Josefina Aranda. 1996. *Decentralization and Rural Development in Mexico.* La Jolla: Center for U.S.-Mexican Studies.

Fung, Archon, and Erik Olin Wright. 2003. "Thinking About Empowered Participatory Governance." In *Deepening Democracy: Institutional Innovations in Empowered Participatory Governance. The Real Utopias Project IV.* London: Verso.

García, Alan. 1982. *El futuro diferente: La tarea histórica del APRA.* Lima: Deza.

García, Victor. 1989. *Estado y regionalización.* Lima: COCOMI.

García de Chu, Ines, and Maria del Carmen Piazza. 1998. *Sociedad y gobierno local.* Lima: DESCO.

George, Alexander. 1979. "Case Studies and Theory Development: The Method of Structured, Focused Comparison." In *Diplomacy: New Approaches in History, Theory, and Policy.* New York: Free Press.

George, Alexander, and Andrew Bennett. 2005. *Case Studies and Theory Development.* Cambridge: MIT Press.

Gerring, John. 2004. "What Is a Case Study and What Is It Good For?" *American Political Science Review* 98(2): 341–54.

Gitlitz, John. 1971. "Impressions of the Peruvian Agrarian Reform." *Journal of Interamerican Studies and World Affairs* 13(3/4): 456–74.

Gitlitz, John, and Telmo Rojas. 1983. "Peasant Vigilante Committees in Northern Peru." *Journal of Latin American Studies* 15(1): 163–97.

Gobierno Regional Ayacucho. 2005. "Registro de organizaciones de la sociedad civil." Ayacucho, Peru.

———. 2003. "Relación de organizaciones sociales inscritas en el registro para el Consejo de Coordinación Regional." Ayacucho, Peru.

———. n.d. "Plan de desarrollo concertado de la región Ayacucho 2004–2006." Ayacucho, Peru.

Gobierno Regional Cajamarca. 2005. "Registro de organizaciones de la sociedad civil." Cajamarca, Peru.

———. 2004a. "El proceso del presupuesto participativo en la región Cajamarca." Retrieved July 12, 2005, from http://www.regioncajamarca.gob.pe.

———. 2004b. "Memoria anual 2003." Cajamarca, Peru.

———. 2003a. "Directiva para la conformación del Consejo de Coordinación Regional." Directiva No. 1-2003-RECAJ/ST-CCR. Cajamarca, Peru.

———. 2003b. "Evaluación final de las organizaciones de la sociedad civil." Cajamarca, Peru.

———. 2003c. "Plan de desarrollo regional Cajamarca, 2003–2006." Cajamarca, Peru.

Gobierno Regional Cusco. 2007. "Balance del presupuesto participativo regional del Cusco." Retrieved June 15, 2008, from http://www.regioncusco.gob.pe/documentos/ppto_2008/balance_coincide.pdf.

———. 2004. "Proceso del presupuesto participativo 2005." Cusco, Peru.

———. 2003a. "Plan estratégico de desarrollo regional concertado a mediano plazo, Cusco al 2006." Cusco, Peru.

———. 2003b. "Relación de organizaciones y representantes de la sociedad civil inscritos en el padrón electoral para el Consejo de Coordinación Regional." Cusco, Peru.

Gobierno Regional Lambayeque. 2007a. "Remite informe anual 2006 sobre proceso de descentralización." Oficio #259-2007-PCM/SD. Chiclayo, Peru.

———. 2007b. "Elección de delegados de la sociedad civil al Consejo de Coordinación Regional –CCR: Padrón de electores." Chiclayo, Peru.

———. 2005. "Libro registro de la sociedad civil." Chiclayo, Peru.

———. 2003a. "Elección de representantes de la sociedad civil al Consejo de Coordinación Regional: Lista de electores." Chiclayo, Peru.

———. 2003b. "Plan de desarrollo regional concertado Lambayeque 2010." Chiclayo, Peru.

Gobierno Regional Loreto. 2007. "Informe anual 2006 sobre proceso de descentralización." Oficio M#047-2006-CND-GGD/P. Iquitos, Peru.

———. 2005. "Relación de participantes de la sociedad civil de la provincia de Maynas para la elección al Consejo de de Coordinación Regional 2005." Iquitos, Peru.

———. 2004a. "Plan estratégico institucional 2004–2006." Iquitos, Peru.

———. 2004b. "Reglamento del proceso de identificación y acreditación de los agentes participativos en el presupuesto participativo." Ordenanza regional 009-2004-CR/GRL. Iquitos, Peru.

———. 2003. "Elección de los representantes de la sociedad civil ante el Consejo de Coordinación Regional 2003." Iquitos, Peru.

Gobierno Regional Moquegua. 2007. "Remite informe anual 2006 sobre proceso de descentralización." Oficio Multiple #947-2006-CND-GGPD/P. Moquegua, Peru.

———. 2006. "Padrón final de los electores representantes de la sociedad civil para el Consejo de Coordinación Regional – periodo 2006–2007." Moquegua, Peru.

———. 2003a. "Plan de desarrollo regional concertado 2003–2021." Moquegua, Peru.

———. 2003b. "Publicación final de la relación de organizaciones representantes de la sociedad civil inscritos en el padrón electoral para el Consejo de Coordinación Regional." Moquegua, Peru.

Goldfrank, Benjamin. Forthcoming. *Deepening Local Democracy in Latin America: Participation, Decentralization, and the Left.* University Park: Pennsylvania State University Press.

———.2009. "The Diffusion of Participatory Democracy and the Rise of the Left." Paper presented at the Midwest Political Science Association Annual Meeting, Chicago. April 3.

———. 2007a. "The Politics of Deepening Local Democracy: Decentralization, Party Institutionalization, and Participation." *Comparative Politics* 39(2): 147–68.

———. 2007b. "Lessons from Latin America's Experience with Participatory Budgeting." In *Participatory Budgeting.* Edited by Anwar Shah. Washington, DC: World Bank.

Gonzales de Olarte, Efraín. 2004. *La difícil descentralización fiscal en el Perú: Teoría y práctica.* Lima: Instituto de Estudios Peruanos.

———. 2000. *Neocentralismo y neoliberalismo en el Perú.* Lima: Instituto de Estudios Peruanos.

Gorriti, Gustavo. 2004. "Yanacocha: El campo y la mina." *IDEELE* 166: 8–21.

———. 1990. *Sendero: La historia de la guerra milenaria.* Lima: Apoyo.

Graham, Carol. 1990. "Peru's APRA Party in Power: Impossible Revolution, Relinquished Reform." *Journal of Interamerican Studies and World Affairs* 32(3): 75–116.

Gray, Virginia. 1994. "Competition, Emulation, and Policy Innovation." In *New Perspectives on American Politics.* Edited by Lawrence Dodd and Calvin Jillson. Washington, DC: Congressional Quarterly Press.

Gret, Marion, and Yves Sintomer. 2005. *The Porto Alegre Experiment: Learning Lessons for a Better Democracy.* London: Zed Books.

Grey Figueroa, Carlos, Maria Guadalupe Hinojosa, and José Ventura. 2003. *Democratizando el presupuesto público: Presupuesto participativo metodologías y herramientas al alcance.* Lima: CARE.

Grindle, Merilee. 2007. *Going Local: Decentralization, Participation, and the Promise of Good Governance.* Princeton, NJ: Princeton University Press.

———. 2000. *Audacious Reforms: Institutional Invention and Democracy in Latin America.* Baltimore: Johns Hopkins University Press.

Grompone, Romeo. 2005a. "Discutiendo la intervención ciudadana en el presupuesto participativo regional." Cuadernos Descentralistas. Lima: Grupo Propuesta Ciudadana.

———. 2005b. "Notas sobre descentralización, relaciones entre estado y sociedad, y participación ciudadana." Desde el foro: Balance y desafíos de la descentralización, Lima, Peru. Accessed December 13, 2010, from http://www.defensoria.gob.pe/programa-gob.php.

———. 2004. "Posibilidades y límites de experiencias de promoción de la participación ciudadana en el Perú." Lima: Instituto de Estudios Peruanos.

———. 2002. "Los dilemas no resueltos de la descentralización." Lima: Instituto de Estudios Peruanos.

Grompone, Romeo, and Carlos Mejía. 1995. *Nuevos tiempos, nueva política: El fin de un ciclo partidario*. Lima: Instituto de Estudios Peruanos.

Grupo Propuesta Ciudadana (GPC). 2009. "Presupuesto Participativo: Boletín de Vigilancia #2." Lima, Peru. Retrieved November 1, 2010, from http://www.descentralizacion.org.pe/vigilaperu-gobiernosregionales.shtml.

———. 2008. "Distribución del presupuesto por niveles de gobierno." Lima: GPC.

———. 2007a. "Vigilancia del proceso de descentralización." Reporte nacional 11, Balance 2003–2006. Lima: Participa Perú.

———. 2007b. "¿Reforma del estado?" Suplemento 38. Lima: Participa Perú.

———. 2007c. "La regionalización y el fortalecimiento de las juntas de coordinación interregional." Cuaderno Descentralista 21. Lima: Participa Perú.

———. 2006. "Las regiones y los gobiernos locales en el presupuesto 2006." Editorial. Accessed February 1, 2006, from http://www.participaperu.org.pe/n-editorial.shtml?x=45418.

———. 2005a. "Nuevo instructivo del presupuesto participativo en consulta." Accessed February 15, 2005, from http://www.participaperu.org.pe/.

———. 2005b. "Sistema Vigila Perú: Balance anual 2004." Reporte nacional 6. Lima: GPC.

———. 2005c. "Vigilancia del proceso de descentralización." Reporte nacional 7. Lima: GPC.

———. 2004a. "Balance del proceso de descentralización." Presented in the VIII Foro Descentralista: La reforma del estado: Experiencias Latinoamericanas sobre descentralización y participación, Lima, Peru. March 29.

———. 2004b. "Nota 38: El presupuesto general de la república 2005 y la (falta de) descentralización." Lima: GPC.

———. 2004c. "Sistema Vigila Perú: Balance del primer año de la descentralización." Reporte nacional 3. Lima: GPC.

———. 2003a. "La descentralización y los gobiernos locales." Participa Perú 3. Lima: GPC.

———. 2003b. "MEF presenta proyecto de reglamento de la ley Marco del Presupuesto Participativo." Notas de información y análisis 7. Lima: GPC.

———. 2003c. Vigila Perú: Reporte nacional. Lima: GPC.

Guerrero Figueroa, Luis. 2002. *Sembrando descentralización y concertación*. Lima: Fondo Editorial del Congreso del Perú.

Habermas, Jurgen. 1975a. *Legitimation Crisis*. London: Heinemann.

———. 1975b. *Communication and the Evolution of Society*. London: Heinemann.

Haya de la Torre, Víctor Raúl. 1936. *El anti-imperialismo y el APRA*. Santiago: Ercilla Press.

Heller, Patrick. 2001. "Moving the State: The Politics of Decentralization in Kerala, South Africa, and Porto Alegre." *Politics and Society* 29(1): 131–63.

Hinojosa, Iván. 2004. "El golpe estoico de Yehude Simon." *Caretas* (March 4): 21–24.

Huber, Ludwig, Karin Apel, Jorge Iván Caro, Lenin Castillo, Enver Quinteros, and Hugo Rodríguez. 2003. "Centralismo y descentralización en Ayacucho." In *Ayacucho: Centralismo y descentralización*. Lima: Instituto de Estudios Peruanos.

Hunther, Jeff, and Anwar Shah. 1998. "Applying a Simple Measure of Good Governance to the Debate on Fiscal Decentralization." World Bank Working Papers, Governance, Corruption, Legal Reform #1894. Washington, DC: World Bank.

Inter-American Development Bank (IDB). 1997. "Latin America After a Decade of Reforms." Economic and Social Progress in Latin America, 1997 Report. Washington, DC: IDB.

Isaac, T. M. Thomas, and Patrick Heller. 2003. "Democracy and Development: Decentralized Planning in Kerala." In *Deepening Democracy: Institutional Innovations in Empowered Participatory Governance. The Real Utopias Project IV*. Edited by Archon Fung and Erik Olin Wright. London: Verso.

Kauzya, John-Mary. 2007. "Political Decentralization in Africa: Experiences of Uganda, Rwanda, and South Africa." In *Decentralizing Governance: Emerging Concepts and Practices*. Washington, DC: Brookings Institution Press.

Kay, Bruce. 1999. "Violent Opportunities: The Rise and Fall of 'King Coca' and Shining Path." *Journal of Interamerican Studies and World Affairs* 41(3): 97–127.

Kenney, Charles. 2004. *Fujimori's Coup and the Breakdown of Democracy in Latin America*. Notre Dame: University of Notre Dame Press.

Krauss, Clifford. 2001. "Tapes Spy Chief Left Behind Scandalize Peru." *New York Times* A1. February 3.

Krishna, Anirudh. 2003. "Do Poor People Benefit Less from Decentralization?" Paper presented at the 2003 annual meeting of the American Political Science Association, Philadelphia, PA. August 27–31.

———. May 2002. "Enhancing Political Participation in Democracies: What Is the Role of Social Capital?" *Comparative Political Studies* 35(4): 437–60.

———. 2001. "Moving from the Stock of Social Capital to the Flow of Benefits: The Role of Agency." *World Development* 29(6): 925–43.

Laos Fernández, Alejandro, Pastor Paredes, and Edgardo Rodríguez. 2003. *Rondando por nuestra ley*. Lima: SER.

Larco, Giovanna, and Carlos Mejía. 1995. *Con los ojos bien abiertos: Reestructuración empresarial y sindicalismo en los 90s.* Lima: PLADES.

Levitsky, Steven, and Maxwell A. Cameron. 2003. "Democracy Without Parties? Political Parties and Regime Change in Fujimori's Peru." *Latin American Politics and Society* 45(3): 1–34.

Leyton, Carlos. 2006. "Nuevas oportunidades para la integración regional en el sur." *Revista Quehacer* 163. Lima: DESCO.

Lijphart, Arend. 1971. "Comparative Politics and the Comparative Method." *American Political Science Review* 65: 691–93.

Llona, Mariana. 2002. "El presupuesto participativo en el proceso de planificación de Villa El Salvador." *Revista Quehacer* (May–June): 78–88.

López, Follega, and José Luis. 2000. *Ilo: Los sueños de una ciudad.* Ilo, Peru: Asociación Civil Labor.

López, Follega, José Luis, Walter Melgar Paz, and Doris Balbín Díaz. 1995. "La concertación en la gestión ambiental urbana: La experiencia de Ilo." Ilo, Peru: Asociación Civil Labor.

López Ricci, José. 2005. "Planeamiento y presupuesto participativo: Tendencias generales analizadas a partir del portal MEF." In *Cuadernos Descentralistas 14.* Lima: Grupo Propuesta Ciudadana. .

López Ricci, José, and Elisa Wiener. 2004. "Lecciones y tensiones de una historia que recién empieza: Balance de los procesos de planteamiento y presupuesto participativo regional 2003–2004 en 11 regiones del Perú." Unpublished working paper. Lima: GPC.

Mahoney, James. 2007. "Qualitative Methodology and Comparative Politics." *Comparative Political Studies* 40(2): 122–44.

Mainwaring, Scott. 1998. "Party Systems in the Third Wave." *Journal of Democracy* 9(3): 647–81.

Malena, Carmen, ed. 2009. *From Political Won't to Political Will: Building Support for Participatory Governance.* Sterling, VA: Kumarian Press.

Manor, James. 1999. *The Political Economy of Democratic Decentralization.* Washington, DC: World Bank.

Manrique, Nelson. 1996. "The Two Faces of Fujimori's Rural Policy." *NACLA Report on the Americas* 30(1): 39–44.

Mansbridge, Jane. 1983. *Beyond Adversary Democracy.* Chicago: University of Chicago Press.

Márquez Calvo, Jaime, and Gerardo Castillo Távara. 2010. *Participación ciudadana y buen gobierno.* Mesa de Concertación para la Lucha Contra la Pobreza, Lima, Peru.

Mauceri, Philip. 2000. "Fujimori's Peru: The Political Economy." *Journal of Latin American Studies* 32: 288–90.

———. 1997. "The Transition to 'Democracy' and the Failures of Institution Building." In *The Peruvian Labyrinth: Politics, Society, and Economy.* Edited by Maxwell A.

Cameron and Philip Mauceri. University Park: Pennsylvania State University Press.

———. 1995. "State Reform, Coalitions, and the Neoliberal *Autogolpe* in Peru." *Latin American Research Review.* 30(1): 7–37.

McAdam, Doug. 1982. *Political Process and the Development of Black Insurgency 1930–1970.* Chicago: University of Chicago Press.

McAdam, Doug, John D. McCarthy, and Mayer Zald, eds. 1996. *Comparative Perspectives on Social Movements.* Cambridge, MA: Cambridge University Press.

McClintock, Cynthia. 2006. "An Unlikely Comeback in Peru." *Journal of Democracy* 17(4): 95–109.

———. 2005. "The Evolution of Internal War in Peru: The Conjunction of Need, Creed, and Organizational Finance." In *Rethinking the Economics of War: The Intersection of Need, Creed, and Greed.* Baltimore: Johns Hopkins University Press.

———. 2001. "Room for Improvement: The OAS in Peru." *Journal of Democracy* 12(4): 137–40.

———. 1999. "Peru: Precarious Regimes, Authoritarian and Democratic." In *Democracy and Developing Countries: Latin America.* 2nd ed. Boulder: Lynne Rienner Publishers.

———. 1998. *Revolutionary Movements in Latin America: El Salvador's FMLN and Peru's Shining Path.* Washington, DC: U.S. Institute of Peace Press.

———. 1993. "Peru's Fujimori: A Caudillo Derails Democracy." *Current History* (March): 112–19.

———. 1984. "Why Peasants Rebel: The Case of Peru's Sendero Luminoso." *World Politics* 37(1): 48–84.

———. 1981. *Peasant Cooperatives and Political Change in Peru.* Princeton, NJ: Princeton University Press.

McNulty, Stephanie. 2003. "Cada vez más fuerte: The Role of Civil Society in Peru's Transition from the Fujimori Regime." Presented at the Latin American Studies Association Conference, Dallas, TX. March 27.

———. 1999. "The Role of NGOs in Latin America's Development: A Case Study of Peru." In *Learning NGOs and the Dynamics of Development Partnership.* Dhaka, Bangladesh: Dhaka Ahsania Mission (Ahsania Books).

———. 1996. "The Role of NGOs in Peru's Development Process." In *Peru: Beyond the Reforms.* Lima: PromPerú.

Meléndez Guerrero, Carlos. 2003. *Último mapa político: Análisis de los resultados de las elecciones regionales de noviembre del 2002.* Lima: Instituto de Estudios Peruanos.

Mendoza, Raúl. 2004. "Los Frentes, la alternativa del 2006." *La Republica*, edición nacional. August 15.

Mesa de Concertación para la Lucha Contra la Pobreza (MCLCP). 2008. "Segundo informe nacional de seguimiento del presupuesto participativo 2007: El cumplimiento de los compromisos asumidos por los gobiernos regionales." Retrieved May 6, 2009, from http://www.mesadeconcertacion.org.pe/contenido.php?pid=87.

———. 2007. "Presupuesto participativo 2007: Informe nacional de monitoreo: Resultados del proceso participativo." Retrieved May 6, 2009, from http://www.mesade concertacion.org.pe/contenido.php?pid=87.

———. 2003. "Propuesta de reglamento para la participación de las organizaciones de la sociedad civil ante el Consejo de Coordinación Regional." Lima: MCLCP.

———. 2002. "Plan de desarrollo departamental concertado de Lambayeque." Retrieved October 29, 2004, from http://www.mesadeconcertacion.org.pe/.

———. 2001. "Plan estratégico de desarrollo: Ayacucho al 2011." Retrieved October 29, 2004, from http://www.mesadeconcertacion.org.pe/.

Meseguer, Covadonga. 2005. "Policy Learning, Policy Diffusion, and the Making of a New Order." *Annals of the American Academy of Political and Social Science* 598: 67–82.

Meyer, David S., and Debra Minkoff. 2004. "Conceptualizing Political Opportunity." *Social Forces* 82(4): 1457–92.

Mill, John Stuart. 1925. *A System of Logic: Raciocinative and Inductive*. 8th edition. London: Longman, Green, and Co.

Ministerio de Economía y Finanzas (MEF). 2006. "Instructivo para el proceso del presupuesto participativo año fiscal 2007." Lima: MEF.

———. 2005. "Instructivo para el proceso del presupuesto participativo año fiscal 2006." Lima: MEF.

———. 2004a. "Instructivo para el proceso de planeamiento del desarrollo concertado y presupuesto participativo." No. 001-2004-EF/76.01. Lima: MEF.

———. 2004b. "Una breve reseña de los avances del presupuesto participativo en el Perú 2003–2004." Lima: MEF.

———. 2003. "Guía general de identificación, formulación, y evaluación social de proyectos de inversión publica a nivel de perfil." Lima: MEF.

Moehler, Devra C. 2008. *Distrusting Democrats: Outcomes of Participatory Constitution Making*. Ann Arbor: University of Michigan Press.

Moffett, Mat. 2006. "Missed Chance: In Latin America, Commodities Boom Has Unlikely Fallout—Many Mayors Flub Opportunity to Help Region's Poor." *Wall Street Journal* A1. March 6.

Monge, Carlos. 2005. "La descentralización y participación ciudadana." In *El proceso de regionalización en el Perú: Realidades y desafíos*. Lima: CEDEP.

———. 2002. "Sociedad civil y participación en la transición Peruana." Monografía. Lima: GPC.

Montero, Alfred, and David Samuels. 2004. "The Political Determinants of Decentralization in Latin America: Causes and Consequences." In *Decentralization and Democracy in Latin America.* Notre Dame: University of Notre Dame Press.

Mouffe, Chantal, and Ernesto Laclau. 1985. *Hegemony and the Socialist Strategy: Toward a Radical Democratic Politics.* London: Verso.

Moynihan, Donald. 2007. "Citizen Participation in Budgeting: Prospect for Developing Countries." In *Participatory Budgeting.* Edited by Anwar Shah. Washington, DC: World Bank.

Navarro Sarmiento, Daniela. 2007. "Entrevista a Marco Arana, presidente regional de la Mesa de Concertación de Lucha Contra la Pobreza." Retrieved August 15, 2008, from http://www.ser.org.pe/index.php?option=com_content&task=view&id=352&Itemid=123.

Nickson, Andrew. 1995. *Local Government in Latin America.* Boulder: Lynne Rienner.

Noriega Davila, Jorge, ed. 1997. *Perú: Las organizaciones no gubernamentales (ONGs).* Lima: DESCO.

Nylen, William. 2003. *Participatory Democracy Versus Elitist Democracy: Lessons from Brazil.* New York: Palgrave.

Oates, Wallace. 1999. "An Essay on Fiscal Federalism." *Journal of Economic Literature* XXXVII: 1120–49.

———. 1972. *Fiscal Federalism.* New York: Harcourt, Brace, Jonanovich.

O'Brien, Eduardo. 2004. "Propuestas participativos regionales: Enfoques consistencias y recomendaciones." Lima: GPC.

O'Donnell, Guillermo. 1994. "Delegative Democracy." *Journal of Democracy* 5(1): 55–69.

O'Donnell, Guillermo, and Philippe C. Schmitter. 1986. *Transitions from Authoritarian Rule: Tentative Conclusions About Uncertain Democracies.* Baltimore: Johns Hopkins University Press.

Ojeda Segovia, Lautaro. 2003. "Balance comparativo de la descentralización en los países de la comunidad Andina." In *Procesos de descentralización en la comunidad Andina.* Quito: FLACSO.

Olowu, Dele, and James S. Wunsch. 2004. *Local Governance in Africa: The Challenges of Democratic Decentralization.* Boulder: Lynne Rienner.

O'Neill, Kathleen. 2004. "Decentralization in Bolivia: Electoral Incentives and Outcomes." In *Decentralization and Democracy in Latin America.* Notre Dame: University of Notre Dame Press.

———. 2003. "Decentralization as an Electoral Strategy." *Comparative Political Studies* 36(9): 1068–91.

Oxhorn, Philip. 2004. "Unraveling the Puzzle of Decentralization." In *Decentralization, Democratic Governance, and Civil Society in Comparative Perspective.* Washington, DC: Woodrow Wilson Center for International Scholars.

Palmer, David Scott. 2000. "Democracy and Its Discontents in Fujimori's Peru." *Current History* (February): 60–65.

——. 1999. "Soluciones ciudadanas y crisis política: El caso de Ayacucho." In *El juego político: Fujimori, la opción y las reglas*. Lima: Friedrich Ebert Stiftung.

——. 1997. "Peru-Ecuador Border Conflict: Missed Opportunities, Misplaced Nationalism, and Multilateral Peacekeeping." *Journal of Interamerican Studies and World Affairs* 39(3): 109–48.

——. 1994. *The Shining Path of Peru*. New York: St Martin's Press.

Panfichi, Aldo. 2007. "Democracia y participación: El Fujimorismo y los gobiernos de transición." In *Participación ciudadana en el Perú: Disputas, confluencias, y tensiones*. Lima: Fondo Editorial de la Pontificia Católica del Perú.

Panfichi, Aldo, and Luis Dammert. 2005. "Participación, concertación, y confrontación en espacios locales. El caso de la Mesa de Concertación para la Lucha Contra la Pobreza del Departamento de Puno." Working paper for the Inter-American Foundation. Lima, Peru.

Panfichi, Aldo, and Lino Pineda. 2007. "De la confrontación a la concertación en las provincias de Huanta en Ayacucho y Churcampa en Huancavelica." In *Participación ciudadana en el Perú: Disputas, confluencias, y tensiones*. Lima: Fondo Editorial de la Pontificia Católica del Perú.

——. 2004. "De la confrontación a la concertación en provincias indígenas del Perú: Comparando las Mesas de Concertación para el desarrollo local en Huanta (Ayacucho) y Churcampa (Huancavelica)." Cuadernos de Investigación Social. Departamento de Ciencias Sociales. Lima: Pontificia Universidad Católica del Perú.

Pariona Arana, Luis. 2004. "En el centro del conflicto: Cocaleros, narcotráfico, y Sendero Luminoso en el alto Huallaga." *IDEELE* 163: 36–40

Partido Aprista Peruano. 2006. "Plan de gobierno 2006–2011." Retrieved August 15, 2008, from http://www.apra.org.pe/neo/plan.pdf.

Pease García, Henry. 2008. *Reforma política: Para consolidar el régimen democrático*. Lima: Pontificia Universidad Católica del Perú.

Peruzzotti, Enrique, and Andrew Selee. 2009. "Participatory Innovation and Representative Democracy in Latin America." In *Participatory Innovation and Representative Democracy in Latin America*. Baltimore: Johns Hopkins University Press.

Peterson, George. 1997. *Decentralization in Latin America: Learning Through Experience*. Washington, DC: World Bank.

Pinglo, Elías. 2007. "Memoria de la actividad del CCR-Lambayeque." Año 2006. Lambayeque, Perú.

Planas, Pedro. 2000. *La democracia volátil: Movimientos, partidos, líderes políticos, y conductas electorales en el Perú contemporáneo*. Lima: Friedrich Ebert Stiftung.

———. 1998. *La descentralización en el Perú republicano (1821–1998)*. Lima: Municipalidad Metropolitana de Lima.

———. 1996. "¿Existe un sistema de partidos en el Perú?" In *Los enigmas del poder: Fujimori 1990–1996*. Lima: Friedrich Ebert Stiftung.

Portes, Alejandro. 2000. "The Two Meanings of Social Capital." *Sociological Forum* 15(1): 1–12.

———. 1998. "Social Capital: Its Origins and Applications in Modern Sociology." *Annual Review of Sociology* 24: 1–24.

Portocarrero, Felipe, Cynthia Sanborn, Hanny Cueva, and Armando Millán. 2002. *Más allá del individualismo: El tercer sector en el Perú*. Lima: Universidad del Pacífico.

Pro-Descentralización (PRODES). 2010. Mapa de Políticas y Normas de la Descentralización. Retrieved June 16, 2010, from http://www.prodescentralizacion.org.pe/ultimas_publicaciones.php.

———. 2009. "Participación y descentralización: Percepciones y expectativas ciudadanas." Evaluación Rápida de Campo. Lima: PRODES.

———. 2007a. "Proceso de descentralización: La agenda a cuatro años de iniciado el proceso." Lima: PRODES.

———. 2007b. "Del CND a la secretaría de descentralización." *Boletín Trimestral* 9. Lima: PRODES.

———. 2007c. "El proceso de descentralización: Balance y agenda a septiembre de 2007." Lima: PRODES.

———. 2006. "La descentralización en la agenda electoral: Aportes para la formulación de propuestas." Lima: PRODES-USAID.

———. 2005. "Proceso de descentralización 2004: Balance y recomendaciones para una agenda pendiente." Lima: PRODES.

Prud'homme, Remy. 1995. "The Dangers of Decentralization." *World Bank Research Observer* 10(2): 201–20.

Putnam. Robert D. 1993. *Making Democracy Work: Civic Traditions in Modern Italy*. Princeton, NJ: Princeton University Press.

Qian, Yingyi, and Barry Weingast. 1997. "Federalism as a Commitment to Preserving Market Incentives." *Journal of Economic Perspectives* 11(4): 83–92.

Ragin, Charles. 1987. *The Comparative Method: Moving Beyond Qualitative and Quantitative Strategies*. Berkeley: University of California Press.

Reilly, Charles. 1995. *New Paths to Democratic Development in Latin America*. Boulder, CO: Lynne Rienner.

Remy, María Isabel. 2005. *Los múltiples campos de la participación ciudadana en el Perú*. Lima: Instituto de Estudios Peruanos.

Roberts, Kenneth. 2002. "Social Inequalities Without Class Cleavages in Latin America's Neoliberal Era." *Studies in Comparative International Development* 36(4): 3–33.

———. 1998. *Deepening Democracy? The Modern Left and Social Movements in Chile and Peru.* Stanford, CA: Stanford University Press.

Rondinelli, Dennis A. 1990. "Decentralization Urban Development Programs: A Framework for Analyzing Policy." Policy and Research Series (P&RS) No. PN-ABD-906. Washington, DC: USAID.

———. 1989. "Decentralization Public Services in Developing Countries: Issues and Opportunities." *Journal of Social, Political, and Economic Studies* 14(1): 77–98.

———. 1981. "Government Decentralization in Comparative Perspective: Theory and Practice in Developing Countries." *International Review of Administrative Science* 47(2): 133–45.

Rondinelli, Dennis A., and Shabbir Cheema. 1983. "Implementing Decentralization Policies: An Introduction." In *Decentralization and Development: Policy Implementation in Developing Countries.* Edited by Shabbir Cheema and Dennis A. Rondinelli. Beverly Hills: Sage Publications.

Rondinelli, Dennis A., and John M. Heffron, eds. 2009. *Leadership for Development: What Globalization Demands of Leaders Fighting for Change.* Sterling, VA: Kumarian Press.

Sabatini, Christopher. 2003. "Decentralization and Political Parties." *Journal of Democracy* 14(2): 138–50.

Sagasti, Francisco, Pepi Patrón, Nicolás Lynch, and Max Hernández. 2001. *Democracy and Good Government: Towards Democratic Governance in Peru.* 3rd ed. Lima: Agenda Perú.

Saldaña, Jorge. 2002. "Decisión multipartidaria." *El Comercio*, edición nacional. March 7.

Samuels, David. 2004. "The Political Logic of Decentralization in Brazil." In *Decentralization and Democracy in Latin America.* Notre Dame: University of Notre Dame Press.

Santos-Granero, Fernando, and Frederica Barclay. 2002. *La frontera domesticada: Historia económica y social de Loreto 1850–2000.* Lima: Fondo Editorial de la Pontificia Universidad Católica del Perú.

Schmidt, Gregory. 2004. *Peru: The Politics of Surprise.* McGraw-Hall Primis On-Line.

———. 2000. "Delegative Democracy in Peru? Fujimori's 1995 Landslide and the Prospects for 2000." *Journal of Interamerican Studies and World Affairs* 42(1): 99–132.

———. 1989. "Political Variables and Governmental Decentralization in Peru, 1949–1988." *Journal of Interamerican Studies and World Affairs* 31: 193–234.

Schmitter, Philippe. 1974. "Still the Century of Corporatism." *World Politics* 36(1): 85–131.

Schonwalder, Gerd. 2002. *Linking Civil Society to the State: Urban Popular Movements, the Left, and Local Government in Peru: 1980–1992.* University Park: Pennsylvania State University Press.

———. 1998. "Local Politics and the Peruvian Left: The Case of el Agustino." *Latin American Research Review* 33(2): 73–103.

Selee, Andrew. 2004. Introduction to *Decentralization and Democratic Governance in Latin America*. Washington, DC: Woodrow Wilson Center for International Scholars.

Selee, Andrew, and Joseph Tulchin. 2004. "Decentralization and Democratic Governance: Lessons and Challenges." In *Decentralization, Democratic Governance, and Civil Society in Comparative Perspective*. Washington, DC: Woodrow Wilson Center for International Scholars.

Shah, Anwar, ed. 2007. *Participatory Budgeting*. Washington, DC: World Bank.

Shah, Anwar, and Theresa Thompson. 2004. "Implementing Decentralized Governance: A Treacherous Road with Potholes, Detours, and Road Closures." Retrieved January 15, 2006, from http://ideas.repec.org/e/psh62.html.

Snyder, Richard. 2001. "Scaling Down: The Subnational Comparative Method." *Studies in Comparative International Development* 36(1): 93–110.

Soberón, Ricardo. 2004. "Cocaleros y Estado." *IDEELE* 164: 25–27.

Solari, Andrés. 2005. "Representantes de la sociedad civil ante el Consejo de Coordinación Regional—CCR. Informe 01." Ayacucho, Peru: Agenda Sur Ayacucho.

Somodevilla Lambright, Gina. 2004a. "Political Meddling or Critical Instruction? The Impact of Central-Local Relations on Local Government Performance." Paper presented at the annual meeting of the Midwest Political Science Association, Chicago. April 15–18.

———. 2004b. "Silence from Below: Testing Social and Cultural Explanations for Good Government in Uganda." Paper presented at the annual meeting of the American Political Science Association, Chicago. September 2–5.

Starn, Orin. 1999. *Nightwatch: The Politics of Protest in the Andes*. Durham, NC: Duke University Press.

———. 1995. "To Revolt Against the Revolution: War and Resistance in Peru's Andes." *Cultural Anthropology* 10(4): 547–80.

Stern, Steve. 1998. *Shining and Other Paths: War and Society in Peru, 1980–1995*. Durham, NC: Duke University Press.

Stokes, Susan. 1997. "Democratic Accountability and Policy Change: Economic Policy in Fujimori's Peru." *Comparative Politics* 29(2): 209–26.

———. 1995. *Cultures in Conflict: Social Movements and the State in Peru*. Berkeley: University of California Press.

Tanaka, Martín. 2007. "La participación ciudadana y el sistema representativo." Lima: PRODES-USAID.

———. 2005. *Democracia sin partidos: Perú 2000–2005: Los problemas de representación y las propuestas de reforma política*. Lima: Instituto de Estudios Peruanos.

———. 2002a. "La dinámica de los actores regionales y el proceso de descentrali-zación: ¿Es despertar del letargo?" Documento de trabajo 125. Lima: Instituto de Estudios Peruanos.

———. 2002b. *La situación de la democracia en Colombia, Perú, y Venezuela a inicios del siglo.* Lima: Comisión Andina de Juristas.

———. 2001. "¿Crónica de una muerte anunciada? Determinismo, voluntarismo, acto-res, y poderes." In *Lecciones del final del Fujimorismo.* Lima: Instituto de Estudios Peruanos.

———. 1998. *Los espejismos de la democracia: El colapso del sistema de partidos en el Perú.* Lima: Instituto de Estudios Peruanos.

Tanaka, Martín, and Carolina Trivelli. 2002. *Las trampas de la focalización y la par-ticipación: Pobreza y políticas durante la década de Fujimori.* Lima: Instituto de Estudios Peruanos.

Tanaka, Martín, and Patricia Zárate. 2000. *Valores democráticos y participación ciu-dadana.* Lima: Instituto de Estudios Peruanos.

Tarrow, Sidney. 1994. *Power in Movement.* Cambridge: Cambridge University Press.

Tendler, Judith. 1997. *Good Government in the Tropics.* Baltimore: Johns Hopkins Uni-versity Press.

Tendler, Judith, and Sarah Freedheim. 1994. "Trust in a Rent-Seeking World: Health and Government Transformed in Northeast Brazil." *World Development* 22(12): 1771–91.

Tiebout, Charles. 1956. "A Pure Theory of Local Expenditures." *Journal of Political Economy* 64: 416–24.

Tilly, Charles.1978. *From Mobilization to Revolution.* New York: McGraw-Hill.

Tulchin, Joseph, and Gary Bland, eds. 1994. *Peru in Crisis: Democracy or Dictatorship?* Boulder: Lynne Renner.

Tulchin, Joseph, and Andrew Selee, eds. 2004. *Decentralization and Democratic Gov-ernance in Latin America.* Washington, DC: Woodrow Wilson Center for Interna-tional Scholars.

United Cities and Local Governance and the World Bank. 2008. *Decentralization and Local Democracy in the World.* Retrieved June 16, 2010, from http://www.cities-localgovernments.org/gold/gold_report.asp.

Van Cott, Donna Lee. 2008. *Radical Democracy in the Andes.* Cambridge, MA: Cam-bridge University Press.

Van Evera, Stephen. 1997. *Guide to Methods for Students of Political Science.* Ithaca, NY: Cornell University Press.

Vargas Chirinos, Raúl. 1989. *Regionalización del Perú y gobierno nacional descentrali-zado.* Lima: Tarea Press.

Wagle, Swarnim, and Parmesh Shah. 2003. "Porto Alegre, Brazil: Participatory Ap-proaches in Budgeting and Public Expenditure Management." Social Develop-ment Note 71. Washington, DC: World Bank.

Wainwright, Hilary. 2003. "Making a People's Budget in Porto Alegre." *NACLA Report on the Americas* 36(5): 37–42.

Walzer, Michael. 1991. "The Idea of Civil Society." *Dissent* 38(2): 296–304.

Wampler, Brian. 2009. "Following in the Footsteps of Policy Entrepreneurs: Policy Advocates and Pro Forma Adopters." *Journal of Development Studies* 45(4): 572–92.

———. 2008. "When Does Participatory Democracy Deepen the Quality of Democracy? Lessons from Brazil." *Comparative Politics* 41(1): 61–81.

———. 2007a. *Participatory Budgeting in Brazil: Contestation, Cooperation, and Accountability.* University Park: Pennsylvania State University Press.

———. 2007b. "Can Participatory Institutions Promote Pluralism? Mobilizing Low-Income Citizens in Brazil." *Studies in Comparative International Development* 41(4): 57–78.

———. 2007c. "A Guide to Participatory Budgeting." In *Participatory Budgeting.* Edited by Anwar Shah. Washington, DC: World Bank.

Wampler, Brian, and Leonardo Avritzer. 2004. "Participatory Publics: Civil Society and New Institutions in Democratic Brazil." *Comparative Politics* 36(3): 291–312.

Warner, Carolyn. 2003. "The Perverse Link Between Decentralization, Democratization, and Political Corruption." Paper presented at the 2003 annual meeting of the American Political Science Association, Philadelphia, PA. August 27–31.

Weyland, Kurt. 2006. *Bounded Rationality and Policy Diffusion: Social Sector Reform in Latin America.* Princeton, NJ: Princeton University Press.

Willis, Eliza, Christopher da C.B. Garman, and Stephen Haggard. 1999. "The Politics of Decentralization in Latin America." *Latin American Research Review* 34(1): 7–56.

Wise, Carol. 2003. *Reinventing the State: Economic Strategy and Institutional Change in Peru.* Ann Arbor: University of Michigan Press.

———. 1997. "State Policy and Social Conflict in Peru." In *The Peruvian Labyrinth: Politics, Society, and Economy.* Edited by Maxwell A. Cameron and Philip Mauceri. University Park: Pennsylvania State University Press.

Wong-Gonzalez, Pablo. 1992. "International Integration and Locational Change in Mexico's Car Industry: Regional Concentration and Deconcentration." In *Decentralization in Latin America: An Evaluation.* New York: Praeger.

World Bank. n.d. "Decentralization Topics." Retrieved March 7, 2006, from http://www1.worldbank.org/publicsector/decentralization/admin.htm.

———. n.d. "Participation and Civic Engagement." Retrieved January 17, 2006, from http://web.worldbank.org/WBSITE/EXTERNAL/TOPICS/EXTSOCIALDEVELOPMENT/EXTPCENG/0,,menuPK:410312~pagePK:149018~piPK:149093~theSitePK:410306,00.html.

———. n.d. "Bank Projects." Retrieved August 13, 2005, from http://www1.worldbank.org/publicsector/decentralization/operations.htm.

———. 2010. "Peru: Evaluación del Presupuesto Participativo y su relación con el presupuesto por resultados." Washington, DC: The World Bank.

———. 2005. World Development Indicators Database. Retrieved August 25, 2005, from http://www.worldbank.org/data/countrydata/countrydata.html.

———. 2002. "Peru: Restoring Fiscal Discipline for Poverty Reduction." Country Distribution Draft Report No. 24286-PE. Washington, DC: World Bank.

Yin, Robert. 1994. *Case Study Research: Design and Methods.* 2nd ed. London: Thousand Oaks.

Youngers, Coletta. 2003. *Violencia política y sociedad civil en el Perú: Historia de la coordinadora nacional de derechos humanos.* Lima: Instituto de Estudios Peruanos.

———. 2000. *Deconstructing Democracy: Peru Under President Alberto Fujimori.* Washington, DC: Washington Office on Latin America.

Youngers, Colletta, and Susan Peacock. 2002. "Peru's coordinadora nacional de derechos humanos: A Case Study of Coalition Building." WOLA Special Report. Washington, DC: Washington Office on Latin America.

Zapata Velasco, Antonio. 1996. *Sociedad y poder local: La comunidad de Villa El Salvador 1971–1996.* Lima: DESCO.

Zárate, Patricia, and Carolina Trivelli. 2005. "Encuesta de percepción ciudadana sobre el proceso de descentralización." Lima: Pro-Decentralization Program.

Zas Friz Burga, Johnny. 2004. *La insistencia de la voluntad: El actual proceso peruano de descentralización política y sus antecedentes inmediatos (1980–2004).* Lima: Defensoría del Pueblo.

———. 2001. *El sueño obsecado.* Lima: Editorial del Congreso del Perú.

———. 1998. *La descentralización ficticia: Peru 1821–1998.* Lima: Universidad del Pacífico.

Zolezzi, Mario. 2004. "Participation in Planning in Budgeting in Villa El Salvador, Peru." In *Citizens in Charge: Managing Local Budgets in East Asia and Latin America.* Edited by Isabel Licha. Washington, DC: IDB.

INDEX

Abers, Rebecca, 13–14
Acción Popular (AP), 17, 18, 69
Ackerman, John, 12
Administrative map of Peru, 84 (figure)
Alianza Popular Revolucionaria Americana (APRA). *See* APRA (American Popular Revolutionary Alliance)
American Popular Revolutionary Alliance (APRA). *See* APRA (American Popular Revolutionary Alliance)
ANGR (National Assembly of Regional Governments), 154
APRA (American Popular Revolutionary Alliance): in CCR design debates, 66, 68–70; civil society organizations and, 29–30; emergence of, 17; García and, 19; in Lambayeque, 87; in 1980s party system, 18; party politics and, 128–129; Toledo and, 57
Arpasi Velasquez, Paulina, 67
Asambleísmo, 31, 68
Audiencias públicas, 37, 75
Avritzer, Leonardo, 9, 14, 64, 129, 141
Ayacucho, 24, 104–110, 122

Barclay, Frederica, 180n58
Belaúnde Terry, Fernando, 18, 54
Blair, Harry, 12
Blondet, Cecilia, 59
Bryan, Frank, 14
Budget. *See* participatory budget; regional investment budgets
Burt, Jo-Marie, 20, 165nn16,22

Cabanillas Bustamante de Llanos, Mercedes, 68
Cajamarca, 24, 33, 97–104, 121–122
Calderón, Walter Alejos, 80
Cameron, John, 77
Campesinos, 17, 18, 98, 104–105, 169, 166n36, 179n43
Capital investment costs, 38, 48, 71, 77–78
Case study method, 23
CCRs (Consejos de Coordinación Regionales). *See* Regional Coordination Councils
Centro de Estudios para el Desarrollo y la Participación (CEDEP), 97
Cheema, G. Shabbir, 12–13
Citizen participation, 8–9, 32–34, 38
Citizen Participation Law (1993), 33
Civil Society Assembly, 89–90
Civil society/civil society organizations: in Ayacucho, 104–107, 107 (table), 122; in Cajamarca, 97–98, 100 (table), 100–102, 101 (table), 122; in CCR design debates, 65–70; communication channels for, 178n41; in Cusco, 110, 111–113, 112 (table), 115, 121; defined, 163n3; education of, 75–76; in first regionalization, 28–29; historical organizational factors, 135 (table); increase in, 166n31; in Lambayeque, 86–90, 89 (table), 91, 121; in Loreto, 116, 118 (table), 122; in Moquegua, 92–95, 97, 122; under Organic Regional Government Law,